REVOLUTIONARY EXILES

REVOLUTIONARY EXILES

The Russians in the First International and the Paris Commune

WOODFORD McCLELLAN

FRANK CASS

First published 1979 in Great Britain by
FRANK CASS AND COMPANY LIMITED
Gainsborough House, Gainsborough Road,
London E11 1RS, England

and in the United States of America by
FRANK CASS AND COMPANY LIMITED
c/o Biblio Distribution Centre,
81 Adams Drive, P.O. Box 327, Totowa, N.J. 07511

Copyright© 1979 Woodford McClellan

British Library Cataloguing in Publication Data

McClellan, Woodford
    Revolutionary Exiles.
    1. International Working Men's Association—
    History 2. Revolutionists—Russia—
    History 3. Paris—History—Commune, 1871
    I. Title
    329'.072   HX11.I/

ISBN 0 7146 3115 9

Photoset in Baskerville by Saildean Ltd
Printed in Great Britain by offset lithography by
Billing and Sons Limited, Guildford, London and Worcester

*To my son, Charles,
and to the
sacred memory of G.H.S.*

Acknowledgments

Friendship may have limits, but five people ignored them in giving invaluable scholarly assistance with this book. I am deeply indebted to that *moguchaia kuhka* of Professors Bert Andréas of Geneva, Loren Graham of Columbia University, Boris Itenberg of Moscow, Cecil Lang of the University of Virginia, and George Vogt of the National Archives in Washington. I am profoundly grateful too to M.G. Sedov of Moscow, Charles Jelavich of Indiana University and Nicholas V. Riasanovsky of the University of California at Berkeley. My senior colleagues in the Department of History at the University of Virginia generously awarded me a semester in the University's Centre for Advanced Studies; it is a pleasure to thank them, and the Centre, for that splendid opportunity to work on the manuscript. In Moscow and Leningrad the staffs of various archival collections and libraries were most helpful. The same was true elsewhere in Europe, but I should like to pay special tribute to the keepers of the Police Archives in Paris and to M. Desneux at the Ministry of Foreign Affairs in Brussels. At the University of Virginia, Martin Davis, Richard Martin and Angelika Powell of Alderman Library have shown me on countless occasions the wonders that skilled professional librarians can perform. To the American Council of Learned Societies and the International Research and Exchanges Board, which together funded several very productive periods of study in the Soviet Union, I am most grateful indeed.

Finally, I must pay tribute to Irina Igorevna McClellan, and to Rabbi Gedalyah Engel of Purdue University. Their contribution to this book was indirect but profound; and than them there are none nobler on this earth.

For such merits as this work may possess, the individuals and organizations named above merit enormous credit. Its shortcomings are mine, and mine alone.

W.M.

Contents

Abbreviations

AEG	Archives d'Etat de la République et Canton de Genève.
AMAE	Archives du Ministère des Affaires Etrangères.
APP	Archives de la Préfecture de Police, Paris.
BL/OR	Biblioteka im. Lenina, Otdel' rukopisei, Moscow.
CMRS	*Cahiers du Monde Russe et Soviétique.*
CP, CPL	*Correspondance Politique; Correspondance Politique, Légations.*
Deiateli	Vsesoiuznoe obshchestvo politicheskikh katorzhan i ssyl'no-poselentsev, *Deiateli revoliutsionnogo dvizheniia v Rossii: Bio-bibliograficheskii slovar',* vols. 1, 2, 3, 5, in 10 parts, Moscow, 1927-1934.
DFI	Institute of Marxism-Leninism of the Central Committee of the CPSU, *Documents of the First International,* 5 vols., Moscow, 1963- -.
Freymond	Jacques Freymond, ed., *La Première Internationale: Recueil de documents,* 4 vols., Geneva, 1962-71.
Herzen	A.I. Gertsen, *Sobranie Sochinenii v tridtsati tomakh,* 31 vols., Moscow, 1954-1966.
HHStA	Haus-, Hof-, und Staatsarchiv, Vienna.
IISG	International Institute of Social History, Amsterdam.

KS	*Katorga i ssylka,* Moscow.
LN	Literaturnoe nasledstvo, Moscow.
MERR	Institute of Marxism-Leninism of the Central Committee of the CPSU, *K. Marks, F. Engel's i revoliutsionnaia Rossiia,* Moscow, 1967.
PSB	*Polski Slownik Biograficzny,* Kraków, 1935--.
SIE	*Sovetskaia istoricheskaia entsiklopediia,* Moscow, 1961--.
TsGAOR	Tsentral'nyi gosudarstvennyi arkhiv Oktiabrskoi revoliutsii, Moscow.
TsGALI	Tsentral'nyi gosudarstvennyi arkhiv literatury i iskusstva, Moscow.
Werke	Karl Marx and Friedrich Engels, *Werke,* 39 vols., Berlin, 1959-67.

Preface

In 1864, the government censor Osip Antonovich Przhet-slavsky retired to his modest estate near Tver to tend his garden and study Freemasonry, a subject that had long fascinated him. Convinced as he was that Freemasons were in league not only with foreign revolutionary and socialist societies but also with terrorists inside Russia, Przhetslavsky spent several years compiling his suspicions, findings and conclusions into a work he called 'The Great Secret of the Freemasons.' He sent the manuscript to his former colleagues in St Petersburg.

For several years Przhetslavsky waited patiently for a reply. Finally in 1879, he wrote directly to General A.R. Drenteln, chief of gendarmes and head of the Third Section (political police), asking him to read 'The Great Secret.' In his letter, the retired censor claimed that the dangerous alliance of Freemasons and revolutionaries dated from the Paris Commune of 1871. Karl Marx himself, he claimed, had told him so.

He had met Marx, wrote Przhetslavsky, in Karlsbad in 1875 when both were taking the cure. Marx had acknowledged that his organization, the International Working Men's Association, was responsible for the Paris Commune, a phenomenon Marx described as the first skirmish in a great campaign to create a 'universal commune.' Przhetslavsky had asked when the 'universal revolution' would commence. Marx replied that he needed ten million 'combatants'; at that time, he had only eight million. Przhetslavsky quoted Marx as saying,

We are only demolitionists; we build nothing. And when we

xi

have wiped out everything that has been condemned, then you, *messieurs les philosophes-philanthropes*, can build what you like—so long as we permit.[1]

Though possibly aware that Marx did in fact visit Karlsbad in 1875, the Russian authorities dismissed the letter as apocryphal nonsense. To humour him, however, Drenteln retrieved Przhetslavsky's manuscript from the archives, kept it in his office for a while, then returned it with thanks, convinced that he was no closer to the sources of the modern European revolutionary movement.[2]

In the 1870's and 1880's, the triumphant continental counter-revolution that followed the Paris Commune forced the socialist and revolutionary movements in various countries onto unprecedented paths.[3] In France, Italy and Spain, the victory of the reaction confronted the radicals with a choice between anarchist terrorism, social-democratic sectarianism or simple capitulation. In Germany, the Bismarckian counter-revolution combined suppression and paternalism to defuse and distort the working-class and socialist movements and turn them back toward Lassalleanism. The fact that those movements clung to Marxist rhetoric did not disguise their shedding of revolutionism.[4]

In Russia, the counter-revolution accelerated the development of *narodnichestvo*, or populism, a trend that had been building up among the radicals since the 1840's. This development obscured the temporary merger, in the period 1863-73, of a significant force within the Russian revolutionary movement with the Marxist tendency in the International Working Men's Association, or First International. It is that temporary merger, which sowed seeds of immense fertility, that constitutes the subject of this book.

It is widely assumed that 'Russian social democracy' dates from the formation, in Geneva in 1883, of the 'Group of the Liberation of Labour.' Five young Russians, led by George Plekhanov, founded this tiny circle, and I know of no historian who does not consider them the first Russian social democrats. That view is, however, open to challenge. The sudden conversion of Plekhanov and his associates smacks too much of Saul's experience on the road to Damascus. It is artificial and contrived, and it slights the important spadework done by the revolutionaries in the period of the First International. It is based—astonishingly enough, in the case of Western historians—upon Stalin's 1937 directive to the compilers of a textbook history of the Communist Party of the Soviet Union,[5] and to a lesser extent upon Plekhanov's own self-serving version of events.[6] It demands an extremely narrow interpretation of Lenin's admission that, around 1869-70, 'the Russian Narodnik [populist] socialists were trying to introduce into Russia the most advanced and most important of "European institutions"—the International.'[7] Populists proselytizing for social democracy? That would have been akin to a Christian effort to propagate Islam. The offhand comment cannot withstand close scrutiny, and the possibility—explored in this book—must be left open that Lenin's 'populists' were in the process of making the shift to social democracy.

Who were the forgotten ancestors of Plekhanov and his group? With few exceptions their names do not loom large in the conventional historiography of the Russian revolutionary movement. Lenin's comment referred to the Russian section of the International, a short-lived group also based—coincidentally—in Geneva. That group was formed by Nicholas and Natalie Utin, Anton Trusov, Victor and Catherine Bartenev, Anna Korvin-Krukovskaya, Elizabeth Tomanovskaya and others; and an unstable young man named Alexander Serno-Solovyovich had helped prepare the way for them by his participation in the Geneva organization of the International. These individuals co-operated with Marx in the International and called him one of their teachers. We note 'one of' both because it is historically accurate and because it helps explain why Lenin, and modern historians, have pinned a populist label upon the Russian section. The other principal teacher of that group was N.G. Chernyshevsky, whom Lenin admired above all pre-Marxist Russian socialists. And Chernyshevsky was unquestionably a populist.

We must therefore concede the populist origins of the Russian section's ideology and indeed of that of other revolutionaries whom we shall discuss here who were not members of the section. But it is a truism that ideology and politics are not the same thing. In political orientation the

Russian section, and several (but by no means all) other
Russians in the International, stood squarely in the camp of
social democracy and therefore of Marxism.

In addition to the Russian section, we shall pursue the
stories of others of Marx's Russian friends such as Herman
Lopatin and Nicholas Danielson, who, partly at the instiga-
tion of their friend Nicholas Liubavin, translated *Capital* into
Russian. We shall examine the complex, confused relations
between the terrorist Sergei Nechaev and Marx's friends, and
we shall trace some of the lesser-known activities of Marx's
great adversary, Michael Bakunin. We shall review, for the
first time in English, the participation of the Russians and
Poles in the Paris Commune.

The early Russian social democrats have been largely
ignored by Western historians, and in the Soviet Union their
history has been distorted for ideological and political
reasons. There exists only one substantial work in a Western
language on the Russian revolutionary émigrés of the 1863-73
period; it does not address the question of social democracy
and is limited to the Zürich colony.[8] The best-known work on
Russian populism, Franco Venturi's monumental *Roots of
Revolution,* virtually ignores the Russians in the International
—perhaps another indication that few of them were populists—and in its references to the Russian section makes some
egregious errors.[9]

In the Soviet Union, the late B.P. Kozmin's work on the
Russian section is a tendentious Stalinist interpretation, and
furthermore neither Kozmin nor any other Soviet scholar has
had access to the Western archives utilized in the present
study (to be sure, this is not their fault).[10] A more reasoned
Marxist argument is that of the Moscow historian M.G.
Sedov, who has argued that the Russians of the 1863-73
period were not social democrats and indeed could not
possibly have been because there was then no working class in
Russia. It was, in Sedov's view, 'historically impossible' for
any Russian revolutionary in that period to be a social
democrat.[11]

This study does not accept the historical determinist argument. It does set out to revise the periodization of an
important phenomenon in the Russian revolutionary move-

ment—the appearance of social democracy—and it does so by integrating that phenomenon into the larger context of European socialist and working-class movements, a novel approach. The results will, I hope, lead the reader to understand that the retired censor Przhetslavsky, who imagined having had conversations with Karl Marx, was sufficiently in touch with reality to express the fears and obsessions of a European generation.

NOTES

1. *TsGAOR*, f. III otd., delopr. 3 eksp., No. 154/1879, 'Svedeniia po Tverskoi gubernii,' 11. 6-7, 8, 9.
2. *Ibid.*, 11. 58, 60-1, 62.
3. See in general on this topic Arno J. Mayer, *Dynamics of Counterrevolution in Europe, 1870-1956,* New York, 1971.
4. The failure to understand this important lesson about German radicalism was an important factor in the Bolshevik triumph of 1917. As is well known, the party dared to launch its armed uprising in no small measure because its leaders believed in the imminence of revolution in Germany.
5. Probably advised by E.M. Yaroslavsky, Stalin directed the compilers of the textbook to take as the first period ('the struggle for the creation of a Marxist social-democratic party in Russia') the years 1883 to 1900-1, i.e. from the formation of the Plekhanov group to the first issues of *Iskra.* See *Krasnyi Arkhiv,* vol. 82, pp. 3-5. This periodization has recently been challenged in L.M. Ivanov, ed., *Rabochii klass i rabochee dvizhenie v Rossii, 1861-1917,* Moscow, 1966, pp. 5-57.
6. Plekhanov, *Sochineniia,* vol. 24, Moscow-Leningrad, 1927, p. 171.
7. 'What the "Friends of the People" Are and How They Fight the Social-Democrats,' *Collected Works,* vol. 1, Moscow, 1963, p. 278.
8. J.M. Meijer, *Knowledge and Revolution: The Russian Colony in Zuerich (1870-1873),* Assen, 1955.
9. *Roots of Revolution,* New York, 1966. Venturi erroneously claimed that Bakunin tried to organize the 'young émigrés' into a section of the International; that Bakunin drew up the programme and regulations for the Russian section; that Anton Trusov's role in the section equalled that of Nicholas Utin; and that the section tried to engage Peter Lavrov as a collaborator (pp. 433-4, 443, 452). These are only a few of the errors.
10. *Russkaia sektsiia pervogo Internatsionala,* Moscow, 1957.
11. *Geroicheskii period revoliutsionnogo narodnichestva,* Moscow, 1966. See also the same author's 'Nekotorye problemy istorii blankizma v Rossii (Revoliutsionnaia doktrina P.N. Tkacheva),' *Voprosy Istorii,* 1971, no. 10, pp. 39-54.

CHAPTER ONE

The Origins of Russian Social Democracy

The brutal Russian suppression of the Polish Rebellion of 1863 helped bring to life a new organization, one offspring of which would, half a century later, destroy tsarism. The West European working class, awakening to a sense of its own latent power and its dignity, readily understood that a tyrant—Alexander II—who shot and hanged Poles seeking freedoms already won in the West posed a threat to all Europe. European labour therefore rose up in protest against the Tsar's brutality, and in so doing took a significant step toward unity. The International Working Men's Association, or First International, would surely have come into existence even without the Polish events of 1863, but the birth would have occurred later and the organization would have taken a different form. Its origins went deep into European history, especially, of course, to the French Revolution. And its first pronunciamento, as one historian has pointed out, 'was not the Inaugural Address [which Karl Marx wrote in 1864] but rather the *Communist Manifesto.*'[1] The *Manifesto* had first proclaimed on a wide and sustained basis the general idea, 'workers of the world, unite!' There had been some hopes that that idea, or rather a broader version embracing all democratically-inclined social groups, might become a reality in 1848-9, but the great uprisings collapsed and a period of reaction

1

and war followed. Out of the reaction came the First
International.

The International Association and the Secret Societies

After the Treaty of Paris wrote an end to the Crimean War,
Louis Bonaparte made a gesture of studied goodwill toward
the French working class, permitting a delegation to go to
England to propose the creation of a 'League of Workers of
All Nations'. The delegation was composed largely of Proudhonists, Parisian skilled workers attracted by the prospect of
reviving the old *sociétés de secours mutuels.*[2] In London, a mixed
group of ex-Chartists, trade unionists, an International Committee (composed of English radicals and various émigré
groups) and other individuals met the Frenchmen. The
International Committee had for some time been thinking
along the lines proposed by the French, whose initiative bore
fruit in August 1856. In that month, a group in London had
organized the International Association, the last important
precursor of the International Working Men's Association.

It remains impossible to piece together anything more than
a sketch of the history of the International Association.[3] In
addition to the groups already cited, the German Workers'
Educational Society, a group of skilled craftsmen, émigrés
who had been in the Communist League in the 1840's, helped
to form the new organization. Also involved were the London
Revolutionary Commune (a Polish émigré group) and the
Commune Révolutionnaire of the radical French émigrés.[4]
The organizational structure of the International Association
followed that of earlier societies, especially the Fraternal
Democrats of the 1840's, and that structure was to reappear
in the IWMA.[5] A central committee of five members of each
nationality in the Association co-ordinated activities and
information. There was to be an annual general meeting, and
the headquarters was to be in London.

A resolution adopted at the first meeting of the International Association stated in part,

> The . . . societies engage themselves to use all their power to
> induce the citizens of all countries to organise socialist and
> revolutionary national societies, to bind them together by

means of the general association, in order to make the international propaganda profit by the strength of the association of all the individuals, and the various national propaganda profit by the strength of the association of all the people, and so prepare the success of the future revolution—success which past revolutions could not achieve, for not having known and practised the law of solidarity, without which there is no salvation either for the individuals or for the people.[6]

These same ideas reappeared in the Provisional Rules and Statutes of the First International.

The dearth of information on the International Association is due in part to the fact that it was only semi-public. Deeply involved in it were Masonic groups, Blanquists in the Commune Révolutionnaire and a clandestine, quasi-Masonic organization known as the Philadelphians. Secret societies had flourished in Europe since the Middle Ages, and one of the most important, Freemasonry, had been a moral and sometimes political force in many countries since the 18th century. It is therefore not surprising that such societies were represented in the International Association, which clearly had a moral and a revolutionary mission. Many of these societies (Freemasonry usually excepted) were sympathetic to terror, applauding, for example, Felice Orsini's attempt on the life of Louis and Eugénie Bonaparte on January 14, 1858.[7]

The International Association did not have a very active public life until late in 1858, when it issued a manifesto rejecting Mazzini's exhortation to the European left to relegate the 'social question' to a secondary role and emphasize the various struggles for national independence, while co-operating with the middle classes. The International Association rebuked Mazzini, but the Poles, the Philadelphians and the Commune Révolutionnaire did not sign its manifesto.[8] Many members withdrew over the Mazzini issue. Some rejoined when a new central committee was elected in 1859, but the organization had clearly outlived its usefulness. It issued a manifesto on the Franco-Austrian War, held a last meeting in June 1859, then disappeared, leaving few clues to its identity.

Toward the Formation of the International, 1859-1863.

'So England celebrated a fresh triumph of her liberty!' Thus Alexander Herzen concluded his account of the rejoicing at the 'not guilty' verdict in the trial of Simon Bernard, Orsini's accomplice.[9] There was more reason for the exiled Russian writer and socialist to applaud later: the 'Conspiracy to Murder' Bill, which would have abrogated the right of political asylum and would have permitted foreign powers to exercise police jurisdiction over their nationals on British soil, died in Parliament. The Palmerston government fell with the bill, and that, coupled with mutiny in India, the T'ai P'ing Rebellion in China and economic crisis at home seemed to bode ill for Great Britain.

But the severe economic depression had reached bottom in 1857 and the nation began to recover. The labour movement in general was making modest gains, and the labour aristocracy—skilled workers and craftsmen—was making unprecedented advances. In 1859, the aristocracy formed the London Trades Council to provide 'mutual aid in disputes.'[10]

The London Trades Council played an important role in the founding of the International Working Men's Association. Before that took place, however, great events once again shook the world. Louis Bonaparte conspired with Cavour, his former partner in the Crimean War, to trick Austria into armed conflict. As a result of that encounter, Italy was united, France took Savoy and Nice, Garibaldi's reputation penetrated even to remote Russian and Polish villages, and the French Emperor came to believe himself invincible. The creation of the Kingdom of Italy took place on March 17, 1861. Two weeks earlier, Alexander II had decreed the emancipation of 22,500,000 Russian serfs, and three weeks later the United States plunged into civil war. Violence, upheaval and rapid change were again testing the stability of the European order and its overseas extensions.

The London Trades Council directed and publicized British labour's support for the Union in the American Civil War. Abraham Lincoln was keenly aware of the sacrifices this entailed: 'I know and deeply regret,' he wrote to a committee of British workers, 'the sufferings which the workers of Manchester are undergoing in this crisis. . . . Under these circumstances their conduct is an exalted example of Christian heroism, which has not been surpassed in any country in any epoch'.[11] The strongly pro-Union stance of labour helped dissuade Palmerston's second ministry (1859-1856) from following its natural inclination to intervene on the Confederate side.

In 1862 the captains of British industry held an International Exhibition in London, and more than mere material achievements were on display. So far had Great Britain come from the labour policies of the early Industrial Revolution that the government invited foreign workers to attend in order to see how splendidly their British counterparts were faring. About 750 French workers and a small Italian delegation (composed exclusively of Mazzinians) responded to the invitation. The British trade unionists regarded the Frenchmen with some suspicion, considering them all too comfortable with Louis Bonaparte's government, but that did not hinder discussion of further and stronger international contacts. George Odger and William Cremer agreed with the leader of the French delegation, Henri-Louis Tolain, to explore sentiment concerning the establishment of a permanent international working-class association. That was as far as things went in 1862; but the crucial first step had been taken. Enter now the Polish issue.

When detachments of the Russian army began breaking down doors in Polish cities and towns during the night of January 14-15, 1863, seizing young men secretly selected for conscription, Polish honour and self-respect—qualities long imperfectly understood by the tsars—demanded a response. Not since the reign of the unstable Paul I, grandfather of Alexander II, had such barbaric conduct occurred in Poland in peacetime. The Poles resisted, but after some initial successes the units of the revolutionary forces that dared to stand and fight were annihilated. The Russian government offered rewards and concessions to those who remained loyal, and few Polish peasants needed much encouragement to turn against the gentry. The successful attempt to split the Poles was accompanied by the introduction in Lithuania and

White Russia, where the rebellion had assumed a particularly serious form, of a regime of terror associated with the name of General M.N. Muravyov. Having earned the *epithetum ornans* 'Hangman' for his work in the suppression of the Polish insurrection of 1830-1, Muravyov proved that he had not forgotten the standards of that inglorious campaign. Alexander II professed distaste for his methods, but when rebellion threatened he gave Muravyov *carte blanche*. (General F.F. Berg, who succeeded the Grand Duke Constantine as viceroy in Poland at the end of the summer, copied the Muravyov 'system.'[12])

Protest against Russian action in Poland began as soon as the news reached the West. French diplomats in Geneva reported that the 'parti démagogique' in that city organized a mass meeting at which Wladyslaw Mickiewicz (son of the famous poet), the German '48-er J.P. Becker, and various Geneva politicians spoke in support of the rebels. The German Workers' Educational Society in London commissioned Karl Marx to write a proclamation on the rebellion. And the London Trades Council, which had planned to organize an international conference on working-class problems in the summer, resolved to include the 'Polish question' on the agenda.

A mass protest meeting attended by British, French, Italian and other working men, and by many émigré intellectuals, took place in London on July 22, 1863.[13] The issue of Poland—where the rebellion was dying—dominated the assembly, but other topics were discussed. A joint Anglo-French committee undertook the task of forming an international organization to advance working-class interests. George Odger was asked to compose a statement of principle. In November he produced a document calling for a 'gathering together of representatives from France, Italy, Germany, Poland, England, and all countries where there exists a will to co-operate for the good of mankind. Let us have our congresses; let us discuss the great questions on which the peace of nations depends.'[14] Odger urged the French and British workers to demand that their governments intervene on the side of the Polish rebels, but it had already become clear that neither London nor Paris would act. If the

European workers were to unite, they would do so in part in memory of Poland and not because there was any real chance they could help her.

The International Working Men's Association

On September 28, 1864, British, French, Italian, German and Polish workers, and several intellectuals who claimed to represent workers, gathered in St. Martin's Hall (owned by a Masonic lodge) in London to witness a formal exchange of messages embodying expressions of class solidarity. Poland figured centrally in those missives though the Polish cause had long since become symbolic and not a matter of practical concern. Several speakers observed that the working classes could have influenced the course of the late rebellion only if they had combined in sufficient strength to bring strong pressure upon governments. Solidarity was what the working class needed; solidarity was what it would have. The delegates resolved to form an international proletarian organization to be called the International Working Men's Association.[15]

Labour had created other such organizations, only to see them expire in the crush of governmental repression, war, or—most often—sheer apathy. There was nothing about that meeting in St. Martin's Hall that indicated the IWMA would be any more successful that its predecessors. And indeed, the factional disputes that had always plagued labour reappeared as Proudhonists, Blanquists, utopian socialists, trade unionists, communists, terrorists, members of secret societies and individuals of other persuasisons competed for supremacy in the fledgling organization.

The organizational meeting established a provisional Central (later General) Council, which began regular weekly meetings on October 5. The Council's first task was to prepare a programme and statutes for the International. Major Luigi Wolff, Mazzini's representative, offered a quick answer in the form of the statutes of the Associazione di Mutuo Progresso. These were, however, not to everyone's taste, and the proposals of a follower of Robert Owen (John Weston) were no more palatable. The Council then directed Victor Le

Lubez, a young French radical, to draw up a synthesis of the various suggestions. Le Lubez, as it happened, was a leading Philadelphian.

Karl Marx, who had been present at the inaugural meeting only (as he wrote to Engels) as a 'silent figure on the platform', was a member of the Central Council, and he was 'truly shocked' by the document Le Lubez presented. He wrote to Engels that it was 'awfully phraseological, badly written and immature ... pretending to be a declaration of principles, where Mazzini was peeping though everywhere, encrusted with vague scraps of French socialism.' Marx succeeded in blocking the proposal and himself drew up new documents.[16]

Marx had seen enough of the old conspiratorial societies—he had been a member of the Communist League—to be convinced that the future of the working class did not lie with them. The Provisional Rules and Inaugural Address he succeeded in passing through the Central Council made no concessions to such groups. Marx likewise gave nothing to the Mazzinians, and there was precious little for the Proudhonists, who constituted the largest single bloc in the founding group. He did give a perfunctory nod to the Owenites and to the co-operative movement, but the cautious documents he produced were clearly from the pen of the co-author of the *Communist Manifesto*. The Central Council unanimously approved those documents on November 1, 1864.[17]

The Inaugural Address would not have been complete without an attack upon Russia, and Marx did not disappoint the Poles and the rest of the Tsar's enemies:

The shameless approval, mock sympathy, or idiotic indifference, with which the upper classes of Europe have witnessed the mountain fortress of the Caucasus falling a prey to, and heroic Poland being assassinated by Russia; the immense and unresisted encroachments of that barbarous power, whose head is at St. Petersburg and whose hands are in every Cabinet of Europe, have taught the working classes the duty to master themselves the mysteries of international politics; to watch the diplomatic acts of their respective governments; to counteract them, if necessary, by all means in their power; when unable to prevent, to combine in simultaneous denunciations, and to vindicate the simple laws of morals and justice, which ought to govern the relations of private individuals, as the rules paramount of the intercourse of nations.[18]

The Address concluded with the famous exhortation, 'Proletarians of all countries, Unite!' But this time it was coupled with yet another revolutionary idea, namely, that the working classes had the right and the class duty to influence governmental policy. A new age of labour militancy was at hand.

Russian Developments

Oddly enough, the author of *The Misery of Philosophy*—the famous attack upon Proudhon—found it necessary temporarily to support the Proudhonists against those (such as Le Lubez and his fellow Philadelphians) who were trying to push the IWMA in a conspiratorial direction. The fate of the old Communist League had disillusioned Marx, who now favoured an open, legal organization of the working class. He supported the Proudhonists in order to eliminate what he considered a greater and more urgent danger.

The followers of Proudhon (who died in 1865) remained the strongest single faction in the International and Marx found them difficult, obstinate opponents. In October of 1865 a new element appeared, or seemed to: Marx suspected that the Russian émigrés, notably Alexander Herzen, were collaborating with the Proudhonists. This belief grew out of Marx's interpretation of an international student congress that took place in Liège. There, a radical Proudhonist minority plunged the assembly into an unexpected political debate, and a tiny Blanquist faction tried to revolutionize the meeting. Herzen had nothing whatsoever to do with either the Liège congress or the International, and the identity of the lone Russian who appeared among the students remains a mystery. Nevertheless Marx wrote to Engels that 'The Russian gentlemen have found their very latest comrades in the Proudhonized part or "Jeune France".'[19] Eleven years earlier Marx had refused to attend an International Committee banquet commemorating the revolutions of 1848 because Herzen would be there. At that time he had told Engels that

'I do not ever, anywhere want to be associated with *Herzen*, because I am not of the opinion that old Europe can be rejuvenated by Russian blood.'[20] And now, misjudging Russians as he often did, Marx thought Herzen was coming back to haunt him.

He might have spared himself the worry. Russian events were moving far beyond Alexander Herzen, whose glorious days in the late 1850's (he had edited the famous *Kolokol* [The Bell] in London) were never to return. The genteel, civilized Herzen, who never wholly extricated himself from some liberal illusions, was as shocked as any Russian at the news, in April 1866, that a young revolutionary named Dmitry Karakozov had tried to assassinate the Tsar. Herzen's surprise was genuine, despite the fact that the official Russian investigation indicated some connection between secret Moscow organizations to which Karakozov belonged and the Russian émigrés, notably Herzen himself. When a few weeks later, in May of 1866, Ferdinand Cohen (stepson of Marx's estranged friend Karl Blind) assaulted Bismarck, police authorities in Berlin and St Petersburg quickly became convinced that a 'European Revolutionary Committee', of which they thought Herzen a member, was planning political assassinations on an international scale.[21]

It was not so. There was no such 'Committee'. Karakozov acted alone, and his deed caused consternation and dismay among his closest friends. Alexander Herzen knew nothing about him. As for Cohen, who committed suicide in prison, even the Prussian police finally accepted the veracity of his last letter to Blind. In that letter, he wrote that his attempt on Bismarck's life would be a protest against the impending war between Prussia and Austria.

Dmitry Karakozov was hanged, after being thoroughly investigated by General M.N. Muravyov, in September 1866. Nicholas Ishutin, leader of the secret circles to which Muravyov had belonged, was sentenced to death, and two dozen other radicals received long prison sentences. Ishutin was on the scaffold when a courier dashed in with the news that the Tsar had commuted his sentence to hard labour 'in perpetuity.' (This obscene charade had a precedent: Nicholas I

had done the same thing to Dostoevsky and some of his
political associates in 1849.)

What the revolutionaries called the 'white terror' descend-
ed upon Russia. Opponents of the regime went underground
into small, secret cells which had little or no influence. This
was a time of despair in Russia, and the mood conveyed itself
to the émigrés in the West. Herzen, caught in the inexorable
grip of his declining years, lost all his influence. Michael
Bakunin, though soon to emerge as the leader of a new and
powerful anarchist movement, vegetated in Italy. None of the
young émigrés had yet won the right to speak for the
democratic left.

Where could the Russian revolutionary movement turn?
The leaders of the late 1850's and early 1860's, the 'men of the
'sixties' associated with the famous Land and Liberty (Zemlia
i Volia) group, were most of them in prison, as was Nicholas
Chernyshevsky, widely acknowledged as the leader of the
young radical generation. The philosopher and radical Peter
Lavrov, along with many others, went to prison or exile in the
aftermath of the Karakozov affair. The Russians were leader-
less and without a programme. They had only a vague and
undifferentiated cause no better defined now than it had been
earlier among the peasant insurrectionaries who, periodically
throughout Russian history, had emerged in incoherent,
desperate protest.

But there was hope, though few Russians knew of it. The
International Working Men's Association was now firmly
established, and it offered radicals of many hues an organizational home. It had two main political tendencies, neither of
which could be said, in 1866, to have triumphed. One was
Proudhonist, numerically superior and soon to become anarchist. The other was Marxist social democracy. It was not
long before the Russians too were to discover the International, and were to confront the need to choose between the two
tendencies.

The Russians needed the International more urgently than
they realized. All the émigrés longed to do something for the
movement inside Russia, as Herzen had done with his
Kolokol. They wanted to marshal their forces, summon up a
united voice and send it across the distances to the homeland.

Most émigrés retain a certain alienation in their new surroundings, but the Russians were worse off than most others. Germans felt reasonably at home in Geneva and London; Italians adjusted to life in the north; even the Poles got along well in the West. All of this testified to the essential unity of European culture. But Russia, though a part of that culture, was as it were a relative once removed who seemed at times an awkward visitor; and those who grew up on her uniquely melancholy soil rarely knew peace and happiness when they left it. The International would soon provide some of them a home.

Michael Bakunin, a hero of the revolutions of 1848-9 and a scapegoat of an ill-fated attempt to aid the Poles in 1863, had few illusions about the chances of implanting his latest organization, the International Alliance of Socialist Democracy, in Russia. And he knew there was no role in that country for the League of Peace and Freedom, a middle-class, pacifist organization (created in 1867) in which he played a showy if essentially impotent role. In any event the European left unanimously held that organization in contempt. Still less chance existed that the International, which Bakunin had joined and promptly forgotten soon after its founding, could operate even clandestinely in the 'dark kingdom'. What then, as Nicholas Chernyshevsky's famous prison novel had asked, was to be done?

Narodnoe Delo

After the 1867 (founding) congress of the League of Peace and Freedom, one of the Russian émigrés in Geneva, Nicholas Zhukovsky, approached Bakunin and requested his collaboration on a new journal. Zhukovsky's sister-in-law, Olga Levashyova, had agreed to put up 1,000 rubles for the enterprise.[22] Bakunin resisted at first, pleading his preoccupation with 'international propaganda'. But in the summer of 1868 he gave in (probably with less reluctance than he later claimed) and plunged into the work with characteristic energy and imagination. He wrote to a German friend:

> The principal work that occupies us is revolutionary propaganda in Russia aimed at the dissolution of that Empire, without which,

we believe . . . there can be no emancipation of the peoples there imprisoned by force. Enemies of panslavism as of pangermanism, as of panromanism and all the pan-isms of the world, we are Federalists, and, as Proudhon said, Anarchists, and above all Socialists.[23]

This was one of the earliest declarations of Bakunin's new politics, anarchism, toward which he had been tending for nearly two decades. He rarely defined his terms, and even when he did so his explanations were so lengthy and abstruse as to obscure precise definitions. There is thus no ready, brief and simple explanation of his anarchism. Suffice it to say that with Bakunin as with his predecessor Proudhon, anarchism was the politics of the rejection of politics.

Bakunin brought to this new concept the experience of the Russian revolutionary movement, segments of which still hoped for a mass peasant uprising, for a jacquerie like Stenka Razin's in the 17th century and Emelyan Pugachev's in the 18th. Such an upheaval, Bakunin and many other Russian radicals hoped, would overthrow the tsarist regime and the entire social system. What would replace them? Bakunin and those who thought like him believed that the natural goodwill and good sense of the people would nurture a new egalitarian, stateless society.

Several of the Russians who lived around Lac Léman agreed to co-operate with Bakunin and Zhukovsky. Notable among them were Bakunin's patroness Zoya Obolenskaya and her Polish lover, Walerian Mroczkowski; Victor and Catherine Bartenev; Nicholas and Natalie Utin; Michael Elpidin, a printer; and of course Olga Levashyova. But despite Nicholas Utin's presence on the unofficial editorial board Bakunin excluded him from participating on the first issue of the new journal. And this created a tense situation that boded ill for the project's future. Utin had been a prominent second-level leader of the old Land and Liberty society, had conspired with the Poles in 1863 and had made a dramatic escape from Russia. He had considerable organizational talent and wrote well, if verbosely. Beyond all that he was the lover of Olga Levashyova; and Bakunin could not bear the sight of him.

Michael Bakunin later wrote of that unpleasant conflict,

> [Utin] cannot even eat or drink simply—he cannot for a
> moment forget that he is a terrible revolutionary, a conspirator,
> that he is part of a great movement, that he is sacrificing
> himself . . . [he is] an industrious little Jew, a Tredyakovsky in the
> study of political and social problems.[24]

Notoriously anti-Semitic, Bakunin was also uncommonly
jealous of sexually vigorous males. He had little if any sexual
drive himself; the revolution consumed all his energies.
Behind his back, people joked that he lacked some essential
masculine accoutrements. And no one in the émigré community doubted the nature of Bakunin's wife's relationship
with Carlo Gambuzzi, an Italian hanger-on in Zoya Obolenskaya's entourage.

A big, burly, unkempt man, Bakunin looked like a seedy
lumberjack. His huge, leonine head held no teeth, for he had
lost them all to scurvy in his Siberian confinement. His voice
was sonorous, the cadences rolling, the pitch higher than one
would expect in a man his size. He smoked incessantly,
cadging cigarettes and cigars from friends, acquaintances and
passers-by. His financial woes were notorious but somehow he
managed to turn them into a virtue, and to convince the
unwary that, in buying him dinner and a bottle of wine, they
were advancing the cause of liberty. His idiosyncracies were
legion; but he was a leader who inspired the kind of
devotion—and hatred—that sometimes changes the course of
history.

His newest adversary and rival revolutionary, Nicholas
Utin, was the second son of a self-made vodka millionaire. A
brilliant student, Utin won a gold medal at St. Petersburg
University in 1861; Dmitry Pisarev, the famous nihilist, won
the silver medal in the same competition. Short, small and
intense, Utin had a quick tongue and manner. Basically petty
by nature, his judgment was often faulty, his sentiments
frequently ungenerous. He had few fixed principles. Nevertheless, he was a talented man who was to play a crucial role
in the émigré revolutionary movement.[25]

On September 1, 1968, the first issue of *Narodnoe Delo – La
Cause du Peuple* appeared at Elpidin's press in Geneva.[26] Of the
four articles published, Bakunin and Nicholas Zhukovsky

each wrote two. In the 'programme' of the new journal, Zhukovsky sought to convince the Russian radicals that their intellectual liberation was inseparable from the 'socio-economic liberation of the people'. He described *Narodnoe Delo* as materialist, atheist, and noted that it advocated the rearing of children not by their parents but by 'free society'. He continued,

> As the foundation of economic justice we advance two funda-mental theses: *The land belongs only to those who work it with their own hands—to the agricultural communes. Capital and all the tools of labour [belong to] the workers—to the workers' associations.*

Nothing less than the 'total destruction of the old society' could realize these goals. And after the abolition of the state, 'the future political organization must be nothing other than a free federation of free agricultural and factory-artel workers.'[27]

In his contributions, Bakunin attacked speculative philo-sophy from a positivist point of view . . . and then lashed out at positivism. He maintained that Hegel and Feuerbach had destroyed metaphysics and that their descendants Büchner, Moleschott and Karl Vogt (Marx's 'vulgar materialists') had advanced the cause of freedom on earth by destroying faith in heaven. But the fate of that cause still hung in the balance:

> The way to the liberation of the people through science is blocked to us; we have left, therefore, only one means, that of revolution . . . Our task is to prepare a general uprising through propaganda.

Declaring 'land and liberty' the goals of the Russian people and of *Narodnoe Delo*, Bakunin extended his hand to the survivors of the organization of that name, i.e. to the followers of Nicholas Chernyshevsky. Recognizing the despair they felt under the conditions of the 'white terror', Bakunin called out to the Russian radicals and urged them to recall the brave sacrifices of their predecessors. He exhorted the revolutionar-ies to be worthy of those who had gone before, and he promised to lead them.

Scattered, fragmentary evidence indicates that *Narodnoe Delo* lifted the spirits of the Russian radicals and brought them a glimmer of hope. Bakunin had issued a ringing summons to unity, to work. He had promised to lead. And he had presented that *sine qua non* of Russian revolutionism, an at least superficially plausible ideological programme.[28]

Narodnoe Delo after Bakunin

When *Narodnoe Delo's* editorial board met at her villa in Vevey in October of 1868, Olga Levashyova demanded that Bakunin and Zhukovsky grant Nicholas Utin an equal share in producing the journal. She was adamant; Bakunin could not stomach Utin; Bakunin and Zhukovsky resigned. Michael Elpidin too indicated his desire to withdraw from the project as quickly as possible.

Utin secured the co-operation of his wife, of Victor and Catherine Bartenev and of a few other émigrés. He summoned Anton Trusov, a printer, from Paris to take Elpidin's place. Edouard Bongard, a Swiss who had spent some time in a Siberian penal colony for revolutionary activities in Poland, also joined the Utin group.[29]

In late October, Utin and his associates published the second *Nardnoe Delo*. On the last page there was a note from Bakunin: 'In order to avoid groundless rumours, I request that you inform the readers . . . that I do not take any part in [the journal]'[30] The new editors referred to this communication in seeking to clarify their policy, claiming that they were 'not under the authority of anyone'. They promised not to change 'either the direction of the journal or its content'. And they noted that

> He who has read our [sic] programme conscientiously must have understood that it can only be realized through the destruction of all obstacles to the material and intellectual well-being of the people and the destruction of obstacles . . . to the creation of a new, free way of life.[31]

This amounted to Bakuninism without Bakunin, and it is this second issue of *Narodnoe Delo* that has confused Venturi and other scholars into an assertion that the programme and statutes of the Russian section of the International were drawn up by Bakunin.[32] Such was not the case. The Russian section, which was to grow out of the new *Narodnoe Delo* staff, was to profess views quite unlike those of the second issue of the journal. It is historically inaccurate to pin the ideological shortcomings of the journal's second issue upon the Russian section. It is true that the 'new, free way of life' resembled, in its meaningless ambiguity, Zhukovsky's 'free society'. Grasping for weighty phrases to describe the goals of the Russian revolutionary movement, one of the Utin group cited 'an entirely new mode of life, an entirely new social system in which everything is the opposite of the present order'.[33] It was in no sense an auspicious beginning; the Utin group's move to social democracy would come later.

For the historian, the most valuable information in the second *Narodnoe Delo* is a lengthy account of the revolutionary movement in Russia in the early 1860's. This was probably the work of Nicholas Utin, who alone in the group had such detailed knowledge of events.[34] He outlined the history of Land and Liberty, then moved on to the Ishutin groups, The Organization and Hell. Obliquely criticizing the martyred Karakozov, he insisted that the overwhelming majority of the radicals rejected political assassination as a policy. He maintained that the 'white terror' that invariably followed such outrages did not, as those who advocated assassination claimed, stimulate popular opposition to the regime. Thus the revolutionaries had no right to ask the masses or their fellow radicals to make further sacrifices of doubtful utility and uncertain benefit. (Among others, Sergei Nechaev and Peter Tkachev would soon expressly reject this argument.) While praising Karakozov as a dedicated revolutionary, Utin called him misguided and noted that his act led to intensification of the repression that had already brought Russia to 'starvation, spiritual and moral bankruptcy'.

Utin went on to urge the 'young progressive party' to educate the people, to make them understand the source of their misery. The radical youth must raise the consciousness of the masses. Groups inside Russia should work with the émigrés, for

the Cause of the Organization, its elements, people and means exist in Russia itself, and only the people there can and must lay

the cornerstone of the social Revolution. The cause of Propaganda can [however] be more conveniently served at present by an
organ published abroad . . . . Such a goal *Narodnoe Delo* wishes to
set itself . . . . [It] depends upon the Russian people to support it
with . . . its thought and counsel, and thereby to give it full
significance as the organ of the Russian revolutionary party.[35]

Though valuable, the Utin article was unremarkable in any
ideological sense, and most of the rest of the issue was, as we
have acknowledged, a mere continuation of the Bakunin-
Zhukovsky line. But the last article contained language that
had not previously appeared in any Russian publication, and
it provided a clue to the direction the Utin group would take.
Praising the International Working Men's Association, a
writer declared that:

> The idea of the complete and radical liberation of the people,
> baptized in blood on the June [1848] barricades, has matured
> and become stronger over the last twenty years. It celebrated its
> coming of age at the Brussels Congress of European workers;
> from Brussels it notified the whole world of the gigantic steps by
> which the new era is replacing the old: [the new era is] the era of
> a new life for all the masses of the working people, and of the
> destruction and disappearance of all the unproductive consumers
> who still oppress humanity, the era of the complete, equal
> development of man in society, the era of meaningful labour and
> complete equality.[36]

This was a translation of an address the Geneva International
had sent to the Spanish workers. J.P. Becker, Marx's friend
and an old '48-er, wrote it and urged Utin to publish it in
Narodnoe Delo. Becker was hardly a leading ideologist, and his
'new life for all the masses of the working people' was not
much of an improvement over Zhukovsky's verbiage. But the
talk of workers, barricades, and the Brussels (1868) Congress
of the International was a new vocabulary for a Russian
journal; in the first *Narodnoe Delo*, Bakunin had merely noted
the forthcoming Brussels meeting and had recommended that
his readers pay attention to the 'development of the labour
question'. Becker, on the other hand, was for all his shortcomings a bona fide social democrat and he was perhaps the most
effective single recruiter in the International. His efforts to

influence the new *Narodnoe Delo* group were to bear important fruit.

Harbingers of Russian Social Democracy

Nicholas Utin and his friends had broken with Bakunin and Zhukovsky over essentially trivial, personal issues, and they seemed for a short time unable to establish an ideological identity of their own. But in a significant document written toward the end of 1868, the group set forth its new politics. That document was the 'Russian Address to the Ghent Student Congress'. The first session of the international student meeting had taken place in Liège in 1865. The second—a purely Belgian affair—was held in Brussels in 1867, and the third (and as events proved, the final) session took place in Ghent in December 1868.[37] The *Narodnoe Delo* group's 'Address' was apparently discussed at the meeting, but it was published by a Brussels socialist newspaper only in January 1869.[38]

The statement contained some Proudhonist phraseology, but this might have been expected from a group that had, only months earlier, proclaimed its adherence to the programme of the first issue of *Narodnoe Delo*. Most of the document, however, indicated that the Utin circle was abandoning that earlier position. It called the new *Narodnoe Delo* and the 'party' it represented 'revolutionary socialist', and it continued,

> The present order is based solely upon the exploitation of the popular masses by a few thousand privileged individuals who, in order to defend their personal interests and make them prosper, have constituted themselves as a caste called the *leisure classes.* Now, this exploitation is itself only a natural consequence that flows from forced ignorance and abasement, in which the *bourgeois* system has condemned the people to stagnate .... [That system] is founded upon the usurpation of the labour, possessions and life of the people .... It is clear that the bourgeoisie would exhaust all its forces and means before letting the most fertile source of its riches, the ignorance of the masses, escape. ... We have seen how the bigwigs of industry in Paris threaten the workers with hunger and death by expelling them from the factories solely because these workers have formed unions ... and because these

gentlemen see in this act the 'subversive' tendency of the liberation
of the proletariat . . . . Brothers and comrades! We will not be so
blind as to fail to see that we are participating in the beginning of
the end, in the beginning of the last act of the bloody drama that is
being played out in the theatre of the war between the two worlds,
between the proprietor and the proletarian, between the world of
capital and that of poverty! Capital is going into its last, convulsive
fury, and poverty is summoning all its forces, dispersed over the
entire world, preparing to deliver a decisive blow to the mortal
enemy.[39]

With this statement, the *Narodnoe Delo* group embraced the
concept of the class struggle and in so doing took a giant step
toward social democracy. The members had obviously read at
least some of Marx's works, and they were clearly familiar
with the teachings of Blanqui. The bits and pieces of
Proudhon's thinking (which we have not quoted here) that
studded this Marxist-Blanquist amalgam were relatively
insignificant.

West Europeans had been discussing the class struggle for a
generation, but to Russians this was a new notion. Only very
rarely had the words 'capital', 'bourgeoisie' and 'proletariat'
occurred in the works of Chernyshevsky and other leftist
writers, and when they did they invariably referred to
developments outside Russia. Chernyshevsky and his disciples
believed that in Russia the great contest was between the
'people' (meaning above all the peasantry) and tsarism.
Capital and the bourgeoisie did not figure in the conflict
because they did not exist, at least not in the Western sense,
in Russia, where land remained the principal form of capital.
And of course without capital and a bourgeoisie there could
be no proletariat.

The new *Narodnoe Delo* group brought to Russian revolutionary theory the contention that, though the form of the
struggle for social justice was different in Russia and the
West, the essence was the same. Russian and Western
socialists fought against different kinds of oppression (tsarism,
capital) to emancipate different kinds of 'working people'
(peasantry, proletariat). The origin of this view lay in
Chernshevsky's theory of the pretermission in Russia of the
capitalist stage of economic development. Russia could

proceed directly to socialism, he had argued, from her existing quasi-feudalism without passing through the 'purgatory' of capitalism. The members of Nicholas Utin's circle adhered to this view.

Adherence to Chernyshevsky's voluntarist theories naturally precluded the adoption of Marxist determinism, and no one can argue seriously that the Utin group had, at this stage, gone over to Marxism. The members knew something of Marx's philosophy and agreed with it in considerable measure, but they did not express themselves in a form that would have won Marx's unequivocal approval and their projections differed from his. For example, they continued to ascribe a revolutionary role to the peasantry; Russian Marxists could do this after 1905 and get away with it, but in the 19th century it was heresy. Further, the Utin group misunderstood the nature and what Marx insisted was the 'historical mission' of the proletariat. Because the Russian proletariat was so insignificant in this period, it was difficult for any Russian radical to understand it. Despite all these caveats, however, we must note that the *Narodnoe Delo* circle basically accepted the teachings of the Marxists in the International, and they summoned their fellow radicals inside Russia to heed the 'voice and advice of socialist democracy'. This was apparently the third time that the term 'socialist democracy' had appeared in the Russian revolutionary movement. Bakunin used it in the formal name of his Alliance, and a young Russian socialist employed it—as we shall see in the next chapter—in a letter to J.P. Becker in the summer of 1868. Bakunin equated social (to use the more common form) democracy with anarchism, and in that he stood virtually alone. The Utin group conceived of the term as the sum of the International's aspirations: revolutionary overthrow of the existing order, nationalization of land and the means of production, creation of a new, democratic state order based upon equality. The Russian document presented at the Ghent student congress urged the students to join the workers in order to earn a role in the new society that the revolution would bring:

Let the students of all lands—openly or secretly—ask the

General Council of the International Working Men's Association, or the local central committee, to accept their adhesion and to authorize them to form sections of the International. Let the youth become aware of the great destiny of the International, of its eminent role in the march of the universal people toward the triumph of its cause; let the youth try to attain the level of these workers who ask only that someone formulate their ideas for them, but who summon all to unite with them and to assist one another in the common labour.[40]

This was a strong commitment, and its significance is not diminished by the fact that the *Narodnoe Delo* group was claiming to speak on behalf of a class, the proletariat, that was just emerging in Russia. Nor is its importance lessened by the group's non-Marxist affirmation of faith in the International, rather than the proletariat, as the vehicle of revolution.[41] That the group had ideological shortcomings is abundantly clear. Nevertheless, its members were refining their views, and they would soon become social democrats, fully-fledged members of the International.

NOTES

1. Gustav Jaeckh, *Die Internationale*, Leipzig, 1904, p. 3.
2. Many artisans, shopkeepers and skilled workers believed that the *sociétés* had never, owing to the restrictive legislation of 1850 and 1851, had a fair trial, hence their enthusiasm for Proudhonism. See Frederick A. de Luna, *The French Republic under Cavaignac, 1848*, Princeton, 1969, pp. 302-3.
3. See A. Müller Lehning, *The International Association, 1855-1859*, Leiden, 1938, and G.M. Stekloff, *History of the First International*, New York, 1928, pp. 30-2.
4. Julius Braunthal, *History of the International, 1864-1914*, London, 1966, pp. 79-80, and Alexander Herzen, *My Past and Thoughts*, 4 vols., pp. 17-28, and Alexander Herzen, *My Past and Thoughts*, 4 vols., London, 1968, vol. 3, pp. 1055-63, 1115, 1199n. On the London Revolutionary Commune see Peter Brock, 'The Socialists of the Polish "Great Emigration",' in Asa Briggs and John Saville, eds., *Essays in Labour History*, London, 1960, pp. 171-2.
5. On the Fraternal Democrats see *DFI*, vol. 3, pp. 268, 436-7.
6. Stekloff, *History of the First International*, p. 31.
7. Boris I. Nicolaevsky, 'Secret Societies and the First International', in M. Drachkovitch, ed., *The Revolutionary Internationals, 1864-1943*, Stanford, 1966, pp. 43-4.

8. Nicolaevsky, 'Secret Societies,' p. 45; Braunthal, *History of the International*, pp. 81-3.

9. *Memoirs*, vol. 3. pp. 1111-23.

10. G.D.H. Cole, *Marxism and Anarchism, 1850-1890* (Vol. 2 of *A History of Socialist Thought*), London, 1957, p. 6.

11. Quoted in Braunthal, *History of the International*, p. 87.

12. Z. Lenskii, 'Pol'skoe vozstanie 1863 g.,' in *Istoriia Rossii v XIX veke*, 9 vols., St Petersburg, n.d., vol. 3, p. 314n.

13. L.E. Mins, ed., *Founding of the First International*, London, 1939, pp. 69-72.

14. *Ibid.*, p. 4.

15. *Ibid.*, pp. 1-17, 53-68; Braunthal, *History of the International*, p. 92; Stekloff, *History of the First International*, pp. 34-50.

16. *Werke*, vol. 31, pp. 9-16, letter of Nov. 4, 1864.

17. Boris Nicolaevsky ('Secret Societies,' pp. 51-4) claimed that nearly a third of the Central Council was composed of Philadelphians, who thus had a 'decisive voice in all questions.' There is no evidence to support this view. See Jacques Freymond and Miklós Molnár, 'The Rise and Fall of the First International,' in Drachkovitch, ed., *The Revolutionary Internationals*, p. 8n.

18. *DFI*, vol. 1, p. 287. Marx wrote to Engels that he had inserted 'two "duty" and "right" phrases, ditto "truth, morality and justice",' but had placed them so that they could do no harm; see *Werke*, vol. 31, p. 15, letter of Nov. 4. 1864. Nicolaevsky ('Secret Societies,' pp. 53-4) argued that these phrases were 'something in the nature of [Philadelphian] slogans,' and that the Philadelphians exerted pressure upon Marx. This seems far fetched; such terms were dear to Owenites, Mazzinians, Proudhonists, co-operativists and sentimentalists of all varieties.

19. *Werke*, vol. 31, p. 169, letter of Jan. 5, 1866.

20. *Ibid.*, vol. 28, p. 434, letter of Feb. 13, 1855. See also E.H. Carr, *The Romantic Exiles*, London, 1968, p. 124.

21. M. Klevenskii, ' "Evropeiskii revoliutsionnyi komitet" v dele Karakozova,"' in B. Gorev and B.P. Koz'min eds., *Revoliutsionnoe dvizhenie 60-kh godov*, Moscow, 1932; M. Klevenskii, ed., *Pokushenie Karakozova. Stenograficheskii otchët po delu D. Karakozova, I. Khudiakova, N. Ishutina i drugikh*, Moscow-Leningrad, 1928-30; Otto von Bismarck, *Gedanken und Erinnerungen*, 3 vols. in one, Stuttgart, n.d., p. 299; 'N.N.,' 'Graf Bismark—organizator russkoi politicheskoi agentury zagranitsei,' *Byloe*, 1907, no. 6(18).

22. R.V. Filippov, *Revoliutsionnaia narodnicheskaia organizatsiia N.A. Ishutina—I.A. Khudiakova (1863-66)*. Petrozavodsk, 1964, pp. 55, 158, 173; *LN*, vol. 62, p. 136.

23. *Archiv für die Geschichte des Sozialismus und der Arbeiterbewegung*, vol. 1, p. 481.

24. Bakunin, 'Intrigi gospodina Utina,' in V. Polonskii, ed., *Materialy dlia biografii M.A. Bakunina*, Vol. 3, *Bakunin v Pervom Internatsionale*, Moscow-Leningrad, 1928, pp. 410-2. Peter the Great's daughter, the

Empress Elizabeth, appointed V.K. Tredyakovsky 'professor of Latin as well as Russian facundity' in 1745.

25. *TsGAOR*, f. III otd., 1 eksp., d. No. 97, 'O vozmutitel'nykh vozzvaniiakh,' ch. 90, 'O byvshem studente Nikolae Utine,' 1863 g.; L.F. Panteleev, *Vospominaniia*, Moscow, 1958, pp. 136, 245, 262, 313.

26. The name seems to have come from a pamphlet Bakunin published in London in 1862, 'Narodnoe Delo: Romanov, Pugachyov ili Pestel,' *Izbrannye sochineniia*, vol. 3, Petersburg-Moscow, 1920, pp. 75-91.

27. *Narodnoe Delo*, no. 1, September, 1868, pp. 6-7. This work appears in Bakunin's collected works, but he denied that he wrote it; see 'Discours prononcés au Congrès de la Paix et de la Liberté à Berne par MM. Mroczkowski et Bakounine,' Geneva, 1869. See also *Narodnoe Delo*, no. 2-3, October, 1868, p. 56 and *CMRS*, vol. 7, no. 4, pp. 659, 669, 695.

28. Varlaam Cherkezov, 'Znachenie Bakunina v internatsional'nom revoliutsionnom dvizhenii,' in Bakunin, *Izbrannye sochineniia*, vol. 1, 2nd edition, Petrograd-Moscow, 1922, p. 26; B.P. Koz'min *P.N. Tkachëv i revoliutsionnoe dvizhenie 1860-kh godov*, Moscow, 1922, p. 143; B.S. Itenberg, 'Rasprostranenie izdanii Russkoi sektsii I Internatsionala v revoliutsionnom podpol'e Rossii,' *Voprosy Istorii*, 1962, no. 10, p. 45; Venturi, *Roots of Revolution*, p. 352.

29. M. Elpidin, *Bibliograficheskii katalog. profili redaktorov i sotrudnikov*, Carouge (Geneva), 1906, pp. 20-1; *LN*, vol. 62, p. 688; B.P. Koz'min, *Russkaia sektsiia Pervogo Internatsionala*, Moscow, 1957, pp. 104-6; *Staatsarchiv* (Zurich), Y 60.27.291, 'Edouard Bongard von Bonnefontaine [*sic*] und Maximilian Syszkowsky aus Polen betr. Betrug. Criminal-Urtheil vom 12 Dezember 1874'; *Bundesarchiv* (Berne), Schweizerisches General-Konsulat in St Petersburg, 1862, 36, 'Bongard, Edouard, de Fribourg'; *AEG*, Etrangers, 1869, Dh 40, p. 8, 45035; *ibid.*, Dh 21. p. 151, 45035.

30. *Narodnoe Delo*, no. 2-3, October, 1868, p. 56.

31. *Ibid.*, p. 25.

32. See the preface to the present work. Venturi was merely careless, but B.P. Koz'min *(Russkaia sektsiia)* deliberately distorted the history of the section to make it appear a Bakuninist organization.

33. *Narodnoe Delo*, no. 2-3, October, 1868, pp. 26-7.

34   *Ibid.*, pp. 26-51. None of the articles were ever signed.

35. *Ibid.*, pp. 50-51.

36. *Ibid.*, pp. 51-56.

37. *La Flandre* (Ghent), December 21, 22, 25, 1868; *Journal de Gand*, December 27, 28, 1868; *Le Nord* (Brussels), December 24, 28, 1868; John Bartier, 'Etudiants et mouvement révolutionnaire au temps de la Première Internationale. Les congrès de Liège, Bruxelles et Gand,' in *Mélanges offerts à G. Jacquemyns*, Brussels, 1968, pp. 53-6.

38. *La Liberté*, January 10, 17, 1869.

39. *Ibid.*, January 10, 1869. The 'Adresse' was signed 'Antoine,' i.e. Anton Trusov, but it represented the combined efforts of the *Narodnoe Delo* staff.

40. These Russians knew their revolutionary history. On the eve of the
     February Revolution of 1848, Pierre Dupont wrote:
     > Eclairons les routes nouvelles,
     > Que le travail veut se frayer,
     > Le Socialisme a deux ailes,
     > L'étudiant et l'ouvrier!
     Quoted in *La Flandre*, December 25, 1868.
41. Marx later wrote in 'Critique of the Gotha Program,' 'In no way does
     the international activity of the working class depend upon the
     existence of the *International Working Men's Association.'* *Werke*, vol. 19,
     p. 24.

CHAPTER TWO

The New Russian Revolutionism

The movement of the *Narodnoe Delo* group toward the International and the earlier (1868) creation of Bakunin's Alliance constituted important steps for the revolutionary movement actually inside Russia because they provided potential new alternatives. In Russia itself, the movement had reached a dead end. The momentum generated by the reaction to the Crimean War and the Government's decision to emancipate the peasants reached a peak in the years 1859-61 and then began to decline. The radical opposition, numerically insignificant and lacking a mass base, could do nothing to bring about the great social change it regarded as the next logical step following the emancipation. The revolutionaries founded secret cells and communes, appealed—in vain—to the peasants to rise up against the Tsar, embraced the cause of Polish freedom, called themselves socialists and democrats. But all this activity little affected the dormant seeds of revolution, which were to mature and blossom only when fresh new winds from the West began to sweep over dark Russia.

Marxism in Russia

Russian intellectuals encountered the works of Marx and Engels in the 1840's. The critics Belinsky and Botkin favourably

26

reviewed Engels's 'Schelling und die Offenbarung'—believing, however, that Bakunin wrote it. They knew the work to be a product of the 'left Hegelian' school of thought, a new trend in German speculative philosophy that intrigued Russian contemporaries. Belinsky also knew the *Deutsch-Französische Jahrbücher* of Marx and Arnold Ruge (on which Bakunin *did* collaborate) and wrote to Herzen that he felt a kinship with the authors.[1]

Tsar Nicholas I clashed with Marx as early as 1842, when he demanded that his brother-in-law, Frederick William IV of Prussia, close down several newspapers hostile to Russia. The worst offender, in the tsar's view, was Marx's *Rheinische Zeitung*, which was published in Cologne. The Prussian government suppressed that newspaper in January of 1843; Marx left for Paris, unable to accept the 'special supervision' that was the king's condition for the revival of his newspaper.[2]

He arrived in Paris a celebrated opponent of the tsar. No one welcomed him more effusively than the local Russian colony. So long as Marx remained in the French capital—he left in 1845—nearly every democratically-inclined Russian traveller who passed through the city came to call upon him. Bakunin assisted with the sole volume published of the *Jahrbücher*; and a Third Section (secret political police) agent wrote to his superiors in St. Petersburg that all those associated with the *Jahrbücher* were dangerous revolutionaries. Had not the government of Louis Philippe expelled Marx and Ruge in 1845, Nicholas I would surely have made strong representations.[3]

Some of the members of the Petrashevsky political circles in the 1840's (including Dostoevsky), disciples of Fourier through the medium of Considérant, studied 'left Hegelian' works including a few early pieces by Marx and Engels. But these people, members of a generation cowed by the most savage tsar of modern times, were disinclined to perceive—let alone act upon—the revolutionary implications of German philosophy.

The period between the Revolutions of 1848-9 and the death of Nicholas I in 1855 was one of brutal reaction, the worst of a reign noted for unrelieved political and intellectual repression. No new ideas could take firm root in that obscurantist atmosphere. For a few brief years after 1855, however, the liberals dared hope that Russia might still enter upon an era of social justice. But as early as 1858, the extreme left denounced the travesty the government and landlords were preparing in the name of the emancipation of the serfs. Herzen on the moderate left, and every liberal in Russia, assailed Nicholas Chernyshevsky and his associates and followers for attacking the government on this issue. His attack upon Chernyshevsky ultimately cost Herzen all influence with the young generation, and the liberals, by supporting the government's version of an emancipation (which left the peasants in juridical, formal freedom and at the same time in economic bondage to the state and the landlords), ensured that their political philosophy would never take hold of the thinking of any significant segment of the population.

Vehemently rejecting the terms of the emancipation, but certainly not—as Herzen and the liberals charged—emancipation itself, Chernyshevsky and the 'men of the 'sixties' pushed the Russian revolutionary ethos to the Left, unwittingly preparing it to accept Marxism and deliberately destroying liberalism at its very birth. They developed a democratic-socialist program oriented toward peasant interests and based upon the social organism of the peasant commune. The teachings of Chernyshevsky, the young Herzen, Peter Lavrov and several other thinkers evolved into populism.[4]

Chernyshevsky knew something of Marxism, although precisely how much remains in dispute. In 1861 he or one of his associates defended western socialists in general and Friedrich Engels in particular against a German economist's attempt to portray them as 'utopians.' N.V. Shelgunov discussed the French and British proletariat in Chernyshevsky's *Sovremennik* (The Contemporary) and in the course of so doing approvingly summarized Engels's *The Situation of the Working Class in England in 1844*.[5]

By the mid-1860's, many Russian radicals had at least a passing acquaintance with Marxism. Peter Tkachev discussed *Zur Kritik der politischen Oekonomie* publicly and sympathetically in 1865. The 'Ruble Society' of Felix Volkhovsky, Herman

Lopatin and others planned, in 1867-8, to translate that and other works of Marx into Russian (the plans did not materialize). Peter Lavrov paraphrased the introduction to the *Communist Manifesto* in an article in 1864 but neither indicated the source nor pursued the argument.[6]

A Russian émigré who briefly played an active role in the Geneva organization of the International, Alexander Serno-Solovyovich, considered translating Marx's works into Russian. At J.P. Becker's urging, Marx had sent a copy of *Capital* to Serno-Solovyovich. The latter promptly wrote to friends in Russia asking whether a publisher could be found for a translation. When the friends replied that someone else already planned to translate the work (nothing ever came of this), Serno-Solovyovich, who did not fully comprehend the importance of Marx's study, simply forgot the matter.[7]

The next Russian enquiry was to bear fruit of historic dimensions. Late in September 1868, a young Russian radical, Nicholas Danielson, wrote to Marx that a St. Petersburg publisher wished to commission a translation of *Capital*. Assuming that Marx would be interested, Danielson pointed out the desirability of acquainting the Russian public with his earlier works. He complained, however, that 'in all Prussia we have found nothing except *Zur Kritik, Misère de la philosophie* . . . and *Manifest der Kommunistischen Partei*. We have not even been able to find your famous *Deutsch-Französische Jahrbücher.*'[8]

Danielson's letter betrayed the gaps in his knowledge. Since he obviously had a copy of *Capital*, he possessed all Marx's most significant works (the *Jahrbücher* belonged to a period Marx had left behind). And there was also a minor element of mystery in Danielson's letter. His reference to Prussia, it would seem at first glance, was a slip of the pen. He had, however, sent his letter not directly but through a friend, Nicholas Liubavin, who was then studying in Berlin, and it was Liubavin who had scoured Prussia for Marx's works.[9]

Liubavin was a friend not only of Danielson but also of Lopatin, Volkhovsky and the other members of the Ruble Society, of which he himself had been a member and in which the idea of translating Marx's works into Russian enjoyed wide support. Whether Liubavin went to prison along

with the other members of the group in 1868 remains
unknown; if he did, he obtained his release in time to go to
Prussia in the summer of that year to continue his studies. In
July he visited Leipzig. Motivated no doubt by his observa-
tion of the vigorous Saxon working-class movement, he wrote
to Geneva asking for copies of *Der Vorbote*, which J.P. Becker
published.[10]

Becker promptly sent Liubavin the periodical and some
literature on the International, suggesting that he join the
organization. After a few weeks' reflection the young Russian
accepted the invitation. He wrote to Becker,

> I agree completely with the goal of your society ... and I
> consider your methods expedient. I even recognize the liberation
> of the working class as the common cause of all peoples; but I
> recognize this *only in principle!* I cannot yet apply this principle to
> my country, where no labour movement whatsoever exists, even
> though we need one more than any other country ... The
> situation of our factory workers is much worse than that of the
> West European workers ... In addition to this there is unchecked
> police tyranny, from which all suffer equally. And there is no
> help for it; we still do not have a popular movement. The reasons
> for this are probably, 1) the apathy of our educated people,
> particularly marked in recent years; and 2) the lack of political
> freedom. We have no freedom of the press, no freedom of
> assembly; if the police take a dislike to someone, they can send
> him away from his residence without a judicial sentence ...
>
> As a consequence of all this, we cannot offer any help to the
> West European labour movement, nor can you help us; in other
> words, international solidarity—the main principle of your
> society—does not presently exist for us Russians. It will appear
> only when an independent social-democratic movement comes
> forth .... And so you see that, for us Russians, there are presently
> no grounds for being in closer touch with the International
> Association. If I [myself] enter into relations ... it is only because
> I ... will have the opportunity to become better acquainted with
> the West European labour movement ... [11]

Liubavin thus became the third Russian—after Bakunin
and Alexander Serno-Solovyovich—to join the International
and the first to proclaim himself a social democrat. And the
project to translate *Capital* into Russian grew out of his
correspondence with J.P. Becker. The latter had encouraged

his young Russian recruit in his study of social democracy and had persuaded him to become a member of the International. Liubavin soon related all this to Danielson, Lopatin and other friends; and within a short time Danielson was writing to Marx himself.

Although the evidence has some gaps, the following sequence of events surrounding the translation of *Capital* is consistent with the known facts. At some point in his correspondence with Liubavin, Becker (whose letters have not survived) suggested that he and his friends undertake a Russian translation of Marx's *chef-d'oeuvre*. Becker had probably suggested the same thing to the unstable Serno-Solovyovich. Liubavin relayed the proposal to St. Petersburg, sending also those of Marx's works he had found in Prussia and a copy of *Capital* obtained from Becker. A trained economist, Danielson immediately recognized the significance of the latter work and persuaded N.P. Poliakov, then the only publisher in Russia who dared touch radical material, to sponsor a translation.

The Liubavin-Becker correspondence, and the prior enquiry of Serno-Solovyovich, supply—with this new interpretation of Danielson's letter to Marx—the missing links in the story of the Russian translation of *Capital*. The work certainly had not become so well known that the public was clamouring for a translation, nor did the publisher have much of a chance of reaping a financial windfall. The intiative had to come from outside Russia, and it did.[12]

Liubavin forwarded Danielson's letter to Marx on October 2, 1868.[13] Two days later (this was an era of superb postal service) Marx had not only received it but had posted it along to Engels, noting, 'It naturally makes me extraordinarily happy to hear that my book will appear in *Russian* translation in St. Petersburg.'[14] Marx replied to Danielson a few days later, urging him to proceed with publication of the first volume. The second, he wrote, would not be ready for six months (in fact, fifteen years elapsed before it appeared). He sent along his photograph and *curriculum vitae* (which Danielson had requested) but he could not send copies of all his works because 'la plus belle fille de France ne peut donner que ce qu'elle a.'[15]

Commenting to a friend upon his success among the Russians, Marx wrote,

> It is an irony of fate that the Russians, whom I have fought without interruption for twenty-five years . . . were always my 'patrons.' In Paris in 1843-1844 the local Russian aristocrats spoiled me. My pamphlet against Proudhon . . . and [Zur Kritik] had nowhere such a large circulation as in Russia [this was incorrect]. And the first foreign nation to translate *Capital* is the Russian. But one must not exaggerate all this. In its youth the Russian aristocracy was educated in German universities and in Paris. They always snatch at the West's extremes. It is pure gourmandism, like that practiced by the French aristocracy in the eighteenth century. Ce n'est pas pour les tailleurs et les bottiers, as Voltaire said of his own enlightenment. This does not stop these same Russians, once they enter state service, from becoming scoundrels.[16]

The Bakunin Translation

Fulfilling the decision to translate *Capital* presented difficulties, not the least of which was Marx's lack of followers in Russia who would willingly go to prison for the cause. The translation project was legal enough, but others in which the members of the former Ruble Society were—or had been— involved were not. Constantly skirting the ill-defined edge of official tolerance, Danielson, Lopatin, Volkhovsky and their colleagues (who never abandoned their chief goal, the forcible liberation of Chernyshevsky) did not widely publicise the plan to disseminate the works of a well-known foreign socialist. The police stepped up their surveillance of subversives real and potential during the student unrest of 1868-9, making caution doubly necessary. Thus, as the initiative to produce a Russian version of *Capital* had come from abroad, so did the translation itself. Enter Michael Bakunin.

Having learned of the project from Becker, Bakunin asked him for the address of the 'nouveau jeune russe, Mr. Danielson.' When he received it, he began writing to the Danielson circle, one member of which (M.F. Negreskul) visited him in Geneva in the summer of 1869. The subject of Bakunin's embarrassing financial situation arose. Negreskul told Liubavin about Bakunin, and Liubavin passed the information along to Danielson. The latter promptly arranged for the latter to do the *Capital* translation for the sum of 1,200 rubles, of which 300 were paid in advance.[17]

The news spread rapidly. At the end of September, 1869, Alexander Herzen wrote to his friend Nicholas Ogaryov,

> God grant Bakunin success with the translation of Marx, but I just do not understand one thing: why did he keep his relations with him on the sly? All my conflict with the Marxites is because of Bakunin.[18]

The last remark was untrue, for Herzen and Marx had cordially detested one another for nearly two decades. But Herzen was morally in the right, for Bakunin had denied their friendship in December of 1868 in order to curry favor with Marx and the International.[19]

The prayers of Herzen and the efforts of Bakunin fell short of fulfillment. Bakunin had undertaken the translation lightheartedly, considering it a relatively painless way to earn a handsome sum. He quit after a few pages; his was not the temperament for sustained, solitary work.[20] He did not return the retainer, having spent it immediately, but that was the least of the complications that followed.

In February 1870 one of Bakunin's new friends wrote to Liubavin in the name of the 'Bureau of Foreign Agents of the Russian Revolutionary Society "The People's Summary Justice".' Signing himself secretary of that body, the friend referred to a communication concerning Liubavin that he had received from a 'Committee' inside Russia. That communication, he reported, noted that 'some Russian lords, liberal dilettantes, who live abroad' had taken advantage of the desperate financial circumstances of 'people of certain convictions' (i.e. Michael Bakunin) in order to exploit those people and deprive them of the opportunity to work for the 'liberation of humanity.' Among those 'lords' was the 'real kulak-bourgeois' Nicholas Liubavin, who had 'recruited the well-known Bakunin to do a translation of Marx's book.' Somehow this project embodied a scheme to prevent Bakunin from 'continuing to take part in the present fiery Russian popular cause, where his participation is indispensable.'

Unable to tolerate this, the 'Committee' directed its 'Bureau of Foreign Agents' to inform Liubavin that, 1) if he and his friends thought the translation desirable, they should do it themselves, and 2) he should inform Bakunin that he was released from the project. The 'secretary' directed Liubavin to telegraph this message to Bakunin at once and follow the telegram with a letter. Should he fail to comply, the writer warned, the 'Bureau' might have to fall back upon measures 'urgent and therefore a little rough.'[21]

Enter Nechaev

The 'secretary,' the 'Bureau,' the 'Committee' and the 'Society' were all one and the same: Sergei Gennadievich Nechaev. And we encounter, in this and subsequent episodes, one of the strangest figures in the Russian revolutionary movement. There exists neither a satisfactory biography of the man nor a definitive study of his role in the movement, and Nechaev's work against the First International has received, by and large, polemical treatment. As a measure of the political and psychological mystery that still confronts us, we note that the character of Peter Verkhovensky in *The Possessed*, though not intended by Dostoevsky as a portrait of the revolutionary *wie er eigentlich gewesen ist*, remains the best approximation of a serious study of Nechaev's personality.[22]

Born in Vladimir province in 1847, Nechaev was the son of a house painter. In 1865 he fled the deadly boredom and inertia of provincial life and went to Moscow to study at a pedagogical institute; how he financed this move is unknown. Failing to obtain a diploma, he went to St. Petersburg to continue his studies. In the capital, he apparently was the beneficiary of a tuition fund established for needy students by the students themselves.[23] In any event he obtained his teaching certificate and became an instructor at the St. Sergius parochial school.[24]

By coincidence Nechaev had arrived in St. Petersburg in the month of Dmitry Karakozov's attempt on the life of the tsar, April 1866. The tension and excitement of that spring and summer made a profound impression upon him as indeed upon most of the youth in the capital and in Moscow.

Nechaev very quickly drew close to radical circles. Fragmentary evidence indicates that an acquaintance, a student at the medical school, using copies of Henri Rochefort's famous *La Lanterne* as a text, taught Nechaev French and along with it a certain amount of the revolutionism that was endemic among medical students.[25]

Nechaev was associated with—we do not know whether he joined—the mysterious 'Smorgon Academy,' one of the post-Karakozov groups that hid so deeply underground that the police learned of its existence only after its demise in 1869. Through that group he entered the student radical circles that appeared during the uneasy winter of 1868-9. The Third Section defined two major categories of students in those circles. The first had purely student motivations and grievances and agitated for changes in the disciplinary system, scholarships for poor students, and the right to hold meetings, wear long hair and associate freely with members of the opposite sex. The other category of participants took up political causes.

The authorities did not like the attitudes and practices of the first group, seeing in them signs of moral decay, but this was an understandable, presumably mangeable problem. The second group posed a danger manifestly more serious, and its members—the Third Section claimed—frequently infiltrated legitimate student organizations and movements in an attempt to transform academic or administrative complaints into political issues. Further, these infiltrators were frequently not students at all but auditors, ex-students and hangers-on.[26]

After his graduation from the pedagogical institute of the University, Nechaev belonged to this latter sub-group. He had no money, dressed like a coachman, and spoke in provincial accents that amused the sophisticated St. Petersburg democrats. Small, thin-lipped and moody, scarred by severe acne, Nechaev was unpopular with women and an unpleasant riddle to most men. But he clung tenaciously to the fringes of the radical movement, and perhaps in compensation for his undistinguished background and unattractive appearance he associated with the extreme left wing, that is, with the groups which were beginning to advocate terror.

Such groups were few in number and they had little

influence. The overwhelming majority of students in St. Petersburg (at the University, the several technical institutes and the Medical-Surgical Academy) adhered to a programme of legal struggle against the regime. They hoped to raise the social and political consciousness of the 'people,' by which they meant the intelligentsia, the student youth, the bureaucracy, professional men, the officer corps and skilled workers. Raising the consciousness of the peasantry still seemed as hopeless as draining the sea. The students advocated peaceful propaganda through the legal press and through their own 'proclamations' and brochures, they urged social service through the *zemstvos* (rural institutions of self-government), and they called vaguely for the 'development of the productive forces of the people and the country,' that is, 'socialism' as they then understood the term.[27]

Nechaev agreed with some of these points but on many issues he stood alone. He was already, in the winter of 1868-9, advocating a programme of terrorism. Not only did he call for the assassination of public officials, he also insisted that anyone who left any of the secret student groups (for example, the Smorgon Academy) should be put to death. In this he had no supporters, although, according to his former colleague George Enisherlov, all the students agreed that all actual traitors should be executed.[28] This policy was soon, in Nechaev's hands, to have tragic consequences.

Nechaev was assigned by the student groups to agitate at the University and at the Forestry Institute.[29] He seems to have had little success, and he made only a tiny handful of friends: Enisherlov, Vladimir Orlov, L.B. Goldenberg-Getroitman (whom he met in the Smorgon Academy) and perhaps one or two others.[30] He was trying, without a great deal of success, to create his own circle, and well might he do so: he alienated the vast majority of those with whom he came into contact with his advocacy of an extreme Jacobin program. At one point in the autumn of 1868 a mass meeting took place at which one student, Stepan Ezersky, vigorously attacked both Nechaev and Bakunin, calling them false prophets and defending the moderate course on which the student movement was set. (Ezersky was able to link the two men because a brochure entitled 'Progam of Revolutionary

Action,' which Nechaev wrote in collaboration with Peter
Tkachev, owed a certain debt to the first *Narodnoe Delo*.[31])
Enisherlov recalled in his memoirs that, of the approximately
150 students at that meeting, not a single one defended
Nechaev.[32]

With his extremism and his insistence upon conspiracy
rather than open, legal protest, Nechaev had become both an
embarrassment and a potential danger to the student movement. Deserted by his associates (Enisherlov went so far as to
urge that he be killed), Nechaev found himself virtually alone
in St Petersburg. He had made some converts among the
Moscow students who occasionally visited the capital but he
had alienated others, notably Felix Volkhovsky. Volkhovsky
was a member of the old Ruble Society, now defunct, and
one of his fellow members, Herman Lopatin, would soon
come back to haunt Nechaev.[33] The St Petersburg students,
rejecting Enisherlov's proposal to do away with Nechaev,
decided to send him abroad. It would, they knew, be easy to
convince him that his arrest was imminent and that he
should flee. Once abroad, the students reasoned, he would
never return: he had compromised himself with them by his
policies and with the government by his flight. In Western
Europe, Enisherlov agreed, he would 'join the Genevans [i.e.
Bakunin] and develop his theories.'[34]

Nechaev had won notoriety and a few followers with his
violent rhetoric and his threats of terrible vengeance against
society. His was a scream of anguished frustration rather than
a reasoned analysis or a coherent plan, but his very stridency
drew an audience. Together with his then colleague, Peter
Tkachev, he mastered the rudiments of communism, conspiracy and terrorism; this was to lead both men, quite naturally,
to the teachings of Blanqui. In the long run those teachings
were to exercise a profound influence upon Russian radicals.

A small group of students arranged matters. Nechaev was
'kidnapped,' given a passport that belonged to N.N. Nikolaev
(a Moscow revolutionary) and some money, and sent out of
Russia on an English ship. A student threw a note out of
the carriage that was purportedly taking Nechaev to prison; it
fell to the lot of Vera Zasulich to 'find' this note and—

together with Nechaev's sister Anna—announce to the rest of
the students that one of their number had been arrested.[25]

Nechaev and Bakunin

Nechaev went first to Brussels, then on to Geneva, where he
promptly sought out Bakunin. He claimed to represent a vast
revolutionary conspiracy, one that would—as the pamphlet
he and Tkachev had written promised—launch an uprising
in February 1870, on the anniversary of the emancipation. He
presented himself to Bakunin, as Enisherlov wrote, as
'Nechaev the sufferer, Nechaev the martyr for his convictions,
the ringleader of a great "party of action", arrested by the
Russian government, a state criminal, finally—a hero who
had escaped . . . from the [Peter-Paul] fortress itself.'[36]

Duly impressed, Bakunin solemnly issued Nechaev card no.
2771 (the first and only in the series) of the 'Russian Section
of the World Revolutionary Alliance.' That organization did
not exist except in so far as Bakunin may have created, in his
own mind, a Russian division of his Alliance. Nechaev said
that his friends in Russia needed money. Bakunin had long
eyed the famous Bakhmetev fund, which an eccentric Russian traveller had given Herzen 'for the revolution' some
years earlier, for himself. Now he helped Nechaev obtain half
the money, about 10,000 French francs.[37]

Alone among the émigrés, Bakunin and Herzen's besotted
friend Ogaryov welcomed Nechaev to Geneva. Herzen himself wanted nothing to do with the new arrival and handed
over the Bakhmetev money only with the greatest misgivings.
The new *Narodnoe Delo* group kept Nechaev at a distance,
probably because Enisherlov had communicated to them his
own conviction that Nechaev was a 'spy, agent and investigator.'[38] That charge did not stick, however, not least because
most of the émigrés could not believe that the Russian
government would hire a man who had (as Ogaryov said) the
'manners of a muzhik.'[39]

Although Bakunin and Nechaev began an intense period of
collaboration, Nechaev played only a very minor role in the
public Alliance, and the evidence suggests that he knew
nothing about the secret wing Bakunin had established. With

the money Bakunin had obtained for him, Nechaev launched an extraordinary propaganda campaign to convince the émigrés that he was the leader of a powerful organization in Russia, and to convince the revolutionaries in Russia that he had overnight become the director of a powerful organization in the West. For five months in 1869 Nechaev bombarded Russia with leaflets, pamphlets, brochures, proclamations, personal letters and other literature. At one St Petersburg post office the police seized 560 items addressed to 387 different individuals. Most of this material bore the signature, 'Your Nechaev.' The name of Bakunin appeared on a few items.[40]

The material that Nechaev and Bakunin (principally the former) sent into Russia was of the most bloodthirsty variety, calling as it did for regicide, popular uprisings, the massacre of the landlords and similar measures. Their opponents later charged that Nechaev and Bakunin were trying, with these incredible measures, to compromise their enemies inside Russia. Such viciousness was alien to Bakunin's nature, but Nechaev was unquestionably guilty as charged. It is not easy to understand how he could have deliberately compromised even his own sister, who received some of the material, but we have already observed that no one has ever explained Nechaev's character. By contrast, Bakunin's role in the scheme is easy to comprehend: gullible, careless and under the sway of his compatriot's powerful personality, Bakunin simply acquiesced in what he thought was the spreading of the message of revolution around Russia.[41]

Many scholars have analyzed the propaganda Bakunin and Nechaev sent to Russia (without, however, enquiring into their motives), and the briefest of summaries must suffice here. The two men urged the revolutionaries to abandon all social and moral standards: 'Day and night . . . [you] must have one single thought, one single purpose: merciless destruction!' The revolutionary must have no interests, no concerns other than the revolution—the utter obliteration of the old society. He should use any weapon, not shrinking from blackmail, deceit, fraud, theft, even murder. Nechaev and Bakunin praised Karakozov and Berezowski for attempting to assassinate the Tsar and they urged the revolutionaries to emulate them.

The unrestrained advocacy of violence and terror distinguished the Nechaev-Bakunin program from its predecessors, and in the Russian context it presented an original contribution to revolutionism.[42] Terror was the instrument that would wake the demon of retribution that slept within the peasant's breast. The false emancipation of 1861 stirred that demon, and the approaching anniversaries of the great Razin (1670-1671) and Pugachev (1773-1775) uprisings justly, Nechaev and Bakunin wrote, filled the landlords and bureaucrats with terror.

And yet the two terrorists had their doubts. Still loyal to the crown, the peasant masses might rise against the landlords and bureaucrats but leave the heart and soul of tsarism untouched. Hence terror had another task: to prolong the orgy of destruction until it embraced all institutions in Russia including the throne. Violence would create its own new, egalitarian forms and 'free' institutions when the old ones had fallen.

This propaganda campaign, which involved about a dozen separate initiatives, was an odd fusion of peasant insurrectionism, terrorism, Blanquism, Proudhonism and a bit of the Hegelian dialectic; all that added up to a peculiarly Russian anarchism. One of the most famous of the campaign's publications, Nechaev's 'Catechism of a Revolutionary,' appealed for the creation of a revolutionary conspiracy to ignite the elemental violence of the masses. This programme had been expressly rejected in 1868 and a more moderate one substituted for it, but now—in 1869—it was espoused by small cells of 'Nechaevists' in the two capitals.[43]

In St Petersburg there was a strange sequel to all this. Some of the students wanted to send assassins to Geneva to kill Nechaev, and others wanted to kill him 'not physically but morally' by exposing his utterly insignificant role in the student movement. It was finally decided, however, that Enisherlov would accept responsibility for the proclamations and would himself go to prison to spare Tkachev, Felix Volkhovsky and other leaders who were sorely compromised by the shenanigans of Nechaev and Bakunin.[44]

It proved, however, more difficult to get oneself arrested than Enisherlov had thought. He went to Moscow, where the police were even more vigilant than their counterparts in St Petersburg, but he found the authorities very patient. He plastered new proclamations everywhere, talked loudly in public of his deeds—but no one came to arrest him. Only after some weeks was he able, practically on bended knee, to convince the police to take him into custody. And even then they did not believe his story.[45]

The 'Communist Manifesto' in Russian.

The best-known work of the Nechaev-Bakunin propaganda campaign of 1869 was neither the 'Catechism' nor indeed any other work from the pens of the two men. It was the *Communist Manifesto*.

Russian was the third major European language into which the complete *Manifesto* was translated. The fact that twenty years elapsed before the appearance of that translation testified to the slight impact the revolutions of 1848-9 had had upon Russia. (A Russian émigré translated half the work into French in 1851, but that insignificant venture had no connection with the spread of Marx's ideas to Russia.) Nicholas Danielson told Marx in September 1868 that his circle knew the *Manifesto*. Early the following year, Nicholas Liubavin twice asked J.P. Becker for the work, apparently intending to send it to friends in Russia. But until Sergei Nechaev came to Geneva, no one considered translating the famous document into Russian.[46]

Most historians have casually assumed that Bakunin first translated the *Manifesto* into Russian.[47] A comparative reading of the 1869 translation and the original, however, casts grave doubts—as Bert Andréas first pointed out—upon the assumption. The translation contains errors that Bakunin, who was fluent in German, simply would not have made. Further, the printer (Czerniecki) did not mention Bakunin when he wrote to Ogaryov about the project, and Bakunin, not a modest man, never claimed to have translated the work. Late in 1872, Nicholas Utin told Marx that Bakunin *and Nechaev* had done the translation. All the available evidence suggests, however, that Nechaev's share of the labour was much the greater.[48]

First, his association with Tkachev would account for a prior knowledge of Marx's works. He knew German imperfectly; this would explain the errors and the fact that several passages are missing. Further, the second issue of one of Nechaev's ephemeral publications, *Narodnaya Rasprava (The People's Summary Justice)*, clearly implied that the *Manifesto* translation could have been his own work. And moreover: Nechaev wrote almost all the items involved in the 1869 campaign, and he used the same printer—Czerniecki—for them as for the *Manifesto* translation. The facts and clues at our disposal strongly suggest that Nechaev did the translation with at the most some minor advice from Bakunin.[49]

The translator's identity is obviously less important than the appearance of the revolutionary classic in Russian. That indicated that the Russian revolutionaries were coming out of the political and social backwaters of Europe, and were making fresh explorations into the international socialist movement. The most famous of their number, a man who had almost no influence in Russia itself, Michael Bakunin, was about to launch a massive anarchist attempt to seize control of the International Working Men's Association. Some of Bakunin's former associates had taken over his journal, *Narodnoe Delo,* and were moving steadily away from Bakuninism toward social democracy. Radicals inside Russia were planning to support a translation of *Capital*. And a fanatical young man who was to become the most notorious 'nihilist' of them all came out of Russia in the spring of 1869 like a revolutionary comet and brushed all too close to his new and former associates.

Previously immured in the shabby student dormitories of St Petersburg and Moscow, in the fashionable homes of reactionary fathers, in the dark eastern steppes and forests, the young Russian radicals were now emerging from their isolation. The period of a unique, separate Russian revolutionary movement was nearing its end. In this realm too, Russia was to join Europe.

NOTES

1. A.L. Reuel', *Russkaia ekonomicheskaia mysl' 60-70-kh godov XIX veka i marksizm,* Moscow, 1956, pp. 180-1; P. Orlovskii, 'K istorii marksizma v Rossii,' in V. Bazarov (V.A. Rudnev), ed., *Karl Marks: K dvadtsatipiatiletiiu so dnia ego smerti (1883-1908),* St Petersburg, 1908, p. 353. On Marxism in Russia see also Sh. M. Levin, *Obschchestvennoe dvizhenie v Rossii v 60-70-e gody XIX veka,* Moscow, 1958; Iu.Z. Polevoi, *Zarozhdenie marksizma v Rossii,* Moscow, 1959; Bernhard Dohm, *Marx und Engels und ihre Beziehungen zu Russland;* Berlin, 1955; Institute of Marxism-Leninism of the Central Committee of the CPSU, *Literaturnoe nasledstvo K. Marksa i F. Engel'sa: Istoriia publikatsii i izucheniia v SSSR,* Moscow, 1969. This list could be extended a hundredfold, but I know of no work that excels the volume edited by Rudnev. Western writers have generally ignored the possibility of pre-1883 Marxist influence in Russia; see J.L.H. Keep, *The Rise of Social Democracy in Russia,* Oxford, 1963; S.H. Baron, *Plekhanov,* Stanford, 1963; Leopold Haimson, *The Russian Marxists and the Origin of Bolshevism,* Cambridge, Mass., 1955. A welcome exception is Richard Pipes, 'Russian Marxism and its Populist Background: The Late Nineteenth Century,' *Russian Review,* vol. 19, no. 4.

2. Marx-Engels-Lenin Institute, *Karl Marx: Chronik seines Lebens* (cited hereafter as *Karl Marx Chronik*), Moscow, 1934, pp. 15-19. The *Rheinische Zeitung* changed after Marx left. A Thomas Mann character, speaking in 1845, said 'But you ought to read other newspapers—the *Königsberg Gazette,* for instance, or the *Rhenish Gazette.* You'll find a different story there entirely. There it's what the King of Prussia says.' *Buddenbrooks,* vol. 1, London, 1936, p. 128.

3. B. Nicolaievsky and O. Maenchen-Helfen, *Karl Marx, Man and Fighter,* Philadelphia, 1936, pp. 83-4.

4. In addition to Venturi's justly famous work see Richard Wortman, *The Crisis of Russian Populism,* Cambridge, 1967; James Billington, *Mikhailovsky and Russian Populism,* Oxford, 1958; W.F. Woehrlin, *Chernyshevskii: The Man and the Journalist,* Cambridge, Mass., 1971; Richard Pipes, 'Narodnichestvo: A Semantic Enquiry,' *Slavic Review,* vol. 23, no. 3, September, 1964, pp. 441-58.

5. Chernyshevsky, *Polnoe sobranie sochinenii,* vol. 16, Moscow, 1953, pp. 656-62. See also A.L. Reuel', *'Kapital' Karla Marksa v Rossii 1870-kh godov,* Moscow, 1939, pp. 46-50, and Reuel', *Russkaia ekon. mysl',* pp. 192-7.

6. Peter Tkachev, *Izbrannye sochineniia na sotsial'no-politicheskie temy v chetyrekh tomakh,* vol. 1, *1865-1869,* Moscow, 1932, pp. 69-70; Reuel', *'Kapital' Karla Marksa,* p. 53; Reuel', *Russkaia ekon. mysl',* p. 206n; L.A. Levin, *'Manifest kommunisticheskoi partii' v Rossii,* Moscow, 1956, pp. 5-6; Bert Andréas, *Le Manifeste communiste de Marx et Engels: Histoire et*

Bibliographie, 1848-1918, Milan, 1963, no. 42. On the Ruble Society (so called after the monthly dues) see N.F. Bel'chikov, 'Rublevoe obschchestvo,' *Izvestiia AN SSSR,* otd. obshchestvennykh nauk, no. 10, 1935, pp. 941-1001; S.S. Tatischev, 'Sotsial'no-revoliutsionnoe dvizhenie v Rossii, 1861-1881. Istoricheskoe izsledovanie,' part 1, 1861-71, in *TsGAOR,* f. III otd., d. no. 407, No. 16100, pp. 832-6; German (Herman) Lopatin, *Avtobiografiia,* Petrograd, 1922, pp. 27-43.

7. Reuel', *Russkaia ekon. mysl',* pp. 244-5n.; *LN,* vol. 62, pp. 259-72.

8. *MERR,* pp. 158-9; *Werke,* vol. 32, pp. 56-5.

9. 'Karl Marks i tsarskaia tsenzura,' *Krasnyi Arkhiv,* vol. 56, pp. 5-32; Panteleev, *Vospominaniia,* p. 689.

10. *LN,* vol. 41-2, p. 152.

11. *Ibid.,* pp. 152-3.

12. Albert Resis (*'Das Kapital* Comes to Russia,' *Slavic Review,* vol. 29, no. 2, June, 1970, pp. 219-37) has overlooked the crucial roles of Becker and Liubavin.

13. This letter is carelessly edited in *MERR,* pp. 158-9.

14. *Werke,* vol. 32, pp. 174, 177.

15. *Ibid.,* pp. 563-5, letter of Oct. 7, 1868.

16. *Ibid.,* pp. 566-7, Marx to Ludwig Kugelmann, Oct. 12, 1868 (quoted also in Resis, *op. cit.,* p. 225).

17. IISG, *Becker,* D I 235a; *MERR,* pp. 257-60; *LN* vol. 41-2, p. 151, E.H. Carr (*Michael Bakunin,* New York, 1961, p. 399) mistakenly has Liubavin meeting Bakunin in Geneva.

18. *Memoirs,* vol. 30, p. 201, letter of Sept. 29, 1869.

19. Part of Bakunin's Dec. 22, 1868, letter to Marx is in *Werke,* vol. 32, p. 757.

20. M.P. Dragomanov, ed., *Pis'ma M.A. Bakunina k A.I. Gertsenu i N.P. Ogarevu,* 1st edition, Geneva, 1896, pp. 246-9; Carr, *Bakunin,* pp. 399-402; *MERR,* pp. 257-60.

21. Institute of Marxism-Leninism of the Central Committee of the CPSU, *Gaagskii kongress Pervogo Internatsionala, 2-7 sentiabria 1872 g.: Protokoly i dokumenty,* Moscow, 1970. Michael Confino attaches greater importance to Nechaev's 'Committee' than the evidence warrants; see his introduction to *Violence dans la violence: le débat Bakounine-Nečaev,* Paris, 1973, pp. 43ff.

22. Confino's introduction to the work just cited and his articles in *CMRS* (see the bibliography of the present work) are, with ch. 15 of Venturi, *op. cit.,* the best sources in Western languages. René Cannac, *Netchaiev du nihilisme au terrorisme,* Paris, 1961, and Michael Prawdin, *The Unmentionable Nechaev,* London, 1961, are unsatisfactory. Slightly better is J. Barrué, *Bakounine et Netchaiev,* Paris, 1971.

23. *BL/OR,* f. 100 (Enisherlov, G.I.), Carton No. II, ed. khr. no. 4, 'Avtobiografiia,' 1. 144. Enisherlov writes, 'With the help of good people, Nechaev was accepted into the university at the public expense.'

24. *Journal de St-Pétersbourg,* July 2(14), 1871, refers to Nechaev as an 'ancien instituteur à l'école paroissiale de St-Serge' in St Petersburg.

25. A. Gambarov, *V sporakh o Nechaeve*, Moscow-Leningrad, 1926, p. 77; Zemfirii-Ralli-Arbore, 'Sergei Gennad'evich Nechaev (Iz moikh vospominanii),' *Byloe*, vol. 1, No. 7, July 1906, p. 137. In his 'Avtobiografiia,' Enisherlov writes than when *La Lanterne* reached St Petersburg, he himself learned to hate 'Badinguet' (i.e. Louis Bonaparte). See *BL/OR*, f. 100, 1. 105.

26. *KS*, 1931, no. 4, p. 77; Venturi, *Roots of Revolution*, pp. 357-9.

27. *BL/OR*, f. 100 (Enisherlov), 1. 141. Another of the students' goals was to undertake a 'polemic' with 'the Geneva press,' i.e. with *Narodnoe Delo* and Bakunin (the journal had not yet changed hands).

28. *Ibid.*, 11. 139-140.

29. *Ibid.*, 1. 140.

30. On Enisherlov see, in addition to his own autobiography, *Deiateli*, vol. 1, part 2, 118-9; on Orlov see *ibid.*, 294-5; on Goldenberg-Getroitman see *ibid.*, vol. 2, part 1, 288-9.

31. The Program of Revolutionary Action' is in B.P. Koz'min, *et. al.*, eds., *Istoriko-revoliutsionnaia khrestomatiia*, vol. 1, Moscow, 1923, pp. 81-5; see also Koz'min, 'P.N. Tkachev,' in Tkachev, *Izbrannye sochineniia*, vol. 1, pp. 14-16. On the debt of this 'Program' to the first *Narodnoe Delo* see *CMRS*, vol. 7, no. 4, pp. 629, 631. Nechaev and Tkachev predicted a peasant uprising in 1870 on the ninth anniversary of the emancipation proclamation.

32. *BL/OR*, f. 100, 1. 148.

33. *Ibid.*, 1. 147.

34. *Ibid.*, 11. 149-50.

35. *Ibid.*, 11. 150, 152-3. Vera Zasulich was not immediately told that the 'note' thrown from the carriage was a fake, and Enisherlov recalls that she 'sobbed hysterically' when she found it. Then only about nineteen, she recovered her composure and told some of her comrades that they must avenge Nechaev.

36. *Ibid.*, 1. 159.

37. Carr. *Bakunin*, pp. 390-8.

38. *BL/OR*, f. 100, 1. 158.

39. See Iu.M. Steklov's introduction to 'Zapiska Semena Serebrennikova o Nechaeve,' *KS*, 1927, no. 3(32), p. 16.

40. The best source for the impact of the propaganda campaign is Enisherlov's autobiography; see *BL/OR*, f. 100, 11. 158, 161, 163, 164. Many of the publications are in *LN*, vol. 41-2, pp. 121-50. See also *Krasnyi Arkhiv*, vol. 14, p. 159, and vol. 15, pp. 151-4, and R.M. Kantor, *V pogone za Nechaevym*, Leningrad-Moscow, 1925, p. 8.

41. Marx, Engels and Paul Lafargue, 'L'Alliance de la démocratie socialiste et L'Association internationale des travailleurs,' in *Freymond*, vol. 2, p. 433; Michael Confino, 'Bakunin et Nečaev. Les débuts de la rupture,' *CMRS*, vol. 7, no. 4, Oct.-Dec., 1966, pp. 606ff, 625.

42. Paul Pestel and the 'Decembrists' who revolted in 1825 were—some of them—advocates of regicide, but not even those children of a generation that had seen the French Revolution remotely approached the level of violence advocated by Nechaev and Bakunin.

43.   *BL/OR*, f. 100, 11. 155-6, 157; V. Burtsev, *Za sto let (1800-1896)*, part
      2, London, 1897, p. 75; Koz'min, *P.N. Tkachev*, pp. 190-3; Venturi,
      Roots of Revolution, pp. 364-5. Nicholas Utin wrote to Anton Trusov in
      1869 that Bakunin had boasted of having money to publish
      brochures and 'various catechisms'; see *TsGALI*, f. 1181 (Utiny, B.I.,
      E.I., N.I.), Utin's undated letter, 1. 6.
44.   *BL/OR*, f. 100, 11. 164-5. Among those who wanted to kill Nechaev
      was his former associate, Ferapontov (whose given name I have not
      been able to determine).
45.   *Ibid.*, 11. 166ff. Enisherlov's account of his interrogation at the hands
      of the Third Section, after he was finally arrested, provides a
      valuable insight into police operations in the late 1860's.
46.   Andréas, *Le Manifeste communiste*, no. 54; *LN*, vol. 41-2, pp. 154-5; B.P.
      Koz'min, 'Kto byl pervym perevodchikom na russkii iazyk 'Manifes-
      ta kommunisticheskoi partii'?' *LN*, vol. 63, pp. 700-1 (Koz'min
      ignored Liubavin's January letter and Danielson's comment to
      Marx).
47.   Typical is Richard Hare *(Pioneers of Russian Social Thought*, New
      York, 1964, p. 206), who has Bakunin not only translating the
      Manifesto but publishing it in Herzen's *Kolokol!*
48.   Andréas, *Le Manifeste communiste*, no. 54; *LN*, vol. 63, p. 700; *MERR*,
      p. 265; Levin, *'Manifest'*, pp. 6-10. Nechaev used the Hirschfeld
      (London) edition of 1848.
49.   *Izdaniia obshchchestva Narodnoi Raspravy*, no. 2, Winter 1870, St
      Petersburg (*sic*—but actually Geneva); Koz'min, 'Kto byl pervym
      perevodchikom?,' p. 701; Venturi, *Roots of Revolution*, p. 384.

CHAPTER THREE

The Russians and the International in 1869

The emergence of Michael Bakunin as a major figure in the International could serve as a crude paradigm of the Hegelian dialectic. As the working-class organization was climbing to an unprecedented peak of influence in Europe and expanding to other continents, it encountered and absorbed what proved to be some of the sources of its own destruction. Having overcome the Proudhonists at the 1868 Congress in Brussels, the International permitted the remnants of that faction and new—only marginally labour—forces to regroup around Bakunin in 1869. The new anarchist movement proved far deadlier than the Proudhonists of the early part of the decade.

The success of Bakunin is not easily explained. He had a certain reputation as a political martyr, but Europe was full of such types and enough controversy attached to him to take some of the lustre off his clashes with the forces of law and order. A great raconteur and master of Hegel, few could match him in debate; but the problem was to build a working-class political organization, not a debating society. Bakunin, however, did not frequent workingmen's company: students, intellectuals and parlour radicals constituted his following everywhere save in Italy and the Swiss Jura. His ideas, not surprisingly, were incompatible with social trends in the advanced, industrialized nations. He had no German or British following, and his strength in France and Belgium was unstable. It was the Italians and Spanish radicals who liked him, and the craftsmen of the Swiss Jura—into whose drab lives he brought a dash of colour—accorded him a hero's status. All this indicates that Bakunin's was a ramshackle organization devoid of significant labour participation. By sheer force of will and personality, however, he made himself a force to be reckoned with.

The Campaign against Bakunin

For a quarter of a century Marx and Engels had been unable to make up their minds about Bakunin. Marx had accepted him as a collaborator in Paris in 1843-4. During the great revolutionary epoch of 1848-9 he and Engels first regarded Bakunin as a tsarist spy, then acknowledged the proof of his innocence that George Sand supplied. On more than one occasion Marx praised his role in the Dresden uprising. Engels derisively called him a 'democratic panslav' and never retracted the charge, but through the 1850's he and Marx maintained an essentially positive attitude toward the Russian revolutionary—who was not yet, of course, an anarchist. In 1864 Marx himself signed Bakunin's admission into the International.[1]

As late as October 1868, Marx was amused when one of his more violently Russophobic associates, Sigismund Borkheim, discovered a 'Muscovite conspiracy' in J.P. Becker's request for a halt to his—Borkheim's—attacks on Bakunin. In November Marx tried to end this by telling Borkheim that Bakunin and Engels were personal friends.[2] But the founding of Bakunin's Alliance changed everything. A furious Marx wrote to Engels in December of 1868. 'This time Schaute [Borkheim] is right. The . . . [Alliance] is to restore the 'idealism' our organization [the International] lacks. L'idéalisme russe!'[3] He told Hermann Jung (secretary for Switzerland) that the IWMA's General Council must deal firmly with the Alliance, and he wrote to his daughter Laura and her husband, Paul Lafargue, what he thought of developments in Geneva:

My old acquaintance, the Russian Bakunin, has schemed a neat

little plot against the International. After he fell out with the
League of Peace and Freedom and left it during the [1868] Bern
congress, he entered the Romande section of our association in
Geneva. Very soon he wrapped up our good old Becker, who is
always eager for exciting deeds but who is not very critical, an
enthusiast like Garibaldi, easy to influence. Bakunin then
hatched the 'International Alliance of Socialist Democracy,'
which is supposed to be simultaneously a branch of our
association and a new independent international association ... [4]

Reports from Leipzig reinforced Marx's suspicions and fears.
Wilhelm Liebknecht wrote early in the new year that, to
avoid a scandal in Germany and Switzerland, Becker would
have to break with Bakunin, who was scheming against the
IWMA. But Liebknecht was known to exaggerate, so Engels
urged Marx to seek further information. This admirable
caution led straight to Borkheim, perhaps the least reliable,
most unscrupulous of all Marx's friends. Marx must have
known that Borkheim would confirm Liebknecht's report.[5]

Having requested a written denunciation of Bakunin, in
February 1869 Marx received notes and materials from
Borkheim resurrecting the 'panslavist' charge. The plan here
was obviously to summon up the 'Russian menace to
Europe': the next IWMA Congress might not find anything
less than that sufficient grounds for excluding the Alliance.
By the summer, however, the situation had become so serious
that Marx and Engels considered more drastic action. Becker
and the Geneva Germans proposed changes in the statutes of
the International, notably the grouping of sections by language and occupation. An outraged Marx roared that 'this
archreactionary system is worthy of the panslavs!' and
everywhere he saw the hand of Bakunin:

> Becker himself is not dangerous. But we hear ... that his
> secretary, Remy, has been imposed upon him by Bakunin. This
> Russian manifestly wants to become dictator of the European
> labour movement. He must be held in check; otherwise he will
> have to be officially excommunicated.[6]

Three years later, Marx made good this threat.
Engels agreed with Marx's assessment and noted that 'old
Becker must have gone completely mad.' He found especially

irritating Becker's claim that trade unions represented the most advanced form of labour organization, and he thought he knew the origin of the heresy:

> It is quite clear that Bakunin is behind all this. If this damned Russian really thinks he can intrigue his way to the head of the labour movement, it is time to fix him properly and to raise the question whether a panslav can under any conditions be a member of our International . . . We can catch the fellow very easily. He must not imagine that he can play the workers off against the cosmopolitan communists and the Russians against the ultra-nationalistic panslavs. A wink to Borkh[eim], who has told tales about him, would be quite useful; B[orkheim] will get the hint.[7]

Having already understood the 'hint,' Borkheim had published the first part of the attack on Bakunin that Marx had commissioned. He claimed (in July of 1869) that Bakunin's 'goose will be cooked' before the Basle Congress of the IWMA. He underestimated his opponent.[8]

Published in Germany, the Borkheim articles did Bakunin no harm because he had no German constituency anyway. But their appearance reflected the growing concern of the Marxists over the Alliance. The eventual admission of that organization into the International appears all the more puzzling in view of the Marx-Engels correspondence during the first seven months of 1869.

Public evidence of German anxiety came on the eve of the August, 1869, congress at Eisenach that witnessed the birth of the Social-democratic party (SPD). Encouraged by Borkheim and perhaps by Marx himself, Wilhelm Liebknecht charged that (1) Bakunin was a Russian police agent; (2) the Russian government had connived in his famous escape from Siberia; (3) he had founded the Alliance to destroy the International; (4) he had duped Becker; and (5) as an agent of Bismarck, he had worked with J.B. von Schweitzer, a Lassallean opponent of Marx.

Bakunin learned of this slanderous nonsense early in August and gave Becker ('as a brother of our Alliance'—Becker was indeed a member), who was about to leave for Eisenach, a letter to the congress. He challenged Liebknecht to repeat his charges before the IWMA Congress in Basle in September; if he declined to do so, Bakunin would brand him 'eine infame Canaille' and 'ein niederträchtiger Schurke.' Finding this threat insufficiently disturbing, Liebknecht ignored it. But Bakunin demanded and received a 'jury of honour'—a common device of the 19th-century Left—before the opening of the Basle meeting. Liebknecht had to withdraw most of his accusations but refused—no doubt on Marx's instructions—to disavow his comments about the Alliance. This organization was by then in the International, making the whole question academic. The 'jury' unanimously acquitted Bakunin, whom Liebknecht at once embraced to socialist cheers. The anarchist momentum continued into the Congress.[9]

Bakunin and the Basle Congress

The most representative (of national working-class movements) meeting in the International's history convened in Basle on September 6, 1869. Seventy-seven delegates from Great Britain, France, the German states, Austria-Hungary, Switzerland, Belgium, Italy, Spain and the United States gathered to discuss and debate labour's trials and triumphs in the year since the Brussels Congress and to plan for the future. Several Russian and Polish radicals attended as observers. Neither Marx nor Engels came, but two General Council delegates (Jung and J.G. Eccarius), and the German delegates, spoke for them. Bakunin had mandates from Naples and Lyon and many friends among the Italian, Spanish, Swiss and Belgian delegates.[10]

The International had won new adherents by the thousand in several West European countries, but, as everyone knew, this was not an accurate index of its strength. In many towns and cities one 'joined' the IWMA as casually as one participated in a café discussion. In the industrialized areas where the International should have been strongest it tended to be weak, and where it was strongest—for example, in western Switzerland—it was frequently isolated from the centres of heavy industry. (To a certain extent, however, this did change in the year 1868-9).

In the Borinage, the Belgian iron-workers and others in heavy industry went on strike and received support from the International. When disorders erupted at the gigantic Société John Cockerill works in Seraing, the government called out troops, who fired on the workers. Belgian labour buried its dead and turned in increasing numbers to the International. A similar affair shattered the peace of the French mining town of La Ricamarie, near St Etienne. There, in the wake of a labour dispute, soldiers shot down fifteen people, including women and children. The 'La Ricamarie massacre' joined the 'St Bartholomew's Night of the bourgeoisie' at Seraing in the revolutionary lexicon and mythology of European labour, much to the advantage of the International, which mounted a Europe-wide campaign of protest and collected funds for the victims' families.

In most German states, the law forbade the formation of sections of the International but permitted individual memberships. A vigorous working-class movement had developed in several areas, particularly in Saxony and parts of Prussia, and again the International made capital out of the situation. Working conditions and hours remained atrocious—a seventy-hour week was not uncommon—in the more reactionary states, and labour was determined to change them. The 'Eisenach party' (which evolved into the SPD) came into being in the summer of 1869 and became one of the Marxist mainstays in the latter years of the International.

Owing largely to the efforts of Bakunin's supporters, the International took root in Italy and Spain, and labour disorders and governmental repression recruited new members in Austria, Hungary and Bohemia. Russia remained largely untouched; as Liubavin had told Becker, no real basis for a modern labour movement existed in that country. But the students and radical intellectuals tested the Russian government again in March and April of 1869, and the embryonic working-class movement was probably a little more advanced than Liubavin realized. The *Communist Manifesto* appeared in Russian and a translation of *Capital* was planned. Bakunin, of whose anarchism the radicals inside Russia knew nothing, became a power in the International almost overnight. Other Russian émigrés joined the organization, a few to support him and others to work with the Marxists against him.

The most representative of the International's Congresses was also one of the least productive. The delegates confirmed past decisions and debated peripheral issues. The 1868 Brussels Congress majority thought it had resolved the IWMA position on landed property (it belonged to society), but the Proudhonist minority had extracted a promise to debate the issue once more in Basle. A listless discussion produced no new arguments, and the delegates overwhelmingly rejected the Proudhonist appeal for the recognition of the peasant's right to own his own land. No agreement was reached, however, on the question of how collective property was to be managed.[11]

The last Proudhonist challenge was easily beaten back, but then co-operation began to break down. At Bakunin's insistence and against the wishes of the General Council, the Congress debated the abolition of the right of inheritance. In the *Communist Manifesto,* Marx and Engels had described how the victorious proletariat would make 'despotic inroads on the rights of property, and on the conditions of bourgeois production.' They had noted ten measures, warning that they appeared 'economically insufficient and untenable, but . . . in the course of the movement, [they] outstrip themselves, necessitate further inroads upon the old social order, and are unavoidable as a means of entirely revolutionizing the model of production.' Their third point was 'abolition of all right of inheritance.' Warning against any tendency to regard these measures as panaceas, Marx and Engels declared that they would in any event follow, not precede, the proletarian victory. Attempting to establish only some vague guidelines for the future, they wished to avoid dogmatic formulations. At the Basle Congress, however, Michael Bakunin tried to transform a relatively obscure revolutionary prescription into a first principle.

Marx wrote the General Council's report to the Congress and argued that the laws of inheritance, 'Like all other civil legislation . . . are not the *cause* but the *effect,* the *juridical consequence* of the *existing economical organization of society,* based upon private property in the means of production.' With the abolition of private property, he declared, the right and practice of inheritance would obviously disappear also.[12]

Securing places on an eleven-member commission that delivered a report on this issue, Bakunin and seven supporters easily prevailed over Liebknecht, Moses Hess and César De Paepe, who spoke for the General Council and Marx. The Bakuninists called abolition of the right of inheritance a practical step toward the overthrow of private property; Marx had argued that this could 'never be the *starting-point* of such a social transformation.' Bakunin declared that the difference between the 'collectivists who find it useless to vote . . . [for] abolition' was one of viewpoint. The first group looked to the future, the second to the present. The right of inheritance, Bakunin insisted, was a fundamental socio-economic regulator, removal of which would deal a powerful blow to the institution of private property.[13]

Here lay a trap for the Marxists. Unable to prevent a discussion, the General Council faction could have submitted a mild proposal, a gentle reaffirmation of the desire to abolish the right of inheritance at some undefined future date. That would probably have satisfied a majority of the delegates. But the General Council's delegates did not take that course. Bakunin's proposal came to the floor and won a plurality (thirty-two to twenty-three, with thirteen abstentions). Under the rules, failure to receive an absolute majority defeated the proposal. Nevertheless, Bakunin won, because by any reasonable standard the General Council and Marx lost. The Council's delegates and supporters then offered an alternative proposition calling for increased legacy duties, the use of those revenues for 'social emancipation,' and the restriction of the right of bequest. A clear majority now voted nay, confirming the defeat of the General Council. Attending a Congress for the first time, Bakunin had bested the founders of the IWMA and the organization's chief theorist, Karl Marx. He had established himself as a major force within the society. The International would never be the same.

Not everyone immediately recognized Bakunin's victory; few could ignore the General Council's setback. The near-unanimity on the last major question on the agenda (the development of the trade-union movement) could not conceal that defeat.

Bakunin's stand on the trade-union issue reflected his knowledge of the fact that the Proudhonists, who had constituted the strongest single faction in the IWMA in its early years, were now drifting aimlessly without a leader. They certainly could not join Marx, and Bakunin hoped they would turn to him. Conserving much of Proudhonism, Bakunin added revolutionism and conspiracy, thus appealing to the dispossessed rural proletariat and to some of the lowest-paid urban clerical workers. His views on landed property and the right of inheritance cost him the support of many of the small proprietors who had been the core of Proudhon's following, but even they, having no other haven to which to repair, began to drift toward Bakunin, who held the rest of Proudhon's constituency and added new elements of his own. Even a few Blanquists wondered whether he might serve as their leader. The Basle Congress thus witnessed Bakunin's discovery of the mass following he had always wanted.[14]

Six weeks later he told Herzen why he wanted that following. Though he praised Marx and claimed he would never attack him personally, Bakunin said that a 'struggle to the death' was imminent over questions of principle and that he would combat the 'statist communism' of Marx and his German and English followers. His earlier co-operation with Marx had been merely tactical. By pursuing a *divide et impera* (he used the term) policy, Bakunin believed he could defeat Marx. He intended to work through the Alliance toward that end.[15]

To Bakunin, the International was a vehicle for revolution. He could not conceive of it as a political organization of the working class because he did not believe in politics. Conspiracies, uprisings, intrigues, sharp sallies, sudden dramatic developments—these formed the sum and substance of his revolutionary thinking. When he praised Marx's twenty-five years of service to socialism, it was one insurrectionist's homage to—he sincerely believed—another.

Though he considered them nonsensical, Marx also saw Bakunin's theories as a mortal threat to the IWMA. Writing privately to the new German 'Eisenach' party, he attacked Bakunin's plans to seize control of the organization. Referring

to the 'barbarism' of the 'Muscovite optimists,' Marx mishan-
dled the facts in claiming that Bakunin utilized false mandates at Basle. He did not give a wholly accurate account of
that meeting, and objective observers might have thought
him foolish to call Bakunin's insistence upon abolishing the
right of inheritance a *'vieillerie Saint-Simoniste'*: the *Communist
Manifesto* had called for the same thing (to follow, however,
not precede the revolution).[16]

As his own letter to Herzen proves, Bakunin was guilty as
charged of plotting to take control of the International. A
great storm was brewing, and the first signs tended to
overshadow some of the positive developments of the Basle
Congress: the healthy controversies, the representative nature
of the meeting and even the rebuke to the General Council
(which reaffirmed the Congress as the organization's chief
authority). All this tended to slide into the background
during the next three crucial years during the conflict
between the supporters of the General Council (loosely but
not wholly incorrectly called 'Marxists') and the Bakuninists.

The *'Narodnoe Delo'* Russians and the International

Some of his compatriots were in Basle as observers and
Bakunin cursed the circumstances of their birth. Nicholas
Utin paraded through the city (Bakunin later wrote) 'sur-
rounded by his female entourage.' At a post-congress banquet
Utin spoke on the emancipation of women; Bakunin wryly
noted that he was indeed an expert in the field. Utin and his
friends (his wife, plus the Bartenevs, Anton Trusov and Olga
Levashyova) made the acquaintance of the General Council
delegates and through them sought an introduction to
Marx.[17]

In March 1870, Utin, Trusov and Victor Bartenev reminded Hermann Jung (as secretary for Switzerland, Jung had
responsibility for their application for admission) that they
had met him in Basle and that they had belonged to the
International in Geneva for some time.[18] These men and
others from the Russian and Polish colony had been participating in the work of the Central section in the city (this was
an omnibus section for intellectuals, non-manual workers

and foreigners). A combination of the labour disorders in Western Europe, renewed student unrest in Russia and Poland, and a general intensification of political activity in émigré circles led the Utin group, Józef Hauke ('Bosak') and some of his fellow Poles and other individuals into the International in Geneva. Bakunin had been in the organization since 1864. In the autumn of 1868 he entered the Geneva Central section—one could be a member of several—and created the controversial Alliance (which joined the IWMA as a separate section). Furthermore, Bakunin and his friends now controlled the Geneva *L'Egalité,* one of the most important of the continental IWMA newspapers.

But Bakunin no longer collaborated on *Narodnoe Delo,* and the new editorial board, reversing its original posture, moved toward the Marxist bloc in the International. In May of 1869 the third issue of the journal, discussing the student disorders in Russia, urged the youth there to study the development of the IWMA and to accept the fact that they were part of a world-wide liberation movement:

> Look at the workers-proletarians in Belgium, Switzerland France, England, Germany, Italy, Spain, Austria, America—everywhere there resounds with revitalized, powerful force the same demand for fundamental changes, and everywhere... many victims fall under the blows... of the contemporary police-social order. There where hunger (a consequence of the conspiratorial closing of factories and workshops, or a consequence of the inevitability of strikes) and eviction from homes still do not take—by the calculations of the bourgeoisie—enough victims among the workers' families, there the bourgeoisie falls back upon the army, and blood flows and corpses are strewn about, and still the world of labour considers it necessary... to go against the troops, although they be their best brothers... because this labour world has already understood that otherwise there would be even greater sacrifices than there have been so far in factories, workshops, and mines... [19]

In Russia, the workers were few in number, poorly organized, and insufficiently aware of their political destiny to act for themselves (Liubavin had made these same points in his letter to Becker). Therefore the student youth had to act for them. Soon the 'revolutionary-liberation' movement, however, would progress beyond student circles to embrace the masses. The Russians had to organize; the writer did not specify how this was to be done, but he (or she) dwelled upon the merits of the International and tried to acquaint his readers with the efforts of Western workers to unite through that organization. Russians had to understand the importance of those efforts:

> Must it be said that all the sympathy of the contemporary honest and intelligent man must gravitate toward the interests of the working class? In it lies all the meaning, all the strength of the modern progressive movement, just as in the camp of its enemy . . . the bourgeoisie, there is collected the whole sum of the pernicious doctrines of stagnation and obdurate planterism; in . . .[the working class] are all the elements and indications of the new life style, exactly as in the bourgeoisie there is all the decay, all the demoralization of a moribund, rotten organism.[20]

The Western workers had learned that disunity meant weakness and defeat. After 1864, therefore, the International had served as a 'concentrated nerve centre' to bring them together 'to oppose the international plot of the capitalists.' Two important tactics the workers employed were the strike and 'mutual aid'; the Russians were attracted to this latter Proudhonist slogan because it seemed a direct translation of the Russian peasant commune custom of *krugovaya poruka,* literally, mutual guarantee.[21] The employers usually retaliated with lockouts and strikebreaking tactics. Thus a monumental struggle between workers and 'bosses' had to come, and the IWMA would be in the vanguard:

> the history of the International . . . is . . . the essence of the history of the contemporary labour movement: in it are expressed the common thinking and the united aspirations of the working masses, in it you see those principles that will become fundamental elements of the new social order when the proletariat liberates itself from the yoke of bourgeois capital. The overwhelming importance and significance of the International . . . consists in this, that it serves as the expression of the movement not of one separate country but of the movement that embraces all European countries and the United States in the name of the *solidarity* of all workers of all lands.[22]

Never had such words as these appeared in the Russian language. The writer went on to observe that in Germany the bourgeoisie—cleverer than its French counterpart—knows how, with its sentimental democratizing, to exploit the working people better.' But the German workers, followers of Karl Marx, 'will in their turn know how to teach the bourgeoisie a lesson, after which its inclination to sentimentalize will vanish.'[23] This was the first mention of Marx in *Narodnoe Delo*—which had, however, been using Marxist slogans earlier. The writer praised the 'outstanding and truly democratic labour' of this 'veteran of German democracy' and identified him as the author of *Capital*.

Unquestionably under the influence of Becker, who would have revealed to them (they were not acquainted with the Liubavin-Danielson group) the plans to translate *Capital* into Russian, the Utin circle gravitated toward the left wing of the International. Still politically unsophisticated, they had not forgotten 'mutual aid' and other Proudhonist-communalist schemes. But they were indeed moving toward the Marxist left and by May 1869 their journal had become the unofficial Russian organ of the International

Origins of the Russian Section

In November of 1869, after the Basle Congress, *Narodnoe Delo* made its status official. In that month, the fourth issue carried Russian translations of the General Council's report to the Congress and the resolutions of that meeting. In a notice, the staff described itself as 'members of the International union of proletarians' who supported the IWMA without reservation and reserved the right to speak in its name. In view of all this, it was clearly only a matter of time until the Utin group assumed a more specific identity and incorporated itself as a separate Russian section of the International.

Alexander Serno-Solovyovich, who had briefly played an important role in the Geneva International, committed suicide in August 1869. *Narodnoe Delo* observed in an obituary that his experience in the Russian revolutionary movement (he had been a member of Land and Liberty) had helped him serve the Geneva workers. Serno-Solovyovich had been popular among those workers, many of whom were, like him, foreigners, and the Utin group wanted to inherit the goodwill 'Serno' had enjoyed. Utin himself probably wrote the obituary that concluded,

> At his grave we promise to hold strongly and firmly to the banner that has been raised up until we can safely give it to new activists who will replace us when we falter or show ourselves less fit than others for the great work of propaganda, or when we die in the struggle for the great cause of the People's Liberation.[24]

A lengthy account of the Basle Congress followed this melodramatic elegy. The delegates, according to the writer, represented the vanguard of the universal proletariat, which had 'realized its historical role and entered upon its fulfillment.' The workers had previously had only the right to toil; the leisure classes luxuriated in the fruits of that toil. Now, through the International, the proletariat would change all that.

In another article, a *Narodnoe Delo* writer contended that the Russian 'party of Popular Liberation'—the most progressive part of the youth—had the task of organizing and propagandizing the masses, of bringing Russian revolutionaries into contact with their Western counterparts. Because these tasks would be especially difficult in Russia, an elite would necessarily lead the party:

> for a long time yet a *progressive minority* will lead the masses; if only this minority really understands the interests of the people, genuinely, sincerely and totally acts in the interests of the masses—then, in such circumstances, this minority, at the decisive moment, will be turned into a majority . . . [25]

Here we see one of the first Russian answers—one that directly anticipated Nechaev, Tkachev and the Bolshevik Party—to an ancient revolutionary dilemma. In the presence of an elite, was not the very term 'mass movement' sheer hypocrisy? Did it really make sense to speak of the elite being 'turned into a majority'? Bakunin was arguing for a strictly limited role for the elite: it should ignite the revolutionary flame in the masses. Nechaev and Tkachev (not to speak of their tactical descendants, the Bolsheviks) went to an extreme and rejected *any* limitation upon the elite. Marx called upon the intellectual elite—the existence of which was hardly in doubt—to become teachers, to educate, propagandize and organize the masses.

The *Narodnoe Delo* Russians considered the International an 'aristocracy of the intelligentsia' and as such a model for the Russian organization they hoped to create. This view had much to recommend it if one considered only the General Council and the Congresses, but there was more to the International. There was indeed a mass organization, the actual size of which no one has ever measured; and that was Marx's International. He attached more significance by far to the mass organization than to the General Council and the Congresses, to which organizations he assigned the responsibility of educating the masses of workers (whether members of the International or not), of developing their class consciousness and their sense of historical destiny.

Attempting to persuade the Russian youth to look to the International for guidance and inspiration, a *Narodnoe Delo* writer declared that the organization shared Chernyshevsky's views on the subject of collectivizing the land and insisted that the institution of the peasant commune was in harmony with the practical and theoretical teachings of Western socialists. Noting that Chernyshevsky had rejected a narrow interpretation of the commune, the writer quoted him to the effect that ' "This communal spirit we are not at all disposed to consider some kind of secret quality possessed exclusively by the Slavic or Great Russian nature." ' Indeed that 'spirit' as it then existed grew out of Russia's backwardness, and only the conservative Slavophiles regarded the patriarchal, oppressive commune as the foundation of a reorganized Russian society. The radicals professed belief in some vague, idealized version of the commune that would harmonize some Russian forms and Fourierist theory; and no Russian radical ever satisfactorily defined exactly what that amalgam was.

Chernyshevsky and his disciples thought—perhaps 'hoped' would be more appropriate—that, with the passage of time and the development of political and social consciousness among the masses, a revitalized commune and modern social theory would show the way to the new socialist society *without the intervening stage of capitalism.* They dreamed of transforming Russia directly from its late-feudalist, early-capitalist stage into a socialist republic. They argued that private property did not have strong roots among the Russian masses, that the Russian peasants were the least materialistic of the world's peoples (partly because of their communal traditions, partly because of their great poverty), and that the ancient customs of jointly extracting and sharing the earth's fruits had prepared the Russian people for socialism.

By advocating the skipping of the capitalist stage of economic development, Chernyshevsky and his followers thus obviously ignored what the classical economists and Karl Marx alike regarded as the progressive features of capitalism. Chernyshevsky and his followers have been accused of condemning Russia to remain an agricultural, backward state, of advocating the inhibition of the growth of the one class that can—modern Soviet Marxists allege—create socialism, the industrial proletariat. Were Chernyshevsky and his followers then utopians, as the Soviet Marxists allege?

To answer this question, we must turn to the man who made 'utopian' a term of opprobrium, Karl Marx. In November of 1877 Marx wrote to the editors of the Russian periodical *Otechestvennye zapiski* (Notes of the Fatherland), 'If Russia continues along the path she has followed since 1861 [i.e. the development of capitalism], then she will miss the best opportunity history has ever given to any people, and will experience all the fatal misadventures of the capitalist system.'[26] And these remarks were made in the context of genuine, sincere praise of Chernyshevsky's views on the Russian peasant commune. Further, in no fewer than four drafts of a March, 1881, letter to Vera Zasulich, who had asked for his views on the commune, Marx wrestled vigorously with the question and finally sent the mildest but still highly suggestive variant: the commune, in his view, could indeed serve as the 'point d'appui' of the social renascence of Russia provided it purged itself of pernicious influences.[27]

The question of the 'utopian' character of Chernyshevsky's thought, and that of his disciples (specifically the soon-to-be-constituted Russian section of the International) is thus largely academic. Marxist exegetes have quoted Marx and Lenin on both sides of the question, to no truly useful purpose. It is enough that we note the *apparent* convergence in the thinking of Marx and Chernyshevsky. We should point out too that the latter, like Marx himself, subjected the capitalist system to rigorous and incisive criticism and in the process moved far beyond all previous Russian analysts—that is, he moved toward advanced Western social theories. Chernyshevsky's followers, notably the Russian section, advanced still further that process through which Russian radicalism learned from the West. And, heeding Chernyshevsky's caveat, they did not let their hatred of tsarism blind them to the necessity of salvaging what they could from the existing social order in Russia; this separated them from Dmitry Pisarev and the 'nihilists' of the early 1860's, from Nechaev, Bakunin and Tkachev. The Russian section of the International did not produce any monumental theory nor accomplish any monumentally significant practical work. But the members of that group did make the first attempt to work out a synthesis of the teachings of Marx and the International, on the one hand, and Chernyshevsky on the other.

Describing the political life of the Geneva exiles around the year 1869, a Russian émigré newspaper noted a few years later that

> Geneva was at that time one of the chief [revolutionary and socialist] centres: the pioneers of socialism held meetings; the international union of socialists came into being; the awakening working class was seething with activity which in time took on truly grandiose dimensions. Anarchists, Marxists and collectivists aroused the people with their polemics against each other.[28]

Nicholas Utin and his associates played a key role in this politicking and became a *de facto*, if still unofficial, section of the IWMA with the publication of the November, 1869, *Narodnoe Delo*. The Russians, Poles and others (e.g., the Serb Svetozar Marković and the Swiss Edouard Bongard) in the group supported Marx both out of conviction and because of their hostility toward Bakunin and his new friend, Sergei Nechaev.

This latest issue of *Narodnoe Delo,* which carried more news about the International than any other Russian-language publication ever had, reached Russia only in small quantities. The journal never approached the success of Herzen's *Kolokol;* to speak of its influence in Russia is thus to salute a rather small flag. But such phenomena are rarely best measured in mere numbers. The newspaper did reach some radical intellectuals, some students, even some workers. Though narrow, and uncertain of both depth and destination, a channel nevertheless now existed for the communication of Marxist ideas to the Russian left.

NOTES

1. *Werke,* vol. 6, pp. 270-86, vol. 9, pp. 294-6; *Herzen,* vol. 12, pp. 118-9.
2. *Werke,* vol. 32, pp. 190, 197, 543; *Demokratisches Wochenblatt* (Leipzig), Feb. 1, 8, April 25, May 16, 1868 (where Borkheim attacks Bakunin).
3. *Werke,* vol. 32, p. 234.
4. *Ibid.,* p. 587 (by 'Romande section' Marx meant the Geneva Central section).
5. *Ibid.,* pp. 250-1.
6. *Ibid.,* pp. 257, 350-1, 758 note 291; *Der Vorbote* (Geneva), July, 1869, pp. 105-6.
7. *Werke,* vol. 32, pp. 353-4.
8. The Borkheim articles appeared in the Berlin *Die Zukunft,* nos. 167, 187, 189 and 256 of 1869, none of which have I seen. There are some relevant Borkheim to Marx letters (July 26, 27, Aug. 2, 1869) in IISG, *Marx-Engels Correspondence.*
9. James Guillaume, *L'Internationale: Documents et souvenirs (1864-1878),* 4 vols., Paris, 1905-1910 (reprinted New York, 1969), vol. 1, pp. 210-3 (cited hereafter as *Guillaume);* Carr, *Bakunin,* pp. 381-3.
10. *Guillaume,* vol. 1, p. 193n; Carr, *Bakunin,* p. 377; *Journal de Genève,* Sept. 12, 1869; *Nouvelliste Vaudois* (Lausanne), Sept. 8, 1869. The British minister to Berne noted Bakunin's presence; see Great Britain, F.O. 100 (Switzerland), 175, Aug.-Dec. 1869, no. 95, Bonar to Clarendon, Sept. 20, 1869.
11. *Freymond,* vol. 2, pp. 71-92; Braunthal, *History of the International,* p. 136; I. Bakh, ed., *Pervyi Internatsional,* part 1, Moscow, 1964, pp. 188-9; *Guillaume,* vol. 1, pp. 196-200; Stekloff, *History of the First International,* pp. 141-2.
12. *DFI,* vol. 3, pp. 322-4.
13. *Freymond,* vol. 2, p. 15.
14. *Ibid.,* vol. 2, pp. 25, 108-29; Stekloff, *History of the First International,* pp. 144-5; Bakh, *Pervyi Internatsional,* part 1, pp. 190-1.

15. Bakunin, *Pis'ma*, pp. 233-8; Carr, *Bakunin*, p. 385; Braunthal, *History of the International*, pp. 177-8.

16. *Werke*, vol. 16, pp. 409-20; *Guillaume*, vol. 1, pp. 292-8.

17. Bakunin, *Izbrannye sochineniia*, vol. 5, p. 142; IISG, *Jung*, 864a; *TsGAOR*, f. III otd., sekr. arkhiv, opis' no. 4, ed. khr. no. 346, 'Zapiska (bez podpisa) ob organisatsii, strukture i deiatel'nosti 'Mezhdunarodnogo obshchestva rabochikh' (Internatsional).' Dated Sept. 18, 1872 (old style), this report relies heavily upon E.E. Fribourg, *L'Association internationale des travailleurs*, Paris, 1871. Fribourg was a spy for the Paris police.

18. IISG, *Jung*, 846a; *Narodnoe Delo*, no. 7-10, Nov. 1869, p. 115.

19. *Narodnoe Delo*, no. 4-5-6, May, 1869, pp. 87-8.

20. *Ibid.*, p. 96.

21. On *krugovaya poruka* see the Brokgauz-Efron *Entsiklopedicheskii slovar'* Vol. 16, part 2, St Petersburg, 1895, pp. 836-9. Plekhanov incorrectly claimed *(Sochineniia*, 2nd edition, vol. 5, Moscow, n.d., p. 92n) that Chernyshevsky opposed *krugovaya poruka*, which can also be translated as 'collective responsibility.'

22. *Narodnoe Delo*, No. 4-5-6, May, 1869, p. 97.

23. *Ibid.*, pp. 98-100.

24. *Ibid.*, No. 7-10, Nov. 1869, pp. 105-12. On Serno-Solovyovich see B.P. Koz'min, 'A.A. Serno-Solov'evich v I Internatsionale i. v zehenovskom rabochem dvizhenii,' *Istoricheskii sbornik*, 1936, book 5. Koz'min, who did not have access to the Geneva archives, exaggerated Serno-Solovyovich's role in the local socialist and working-class movement.

25. *Narodnoe Delo*, no. 7-10, Nov. 1869, p. 137.

26. *Perepiska K. Marksa i F. Engel'sa s russkimi politicheskimi deiateliami*, 2nd edition, Leningrad, 1951, p. 221.

27. *Ibid.*, p. 310, and *Werke*, vol. 35, p. 167.

28. *Obshchee Delo – La Cause Générale* (Geneva), no. 47, March, 1882. These comments appeared in an obituary of V.A. Zaitsev, who visited the city in 1869 and who later (1870-1) helped found a section of the International in Turin.

CHAPTER FOUR

Sergio Furioso: Nechaev in 1869-70

Never having had any unity, the Russian émigrés in the West enthusiastically began to choose sides between the two factions that were struggling for supremacy in the International. In part this reflected the passion—always pronounced in Russia—of the politically-minded intellectual for disputation. Such zealotry flourishes (little else can) in periods of repression, and in Russia the government reintroduced the 'white terror' to curb the student disorders of early 1869 in St Petersburg and Moscow. Many revolutionaries went to prison or to exile in Siberia; a few fled abroad. Underground organizations quietly disbanded. Russia again fell silent, but in that brooding, sullen stillness she was more troubled than ever.[1] Those who escaped to the West, and those already there, searched desperately for the instruments with which to perform radical surgery upon a discredited political and social system. That search led to the International.

Labour strife, combined with organizational work and intelligent propaganda, had brought the International many successes. The organization emerged as an important factor in the political and economic life of several countries, notably, France, Belgium, Switzerland and Saxony. The socialist movement enjoyed a certain tenuous prestige in Italy and Spain and was making steady if unspectacular progress in Great Britain. All this influenced the Russian and Polish

66

émigrés as did other developments in the West. A Church Council shook the Roman Catholic world with formal debates on the question of papal infallibility. Louis Bonaparte, tottering on his throne, quickened his search for an easy escape. New labour clashes brewed in many countries. The International gained strength daily, and even conservative newspapers in the West expressed contempt for a Russian government that passed a law making the lampooning of the tsar a major crime.[2]

Nechaevschina (the Nechaev Affair)

The November, 1869, issue of *Narodnoe Delo* concluded with an 'enquiry' directed at Herzen, Nicholas Ogaryov and Bakunin asking whether they would dissociate themselves from the revolutionary proclamations that had come out of Geneva in the spring and summer of that year. That propaganda campaign had seemed to hand the revolutionary initiative among the émigrés to Bakunin and Nechaev, and Utin and his circle were determined to recapture it. Their journal dismissed the campaign as an 'obscene game' played with the 'great, holy cause of Revolution' and called the propaganda the 'gibberish of toothless senility coupled with the mumbling of home-bred Mitrofanovs.'[3]

The item that aroused the greatest resentment was the first issue of *Narodnaya Rasprava* (The People's Summary Justice), which had praised Bakunin and Nechaev, condemned the 'doctrinaire' *Narodnoe Delo* group, exalted Karakozov and ignored Chernyshevsky. It did not (as the 'enquiry' charged) claim any affinity with Herzen and *Kolokol,* but it did express the hope that co-operation would be possible in the future. Strangely enough, Bakunin had not escaped criticism; indeed one can see here a hint of Nechaev's impending break with him:

> Bakunin was right in urging you to overthrow the academies, the universities and schools and go to the people. This thought is correct, but it is far from new. The thing is, *how to go to the people and what to do among the people?* Bakunin did not say a word about this ... the most important task of all honest revolutionaries in Russia ...[4]

Obviously, going 'to the people' meant different things to different people. When he first enunciated this significant general idea a decade earlier, Herzen had never said what he meant, and later revolutionaries who literally *went* 'to the people' usually did not know what to do when they got there. As a vade-mecum, Nechaev recommended a couple of his own tracts and an article in the first *Narodnoe Delo* ... apparently ignorant of the fact that Bakunin wrote it.

In its concern with Nechaev's insults, the Utin group overlooked the ominous passages on regicide in *Narodnaya Rasprava*. Now, widespread sympathy for Karakozov, and for the Ishutin groups that had spawned him, flourished among the revolutionaries. Had Nechaev paid the usual respects and nothing more, his comments would not have been specially significant. But he earlier had said to his erstwhile colleague, Enisherlov, 'Just wait. This is merely the prologue to the great drama of which I shall be the creator.'[5] And now, from the safety of Geneva, he spelled out what he had meant: 'The Karakozov deed must be regarded as a prologue! Yes, it was a prologue! We shall try, friends, to hasten the beginning of the drama itself.' This would involve the assassination of government officials, the rich, 'journalists-apologists' and a host of others, especially the police: 'It must be said that the members of the Third Section and of the police in general ... must be put to death in the most agonizing manner, and they must be dealt with early.'[6]

Nechaev returned to Russia in the late summer of 1869 to keep a rendezvous with his associates and mobilize his revolutionary assassins. He took a route that led through Hamburg, Leipzig, Vienna and Bucharest. At each stop he mailed considerable quantities of revolutionary materials to Russia; the tsarist archives reveal the ease with which those items penetrated into the country.[7]

In Bucharest, Nechaev obtained (probably with the aid of a Bulgarian friend, the revolutionary Liuben Karavelov) a passport from the resident consul of Serbia.[8] With that travel document he went on to Odessa and from there to Moscow; he later told the Zürich police that he had travelled around Russia 'looking for relatives or acquaintances of my father.'

Failing in that search, he eventually arrived in Oryol and presented his passport to the police. Finding no grounds for detaining him, they permitted him to travel on to Prussia. Safely back in the West, he published an immodest account of his activities:

> Our fellow member, Nechaev, returning from abroad ... under the noses of Russian spies, conducted agitation of all kinds during a five month period in the south, and was in this period several times in Kiev, and in Moscow and St Petersburg. He collided with the police frequently but always skipped away safely.[9]

Wherever Nechaev went in Russia, he claimed that his society (also called Narodnaya Rasprava) was part of the International, which he identified as a secret European revolutionary organization. In his mind, it was precisely that. And he knew that the prospect of co-operation with a powerful conspiratorial organization in the West was certain to appeal to many Russian radicals.[10] Nechaev did much to revive the revolutionary optimism that those radicals had lost when the new 'white terror' struck in the spring of 1869. Although not equipped intellectually to play a major role in the revolutionary movement, Nechaev came along at a time when the competition was weak and to some he did indeed appear as a leader. He left no one unmoved; his was the kind of bearing and presence that inspires extreme reactions. Those who responded positively joined the cells or 'fives' he created in the autumn of 1869, pledging their devotion to the cause of revolution. Many others conceived a deep and abiding hatred of the man.

The materials that Nechaev published separately or with Bakunin reached a wide readership. The 'fives' mastered their contents, spread their ideas wherever they could, collected arms, learned codes, studied the techniques of arson, sabotage and murder, preparing for the upheaval that was coming— Nechaev assured them again—on the ninth anniversary of the emancipation, February 19, 1870 (old style).[11]

Some of the politically more sophisticated radicals considered Nechaev a lunatic, charlatan, and worse. M.F. Negreskul and Vera Zasulich (whom Nechaev unsuccessfully courted) found him 'difficult' and wanted nothing to do with him. Nicholas Mikhailovsky, soon to emerge as an important populist ideologist, called him a 'monster.' We have already seen how Stepan Ezersky rallied the St Petersburg students against him; Ezersky went to prison, but opposition to the Nechaevist extreme left continued. Nicholas Chaikovsky and Mark Natanson formed a group to act as a formal counter-weight to the Nechaev-Tkachev faction, and by 1870 a large, stable and moderate organization called the 'Chaikovtsy' (Chaikovskyites) had taken definite shape. The members of the former Ruble Society (Danielson, Liubavin, Lopatin, Negreskul and others) likewise detested Nechaev and his methods, and one of their number, Lopatin, was to play a major role in discrediting him.[12]

The Ivanov Murder

Nechaev knew that he had enemies in abundance and that made him demand unquestioning obedience from his followers. He firmly believed (as he wrote in *Narodnaya Rasprava*, no. 2) that 'he who is not with us is against us.' Being 'for' Nechaev, however, involved a degree of blind trust and faith that an educated individual does not easily attain. To stiffen the resolve and tighten the discipline of his Moscow followers, Nechaev decided in November of 1869, shortly before his return to the West, to make an example of I.I. Ivanov, whose dedication to the cause and to Nechaev personally had begun to waver. Ivanov challenged the leader's authority and refused to turn over any more money to him. Nechaev thereupon persuaded the other members of Ivanov's 'five' that their fellow conspirator was about to inform the police of their activities in order to purchase immunity from prosecution for himself.

The four men accepted this story despite Nechaev's refusal to provide concrete proof of Ivanov's intentions. The group lured its hapless colleague to a deserted spot on the grounds of a Moscow academy and set upon him in a fury with rocks and fists. Ivanov was probably already dead when Nechaev pulled out a revolver and fired several shots into his head. The assassins dumped the body into a pond. Thirteen years later to the day, Nechaev died in prison serving out a 'perpetual' sentence which was only ostensibly for the murder.[13]

Someone soon discovered the body. A police investigation turned up the existence of several Nechaevist 'fives.' A conspiracy of uncertain dimensions, the authorities reasoned, was clearly afoot. Arrests commenced; and Nechaev, accompanied by Barbara Aleksandrovskaya, a young revolutionary, fled to Switzerland by way of Prussia.[14]

The affair became a sensation all over Europe, in part because the 'white terror' had proved ineffective against the revolutionaries. Nechaev's unrestrained language (some of which the Russian government publicized in order to influence the public) generated excitement: the British ambassador informed his government that the conspirators planned the 'wholesale murder of the higher class of society.' Viennese newspapers referred to 'socialist' and 'Karakozov-Ishutin' plots. It was said that the Russian conspirators were in league with the émigrés in Geneva.[15]

Under intense pressure to root out the conspiracy, the Russian police struck out in all directions. What began as a search for some common murderers became a political witch-hunt. Hundreds of people suffered arrest or detention without charge. Among them were several 'Nechaevs,' including one innocent whom the police accused not only of murder and—worse—conspiracy, but also counterfeiting. Having discovered several instances of counterfeiting among the Polish rebels and one or two among the Russian radicals, the authorities imagined a major threat to the financial stability of the Empire.[16]

The Death of Herzen

Nechaev returned to Geneva early in January 1870. This time a different reception awaited: the Russian and Western press had helped the Russian government make him notorious. That, in the beginning, was what he had wanted. Descriptions of him as a dangerous revolutionary, a terrible opponent of the tsar, a leader of men—all this fed his ego. And such a reputation would be useful if ever he had to request political asylum.

Descending upon the bibulous Nicholas Ogaryov, Herzen's friend, Nechaev audaciously demanded the half of the Bakhmetev fund still under Herzen's control. Unable to refuse anything to 'Boy' (as he and Bakunin affectionately called him), Ogaryov wrote to Herzen—who lay ill in Paris—asking him to send 'as much as you like' from the fund. He also asked his old friend to see Nechaev. Surprisingly, in view of his earlier hostility, Herzen agreed to see the notorious young radical, and, although he was resigned to seeing the Bakhmetev fund frittered away, he refused to decide the amount Nechaev should get.[17]

Meanwhile, Ivan Turgenev came to see Herzen in mid-January to regale him with anecdotes and brighten his mood. That Herzen took such pleasure in the visit and remained alert seemed cause for optimism; he even weathered the receipt of Ogaryov's telegram setting the sum he should give Nechaev at 5,000 francs. His condition appeared to stabilize. He telegraphed a friend, 'The worst has passed. I am like everyone dissatisfied with the doctors. Tomorrow I shall try to write.'[18]

The next day, however, one of the noblest Europeans of the time passed into history. The voice that had 'sounded out of the English mists' in the 1850's to bring hope to a despairing generation of Russians now fell silent. With Herzen's death, leadership of the Russian revolutionary movement formally passed into more capable, but cruder, hands.[19]

Their task complicated by the late arrival from Florence of the eldest son, the family arranged for the funeral. It was to be a civil ceremony, with no speeches. Obituaries began to appear; letters, telegrams and visitors deluged the Paris apartment. Overcome by grief, Ogaryov could not travel to Paris from Geneva. And a stunned Bakunin cried out from Locarno in a telegram

Ogaryov! Can it be true? Can he be dead? It seems he is; your terrible telegram can mean nothing else ... you poor man! the poor Natalies! poor Liza! Friend, there are no words for such a misfortune. Maybe one word: we'll die in the cause. If you can, write to me, if only a line.

Your now sole remaining old friend, M.B.[10]

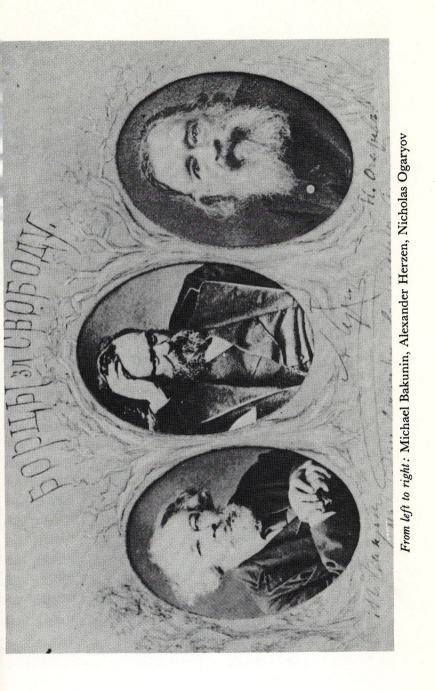

From left to right: Michael Bakunin, Alexander Herzen, Nicholas Ogaryov

Anna Jaclard, *nee*
Korvin-Krukovskaya

Nicholas Utin

Jaroslav Dombrowski

Peter Lavrov

'Elizabeth Dimitrieff'
(Elizabeth Tomanovskaya,
nee Kusheleva)

Herman Lopatin

Peter Tkachyov

Alexander Serno-Solovyovich

The Shooting of the Hostages by the Government of the Paris Commune at the Prison de la Roquette. This photograph may be faked, or may be a staged re-enactment of the shootings.

Not all the attention paid the passing of the great writer and democrat was affectionate and admiring. The notorious triple or quadruple agent of whom we shall hear more later, Apollon Mlochowski, wrote in the Paris *La Liberté* that Herzen had in his last years made his peace with the Alexandrine reforms and had come to favour the creation of a 'free Poland within a free Russia.' Similar distortions of Herzen's views appeared elsewhere in the conservative Western press. Bakunin sought to rebut them in a letter to Henri Rochefort's *La Marseillaise*.[21]

The death of Herzen, which marked the end of a major chapter in the history of Russian revolutionism, soon sank from view beneath the exploits and escapades of Sergei Nechaev. The body had not even reached its final resting place—the family vault in Nice—when Nechaev's intrigues, to which Bakunin and Ogaryov foolishly lent themselves, commenced. The immediate objective of those machinations was the remaining portion of the Bakhmetev fund, control over which now lay with Herzen's son. The latter (also named Alexander), however, had no stomach for a fight over money he merely held in trust. In a formal ceremony he transferred the funds to Ogaryov, who at once turned them over to Nechaev. Promising to revive *Kolokol* in Geneva and to publish another newspaper in London (promises which, after a fashion, he kept), Nechaev declared that the rest of the money would finance other projects of his own choosing.[22]

Crime and Revolution

In February of 1869 a young Russian diplomat, Nicholas Giers (who eventually became foreign minister), arrived in Berne to represent the Tsar. Relatively little political activity was then stirring among the Russian émigrés in Switzerland—things picked up later in the year—and the appointment was regarded as a routine one. But in September, Giers moved his legation to Geneva. He had received orders to discover and destroy the source of the revolutionary propaganda that had flooded into Russia during the summer.[23]

After the Ivanov murder (to which such interest attached because revolutionaries were involved) and Nechaev's second escape from Russia, the tsarist government stepped up its efforts to eradicate the conspiracy at home and abroad. The French embassy in St Petersburg believed that the plot which the Russians sought to smash was aimed at the overthrow of both the political and the social regime. According to French reports, Russia—'pays traditionnel de conspiration et de silence'—was bracing herself for another of the periodic convulsions that revealed the true state of her affairs. These diplomats confirmed the widely-held belief that revolutionaries inside Russia were receiving material aid from émigré circles in Switzerland.[24]

Even before the outbreak of the Nechaev affair, the Russian government had intensified surveillance—by Third Section agents—of the émigrés and it had redoubled its efforts to secure the co-operation of the Swiss authorities. Soon after the appointment of Giers, Swiss and Russian officials began to co-ordinate their attempts to track down a counterfeiting ring that was operating in Warsaw and Geneva. In the spring of 1869, cantonal police arrested some suspects in the latter city. The counterfeiters' base was discovered to be Paris, to which city the Swiss sent the arrested individuals—all of them Poles—to await justice.[25]

Since 1865 Russia had maintained an investigator in Paris whose duty it was to break counterfeiting rings. That sleuth helped, in the summer of 1869, to uncover evidence linking Jaroslaw Dombrowski, a leader of the 1863 Polish Rebellion and future general of the Paris Commune, to still another band of counterfeiters. French police arrested Dombrowski and several associates and held them for more than a year pending trial.[26] Early in 1870, acting upon information supplied by this same agent, Gabriel Kamensky, the Geneva police arrested still another Polish émigré and charged him with counterfeiting. The authorities learned that the man was a member of a gang based in France and promptly sent him to Paris. The case seemed to confirm Kamensky's claim that the Geneva Poles planned to flood western Europe with false banknotes.[27] Apollon Mlochowski sent a similar report to one of his employers, the Vienna police (and presumably to the Russians as well), and claimed that Nechaev and Bakunin were involved in these interlocking criminal rings. The

Habsburg minister to Berne confirmed this intelligence.[28] A group of counterfeiters went on trial in St Petersburg early in 1870. The Geneva government extradited some Italian forgers at about the same time. In the provinces of Kiev, Podolia and Volynia, officials discovered that archivists were fabricating Polish patents of nobility. About sixty counterfeiters—many of them Poles—awaited trial in France and Great Britain.[29]

When the Russian authorities realized that their search for some run-of-the-mill crooks might lead them to Nechaev, their zeal knew no bounds: 'None of the prominent revolutionaries of that time was hunted as they hunted the mysterious Nechaev.'[30] Rumours of the government's tactics reached the émigrés in January 1870. In that month, Ogaryov published a letter in the Geneva press asking whether the local police, acting in concert with Russian agents, were going to conduct searches of the printing presses belonging to the émigrés. A few days later the Geneva police did in fact search the establishments of Czerniecki, Elpidin and *Narodnoe Delo*; and for good measure they invaded the homes of several of the émigrés, claiming to be looking for evidence of counterfeiting. That was at best half true: they were searching *at Giers's request* for revolutionary propaganda and for Sergei Nechaev.[31]

They found nothing incriminating. (Their search was not very skillful; Edouard Bongard was a criminal, but his activities remained unknown to both the police and to Utin for several years.[32]) A great uproar arose among the émigrés and the local opposition party. Bakunin complained that the police, following ugly precedents set elsewhere in Switzerland, had become part of the 'gendarmerie of the All-Russian tsar.' The Geneva agents had shown such an interest in the papers and correspondence of the émigrés that Bakunin wondered if they were hoping to restock the Swiss national library.[33]

Sergei Nechaev knew what, or rather whom, the police were seeking. Hiding in the Jura, he sent a frantic note to Bakunin asking him to protest against the *visites domiciliaires*. An outraged letter appeared over Bakunin's signature in the newspapers; it was probably Nechaev's own handiwork.[34] There was plenty of reason for worry. Rumours circulated among the émigrés concerning the activities of Nechaev and Bakunin;

one version held that the old anarchist had promised obedience to 'Boy' even to the point of agreeing to make counterfeit currency. Nechaev had perhaps discussed that, but Bakunin almost certainly would not have taken such a risk. Nonetheless, the Russian government's attempt to cast Nechaev as a common—if versatile—criminal made headway.[35]

Further Adventures of Nechaev

Nechaev cared nothing for the opinion of the émigrés. His chief concern now was to establish a claim to political asylum, and for that he relied upon his wits, a few friends (chiefly Bakunin and Ogaryov), and Swiss hostility toward Russia. Sometimes, however, he seemed to go out of his way to make enemies, and to alienate people who might have helped him. His January, 1870, letter to Liubavin in the name of *Narodnaya Rasprava* was an example of such conduct. His threat of revenge, should Liubavin refuse to release Bakunin from the translation of *Capital,* contributed to the decline of what little regard for him still existed among the émigrés. The latter became all the more uneasy when they learned that the Tsar himself had ordered a special investigation of the whole Nechaev affair.[36]

Against this background, the Havas press agency reported from Berne on February 14, 1870, that Russia had asked the Swiss government to help track Nechaev down and to extradite him to face murder charges in Moscow. Many people in Europe thought that Russia was co-operating with Prussia in this affair; rumour had it that the two powers had agreed to co-ordinate their fight against revolutionism and subversion mounted from Swiss territory.[37] A Geneva newspaper correctly guessed that the Havas report originated not in Berne but in Berlin and that the Russian authorities had planted it.[38]

When the Third Section learned that Nechaev had crossed into Prussia during his second escape, a special agent went to Berlin to co-ordinate the search. That individual met with high officials including Bismarck himself. A formal agreement was reached; it specified that Russian agents could operate in Prussia during the hunt for Nechaev. The Prussian authorities, for their part, would publish photographs and detailed descriptions of Nechaev and his alleged accomplices in the *Polizei-Anzeiger*, and the Prussian police would of course arrest the fugitives on sight.[39]

No longer the Russian client state of the 1830's and 1840's, Prussia nevertheless had a Russophile minister-president, Bismarck, whose views coincided on most issues with those of the Prussophile Tsar. Since the Polish Rebellion of 1863 the two countries had moved even closer together in an attempt to maintain order in Eastern Europe. The rebirth of the old Holy Alliance seemed a distinct possibility. If such an event came to pass, Franz Josef, having offended both St Petersburg and Berlin more than once since 1848, would have to apply for admission cap in hand. But the chances were good that his request would receive favourable attention. In the eyes of Alexander II and Bismarck, the Habsburg emperor's most recent sin, capitulation to the Hungarians, had at least the merit of increasing the power of a nation still more reactionary than the Austrian.

Hard on the heels of the Havas report, Nicholas Giers requested the Swiss government to prepare papers for the extradition of Nechaev. This was doubly presumptuous: Nechaev had not been found, and Switzerland had no treaty of extradition with Russia. The federal government in Berne sent the request along to cantonal authorities in Geneva— where the search was concentrated—who alone, under existing law, could make a decision about extradition. Giers then complicated matters by reporting to Berne that Nechaev had probably left Geneva. And this lent credence to the belief in some quarters that the mysterious terrorist in fact did not exist but had been created by the Russian government.[40]

At this juncture a letter signed 'Netchayeff' and dated London, February 22, 1870, arrived at the *Journal de Genève*, which published it over official Russian protests early the next month.[41] The letter, if not necessarily the London address, was genuine. Nechaev wrote that he had learned of the attempts of the 'hangman of Russia, Alexander II,' to charge him with murder and have him extradited to Russia. He lamented the *visites domiciliaires* that had caused his compatriots in Geneva anguish and offered his letter as proof that he was no longer in Switzerland. All efforts to track him down, he wrote, would fail; he had taken the necessary precautions to ensure his safety.

A few days earlier Nechaev had sent letters bearing widely scattered postmarks to several European leftist newspapers trying to generate sympathy and incidentally to throw the Russian and Western agents off his track. He described his persecution at the hands of the 'Tatar-German' regime in St Petersburg, his first flight abroad, and his return to Russia at the request of his comrades. He claimed that the Third Section had ordered its agents to kill him on sight, that he had suffered arrest and torture, that he had miraculously escaped. He denied having killed Ivanov. He likewise maintained that he had not engaged in counterfeiting but he defended the right of the revolutionaries to fabricate the tsar's coin should they wish to. In conclusion he wrote that he was prepared to give his life to unite the Russian revolutionary movement with 'that of the West.'[42] He had, as Enisherlov later wrote of him, 'created his own legend—and he believed it.'[43]

The letter reflected Nechaev's attempt to associate himself with the International. He had only the most limited success; most Internationalists with whom he came into contact were deeply suspicious of him, and the Germans wrote that he was 'playing with fire . . . that could lead to catastrophe.'[44] Nechaev persisted in misjudging the International. The stories he had heard from Bakunin about the organization, his experience in the Russian underground and his psychological constitution convinced him that the IWMA was essentially a conspiracy, and he appropriated for himself Bakunin's dream of seizing control. But there was no chance he could realize his hopes. Indeed, his letters of early 1870 marked the beginning of his downfall in the West. Attacks upon him came from two sides. Sigismund Borkheim, Marx's friend whose unscrupulousness matched Nechaev's own, launched a polemic that despite its crude nature did much to discredit Nechaev in Western socialist circles. Borkheim pointed to the connection between Nechaev and Bakunin (who indeed came to rue the day he had sheltered 'Boy') and hinted darkly that the association was politically and morally reprehensible.[45]

The other attack came from the camp of the Russian émigrés. The *Narodnoe Delo* group, for several months now an unofficial section of the International, was still trying to recapture the revolutionary initiative that Nechaev and Bakunin had seized in the summer of 1869. The group made its status official in March of 1870, when it entered the IWMA. Learning of the whereabouts of Nechaev, the leaders of the new Russian section told Marx that 'We consider it our duty to warn you that under no circumstances whatsoever could we agree to having as our representative anyone among the Russians presently in London.'[46] Marx's new Russian friends had unwittingly given him a powerful weapon to use within the International against Michael Bakunin.

NOTES

1. *BL/OR.* f. 100, 1. 161
2. *Neue Zürcher Zeitung,* October 12, 1869. The same law prescribed exile to Siberia for five to fifteen years for smuggling or distributing forbidden literature. The *Neue Zürcher Zeitung* commented, 'Echt Moscowitisch!'
3. *Narodnoe Delo,* no. 7-10, pp. 167-8. The eponymous central character in D.I. Fonvizin's 'The Minor' (1782), Mitrofanov was an archetypal shiftless, dull-witted young man.
4. *Izdaniia obshchestva Narodnoi raspravy,* No. 1, Summer 1869, Moscow (actually Geneva), p. 3.
5. *BL/OR,* f. 100, 1. 160.
6. *Izdaniia obshchestva Narodnoi raspravy,* no. 1, pp. 12-16.
7. Confino, 'Bakunin et Nečaev. Les débuts,' p. 615 *TsGAOR,* f. III otd., 3 eksp., d. No. 110/1869, 'O vozzvaniiakh poluchaemykh iz za granit- sy na imena raznykh lits, i o sobranii po onym svedenii.' Especially useful are 11, 15, 18, 30, 39, 53, 64, 71, 76, 89. See further France, Bibliothèque Nationale, Division des Manuscrits, *Slave 109,* 'Natalie Herzen, Correspondance. Michel Bakounine, Hermann Lopatine, Pierre Lavrov, Serge Netschaeff, etc.' See especially *pièces* 827-33.
8. *Krasnyi Arkniv,* vol. 43, p. 143; *TsGAOR,* f. III otd., 3 eksp., d. no. 110/1869, 11. 256, 258-259 *ibid.,* f. III otd., 3 eksp., d. no. 514/1878, 'Ob ustroistve v Moskve osoboi sekretnoi agentury,' 11. 38, 56, 95-103; Bakunin, *Pis'ma,* pp. 250, 269; Marx-Engels-Lafargue, 'L'Al- liance,' pp. 441-2; Koz'min, *P.N. Tkachev,* p. 168; B.P. Koz'min, ed., *Nechaev i nechaevtsy,* Moscow-Leningrad, 1931, p. 9.
9. *Izdaniia obshchestva Narodnoi Raspravy,* no. 2, p. 7; Zürich, *Staatsarchiv,* Fremdenpolizei, 'Auslieferung des Sergeius Netschajeff, 1872-1873,' *pièce* 50a.

10.   Iu. Steklov, *Istoricheskoe podgotovlenie russkoi sotsial-demokratii,* St Peters-
       burg, 1906, pp. 17-8; V.I. Zasulich, 'Nechaevskoe delo (posmertnaia
       rukopis'),' in *Gruppa 'Osvobozhdenie Truda' (Iz arkhivov G.V. Plekhanova,
       V.I. Zasulich i L.G. Deicha,* sbornik no. 2, Moscow, 1924, pp. 38, 44;
       Gambarov, *V sporakh,* p. 11; Marx-Engels-Lafargue, 'L'Alliance.' pp.
       433, 436-7; *TsGAOR,* f. III otd., 3 eksp., ed. khr. no. 144, ch. 5/1874,
       'O rasprostranenii molodymi liud'mi knig sotsial-revoliutsionnogo
       soderzhaniia i propagande ikh v narode,' 1. 38.
11.   Tatischev, 'Sotsial'no-revoliutsionnoe dvizhenie,' pp. 1021-91; Marx-
       Engels-Lafargue, 'L'Alliance,' p. 443; *Izdaniia obshchestva Narodnoi
       Raspravy,* no. 2, p. 1; *La Marseillaise* (Paris), Jan. 4, 1870; *Journal de
       Genève,* Jan. 5, 1870. For a hostile caricature of the 'fives' see
       Dostoevsky's *The Possessed,* part 2, ch. 7, part 3, ch. 4.
12.   Koz'min, *Nechaev i nechaevtsy,* pp. 3, 26-7; Zasulich, 'Nechaevskoe
       delo,' p. 61; V.I. Zasulich, 'Vospominaniia V.I. Zasulich,' *Byloe,*
       1919, no. 14, pp. 96-7. Alexandra Zasulich thought her sister Vera
       had been unfair to Nechaev; see Aleksandra Uspenskaya, 'Vospo-
       minaniia shestidesiatnitsy,' *Byloe,* 1922, no. 18, pp. 37-40. Nechaev
       also courted Natalie Herzen in his own fashion; see his May 27, 1870,
       letter to her (edited by Tatiana Bakounine and Jacques Catteau) in
       CMRS, vol. 7, no. 2, April-June 1966, pp. 260-1, and see also
       Natalie's diary (edited by Michael Confino) in *CMRS,* vol. 10, no. 1,
       Jan.-March, 1969, pp. 141-5.
13.   See Herman Lopatin's Aug. 1, 1870, letter to Natalie Herzen (and
       Michael Confino's introduction to it) in 'Nečaev et le meurtre de
       l'étudiant I. Ivanov,' *CMRS,* vol. 8, no. 4, Oct.-Dec. 1967, pp. 628-36;
       Zasulich, 'Nechaevskoe delo,' pp. 65-6; Venturi, *Roots of Revolution,*
       pp. 380-1. Dostoevsky's brother-in-law was a fellow student of Ivanov
       and he related the gossip about the murder to the novelist; see *The
       Possessed,* part 3, chs. 6 and 8.
14.   Kantor, *V pogone,* p. 11; Tatishchev, 'Sotsial'no-revoliutsionnoe
       dvizhenie,' p. 1227; Marx-Engels-Lafargue, 'L'Alliance,' p. 442. On
       Barbara Aleksandrovskaya see *Deiateli,* vol. 1, part 2, p. 13, and
       TsGAOR, f. III otd., 1 eksp., d. no. 97, ch. 90, 1863, 1. 2.
15.   Great Britain, F.O. 65 (Russia), 800, no. 15, Jan. 12, 1870; *Journal de
       Genève,* Jan. 5, Feb. 4, 1870; *Der Bund* (Berne), Jan. 30, 1870; *Izdaniia
       obshchestva Narodnoi raspravy,* no. 2, p. 4.
16.   *Le Nord* (Brussels), Jan. 17, 21, 1870 (this newspaper received a large
       annual subsidy from the Russian government); *La Marseillaise,* Jan.
       27, 1870; *Neue Zürcher Zeitung,* no. 120, Mar. 7, 1870. Bakunin
       discussed the charge of counterfeiting made against Nechaev in 'The
       Bears of Berne and the St Petersburg Bear,' *Izbrannye sochineniia,* vol.
       3, pp. 18-9.
17.   *Herzen,* vol. 30, part 1, pp. 297, 299; T.I.Passek, *Iz, dal'nykh let,* 2
       vols., Moscow, 1963, vol. 2, pp. 560-1.
18.   *Herzen,* vol. 30, part 1, pp. 300-1; *LN* vol. 63, p. 531; N.A.
       Tuchkova-Ogareva,, *Vospominaniia,* Moscow, 1959, pp. 248-57.
19.   Bakunin, *Pis'ma,* p. 252. Herzen had lost most of his influence much

earlier, when he had quarrelled with Chernyshevsky, but nevertheless he remained an important symbol until his death.

20.   *Ibid.*, p. 256. The two Natalies were Ogaryov's wife (Tuchkova-
Ogaryova, for a time Herzen's mistress) and Herzen's eldest daughter.
The list of obituaries given in *LN*, vol. 63, pp. 523-540, overlooks those
in *Journal de Genève*, Feb. 2, 1870, and *L'Egalité* (Geneva), Feb. 12, 1870.
The latter was probably written by Bakunin.

21.   *La Marseillaise*, Mar. 2, 3, 1870. In *La Liberté*, Jan. 23, 1870,
Mlochowski used the name 'de Belina,' not for the last time. The
émigrés had exposed him as a spy in 1868; it is astonishing that
Bakunin remained unaware of this (as did the editors of *LN*, vol. 3,
pp. 525-7). Mlochowski's activities received detailed attention in *Le
Peuple Polonais* (Geneva), May 15, July 15, 1868.

22.   Confino, 'Bakunin et Nečaev. La rupture,' pp. 59ff.; Carr, *Bakunin*,
pp. 402-403; Passek, *Iz dal'nykh let*, vol. 2, p. 561; B.P. Koz'min, *Iz
istorii revoliutsionnoi mysli v Rossii*, Moscow, 1961, pp. 562-3; and see
Natalie Herzen's diary in the original Russian, *LN*, vol. 63, pp. 488ff.
A French translation of the diary is in *CMRS*, vol. 10, no. 1, pp. 93ff.

23.   *Le Nord*, Oct. 4, 1869; *Neue Zürcher Zeitung*, Oct. 29, 1869.

24.   France, *AMAE*, CP, Russie, vol. 243, Jan.-May 1870, 60, Fleury to
Paris, Feb. 5, 1870; *ibid.*, 61-73, de Gabriac's Feb. 5, 1870, report.

25.   Switzerland, *Bundesarchiv*, Protokoll des schw. Justiz- u. Polizeide-
partments, 1869, Dep. no. 149, 141, report of Mar. 24, 1869; *Ibid.*,
166-7, report of Apr. 7, 1869. (I was not permitted to see Dep. No.
276, also relevant.) See also K.G. König, *Die polnischen Banknotenfälscher in der Schweiz. Kritik der in Yverdon geführten Untersuchung*, Berne,
1875, p. 13.

26.   *APP*, B/A 1,039, 'Dombrowski, Jaroslaw,' *pièces* 14, 69; *ibid.*, E/A
102.13, 'Dombrowski, Jaroslaw'; *Le Nord*, Apr. 15, July 15, 16, 1870;
Journal de Genève, Apr. 28, 1870; *Der Volksstaat* (Leipzig), Feb. 26,
1870.

27.   *AEG*, Registre du Conseil d'Etat, 1870, 1er sem., R.C. 425, 14, 60,
115; *ibid.*, A.F., no. 20; *ibid.*, 1871, 2e sem., R.C. 428, 141-2; *ibid.*,
O.D. no. 106, suppl.; *Bundesarchiv*, Protokoll des Bundesrathes, 1870;
Jan., 390; Feb., 596; *ibid.*, Protokoll des schw. Justiz- u. Polizei-
departments, 1870, 49, no. 84, Jan. 27, 1870, 76, 144. See also
Konrad Wysotzki et al *'Die polnische Fälscherbände' und die russischen
Staatsräthe und deren Agenten. Zur Aufklärung der öffentlichen Meining*,
Zürich and Leipzig, 1874, pp. 12, 74 (Tkachev and Elpidin
translated this work into Russian: *Fal'shivye monetchiki ili agenty
russkago pravitel'stva*, Geneva, 1875).

28.   *HHStA*, PSMA, 1870, Departement II, no. 496; *ibid.*, no. 588,
Ottenfels to Beust, Apr. 19, 1870.

29.   *Le Nord*, Feb. 3, 1870; *Neue Zürcher Zeitung*, nos. 73, 88, 116 of Feb. 10,
18, and Mar. 5, 1870.

30.   Kantor, *V pogone*, p. 11.

31.   *Journal de Genève*, Jan. 28, Feb. 25, 1870; *La Suisse Radicale* (Geneva),
Jan. 27, 1870.

32. Zürich, *Staatsarchiv,* Y 60.27.291.
33. See Bakunin's article, 'La police suisse,' *Progrès* (Le Locle), which he later expanded into 'The Bears of Berne . . . ' The original *Progrès* article is reproduced in A. Lehning, ed., *Archives Bakounine,* vol. 4, *Michel Bakounine et ses relations avec Sergej Nečaev, 1870-1872,* Leiden, 1971, pp. 43-5
34. Bakunin, *Pis'ma,* p. 257; *La Suisse Radicale,* Feb. 9, 1870 (the letter was signed 'Ouragoff').
35. See the editor's notes in Bakunin, *Pis'ma,* p. 343, and E.H. Carr, *The Romantic Exiles,* London, 1968, p. 257.
36. Koz'min, *Nechaev i nechaevtsy* p. 4. The émigrés feared that the search might lead to Russian pressure upon them all; see L. Haas, 'Njetschajew und die schweizer Behörden,' *Schweizerische Zeitschrift für Geschichte,* vol. 17, 1967, pp. 316-17.
37. *Neue Zürcher Zeitung,* nos. 101 and 103 of Feb. 25, 26, 1870; *Der Volksstaat,* Feb. 19, 1870; *Le Nord,* Feb. 22, 1870.
38. *Journal de Genève,* Mar. 2, 1870.
39. Kantor, *V pogone,* pp. 12-14. The authorities thought that N.N. Nikolaev, whose passport Nechaev had originally used, was now with him.
40. *AEG,* Registre du Conseil d'Etat, 1870, 1er sem., A.F. No. 99; Great Britain, F.O. 100 (Switzerland), 177, no. 21, Bonar in Berne to London, Feb. 26, 1870; Bakunin, *Pis'ma,* pp. 264-265; Haas, 'Njetschajew,' p. 317.
41. *Journal de Genève,* Mar. 2, 1870; Kantor, *V pogone,* p. 76.
42. The letter appeared in nearly identical form in *La Marseillaise,* Feb. 20, 1870; *L'Internationale* (Brussels), Feb. 20, 1870; *Der Volksstaat,* Feb. 26, 1870; *La Suisse Radicale,* Feb. 26, 1870. A Russian translation appeared in the Nechaev *Kolokol* (Geneva, Apr. 2, 1870). *Le Nord* attacked the letter (which is reproduced in *Archives Bakounine,* vol. 4, pp. 39-43) on Feb. 21, 1870.
43. *BL/OR,* f. 100, 1. 229.
44. *Der Volksstaat,* Feb. 23, 1870. The Zürich *Die Tagwacht* (which Herman Greulich edited) called Nechaev a 'patriot' (Mar. 2, 1870) but later changed its views. The Swiss Bakuninist Charles Perron defended Nechaev in *L'Egalité,* Mar. 19, 1870.
45. On the polemic between Borkheim and Nechaev see ch. 6 of the present work.
46. *MERR,* p. 169.

CHAPTER FIVE

The Russian Section of the International

The sudden appearance of Sergei Nechaev as an international renegade seemed to confirm the belief of many tsarist officials in the existence of a vast European revolutionary conspiracy. Despite Nechaev's claims to be a member of the International, however, the Russian government did not make any serious effort to combat or even investigate that organization until 1871, the year of the Paris Commune. Then, as the power most hostile to revolution, Russia would take the lead in forming a new Holy Alliance against it. But in 1870 the police and the Third Section concentrated on rooting out the 'fives' inside Russia. Nechaev had, with criminal disregard for the safety of others, communicated with or referred in writing to literally hundreds of people; the new witch-hunt crippled the revolutionary movement as those unfortunates fell into police hands.

The persecution of the radicals that followed the Ivanov murder muted the revolutionary optimism that Nechaev had spread for a few brief weeks in the summer and autumn of 1869. In a desperate search for a leader to reunite their internally fragmented and externally decimated ranks (and to combat the degeneration of the movement engendered by Nechaev), some of the revolutionaries revived the old schemes of forcibly liberating Chernyshevsky, but those proved impossible of fulfillment. In the midst of the general gloom and frustration, the *Narodnoe Delo* group in Geneva officially constituted itself as a section of the International and proclaimed its solidarity with Marx and the General Council. If not a new Russian leader, the Russian radicals had, at least potentially, a new organizational base.

Becker and the Geneva Russians

At some point in the winter of 1869/70, J.P. Becker realized that he had to make a choice between Marx and Bakunin. No doubt word of Marx's anger over his participation in Bakunin's Alliance reached him; any question he might have had about Marx's views certainly disappeared at the Basle Congress. We note in passing here that the man whom everyone called 'Papa' Becker was one of the most popular figures in the IWMA. He kept his door open and his table set for every socialist, political refugee and workingman who passed through Geneva. Occasionally some of his guests abused his hospitality, and Michael Bakunin took advantage of his gullibility to lead him down an unfamiliar political path. But Becker's errors were on the side of generosity and decency, his greatest weakness a belief that he could please everyone.

In a pathetic attempt to regain Marx's favour and still hold Bakunin's, Becker resolved to create an anti-Bakuninist organization within the International and yet remain a member of Bakunin's Alliance. Had Alexander Serno-Solovyovich lived, Becker would probably have turned to him, but Serno committed suicide on the eve of the Basle Congress. That left Nicholas Utin, who was after Bakunin the most prominent of the active Russian revolutionaries in Switzerland. We have mentioned earlier that Utin moved quickly to win for himself and his group some of Serno's prestige among the Geneva Internationalists. Bakunin found this extremely irritating and claimed that Serno had told him, shortly before his death, 'With his disgusting revolutionary phrases, Utin has made me hate the very word "revolution".'[1] Whether Serno had actually said that made very little difference: Utin had principles sufficiently flexible to permit him to make use of Serno's reputation no matter what their personal relations had been.

As for Bakunin, Utin had publicly called him 'compatriot and friend' at the Basle Congress, then scurried up to enquire whether he had taken undue liberties. Basking in his victory over the General Council, Bakunin refused to allow the insignificant little man to disturb him; he dismissed Utin and returned to Geneva to attend to several matters, among which was his resignation from the editorial board of the International's newspaper, *L'Egalité*.[2]

The decision to resign proved a costly mistake. Bakunin's friends quickly lost control of the journal and were supplanted by Nicholas Utin and a group friendly to the General Council and Marx. That left Bakunin with only one press voice, James Guillaume's obscure *Progrès* (succeeded by *Solidarité*), published in Le Locle. Utin, on the other hand, now had great influence on one of the biggest and best of all the Continental socialist newspapers and he also controlled *Narodnoe Delo*. Bakunin realized too late what he had done. He wrote to Ogaryov that they should 'destroy' Utin, who unfortunately, however, had 'the money and the old women [i.e., Olga Levashyova and Zoya Obolenskaya, both of whom supported Utin's projects]'.[3]

Utin's star was indeed rising. In the November, 1869, *Narodnoe Delo* he or one of his colleagues paid tribute to their new found friends:

> of the participants of the revolution of '48 ... two were especially distinguished, K. Marx and P. Becker, who almost alone in the course of twenty years, and in the midst of a general reactionary era, never once soiled themselves by making common cause with the petty bourgeoisie; they always understood the true aspirations of the popular masses and went inseparably with them, at times ahead of them.[4]

Utin could not have failed to translate this passage for Becker, in whose *Der Vorbote* the following notice appeared two months later: 'There has also arisen here [Geneva] a Russian section, which has set as its tasks the combatting of pan-slavism and the turning of the Slavic-speaking workers, especially those in Austria, toward the international movement.'[5] The IWMA did not officially admit the Russian section until March 1870, but Becker's announcement made it clear both that the group existed in late 1869 and that Becker personally was delighted and relieved to make that fact known. One reason for the delay in the official admission of the section was the confusion in the Utin circle over the attitude of Becker and Marx toward Bakunin; the members knew next to nothing of Marx's hostility toward their countryman or of Becker's own dilemma.[6]

On the basis of Bakunin's June or July, 1870, letter to Nicholas Zhukovsky, some scholars have argued that (1) Bakunin himself planned to create a Russian section of the IWMA and even drew up a programme for it, and (2) Utin and his associates appropriated this programme and pre-empted Bakunin's plans.[7] There are indeed some elements in the Russian section's programme that indicate the difficulty the group had in shedding Bakunin's influence, but it is an egregious oversimplification to call the section a collection of disguised Bakuninists which deceived Karl Marx himself. Even if we accept as truth Bakunin's comments to Zhukovsky (these may well have been sour grapes, for Bakunin had had six years to create a Russian section and had not done so), that still cannot serve as proof of the Bakuninist origin of the Russian section. The latter's assertion that a 'free federation of agricultural and industrial associations' would replace the tsarist state reflected an old Proudhonist concept espoused by Bakunin; but the same idea lay at the root of the Basle Congress's resolution on trade unions and the future organization of society. That resolution, not any of Bakunin's comments, inspired the Utin group. Marx would hardly have urged approval of the program and rules of the Russian section had he considered them Bakuninist. The Alliance had burned him badly, and he was not a man to repeat his mistakes.

Analyzing the situation from his Locarno retreat, Bakunin knew that something inimical was going on in Geneva. He read Becker's *Der Vorbote* and realized that the Russian section's promise to fight panslavism was directed against him; he encountered such attacks constantly but usually they came from Germans. By early February, 1870, Bakunin accepted the fact that he could no longer deal openly with Becker. He advised Ogaryov to keep from Becker the origin of some articles which Herzen's son wished to publish in *Der Vorbote*.[8]

The members of the Russian section, announcing that they would attempt to bring other Slavs into the IWMA, thus flung down another challenge to Bakunin and Nechaev. Bakunin had a European-wide reputation and following; Nechaev, through Liuben Karavelov and others, was trying to establish himself as an 'all-Slav' revolutionary. The *Narodnoe Delo* group knew this and knew too that Becker, their patron, especially wanted to bring the Slavs into the fold. They therefore prepared to combat their enemies on a multi-national level.

Formation of the Russian Section

On March 3, 1870, Nicholas Utin requested Becker's assistance in regularizing the status of the Russian section. He gave the German revolutionary copies of the group's statutes and programme and asked for a 'petite lettre d'introduction auprès de Marx.' Utin urged expedition of the application: he wanted to publish a translation of Becker's 'Manifesto to the Agricultural Population' and thought it would have more authority and impact emanating from the journal of a regularly constituted section of the International.[9] Becker promptly wrote to Jung and Marx recommending admission of the section. Claiming credit for having helped establish it, he said that the group would serve the IWMA well because it resolutely opposed panslavism. Beyond that, he told Marx privately, the section was decidedly hostile to Bakunin.[10]

Becker found nothing controversial in the Russian section's documents, not least because he had helped to write them. He advised Utin to communicate directly with Jung. This Utin and his associates did, telling the secretary for Switzerland that their views and goals entitled them to 'join in the common work of the universal proletariat.' Because the International was illegal in Russia, the section would for the present consist of émigrés. But it would not be difficult, the Utin group claimed, to conduct propaganda among the workers in Russia and in time sections would be established there. The founders of the new section warned Jung against 'imposters' who might falsely claim to represent them; by this, they meant Nechaev and his friends.[11]

Utin, Victor Bartenev and Anton Trusov wrote to Marx soliciting his support and asking him to represent their section on the General Council. They saluted him as 'Dear and venerable citizen'; reasonably vigorous at fifty-two, the irritated Marx asked Jung why the Russians took him for an old man. An apology was quickly forthcoming from Geneva.[12] They had formed their section, the Utin group wrote in their first letter, 'because the great idea of this international movement of the proletariat now penetrates into Russia, too.' They planned to disseminate their principles in Russia, unite the workers, and 'expose panslavism, bringing the youth of the Slavic countries into the fight against these old ideas that render service only to the tsarist empire.' That empire would 'inevitably' be replaced by a 'free federation of agricultural and industrial associations that will unite the workers of the whole world through common interests and similar aims.' They already had had some success, the Russians wrote, finding 'adherents of the International's propaganda among Czechs, Poles and Serbs.' They told Marx that 'your name is deservedly esteemed by the Russian student youth, which is . . . of working-class origin.' (This latter claim was patently false.) The letter continued,

> Brought up in the spirit of the ideas of our teacher Cherny-shevsky . . . we have joyfully welcomed your exposition of socialist principles and your critique of the system of industrial feudalism. These principles and this critique . . . will shatter the yoke of capital, which supports the state—the hireling of capital.

(The news that *Capital* would appear in a Russian translation had obviously made an impression upon the members of the section, who had by now studied the work.)

The Russians formally asked Marx to represent them on the General Council, 'warning' him (as we saw in the last chapter) that no Russian in London could speak for them. This comment, and the following statement, must have perplexed Marx:

> In order not to mislead you and to spare you any surprises in the future, we also consider it our duty to warn you that we have

absolutely nothing in common with Mr Bakunin and his handful of accomplices. On the contrary, in the very near future we shall have to render a public appraisal of this man, so that in the world of the workers—and for us only their opinion matters—it will be made clear that there are persons who, preaching one set of principles among the workers, wish to make something else of themselves at home in Russia, something fully deserving to be stigmatized. It is urgently necessary to expose the hypocrisy of these false friends of political and social equality who in fact dream of a personal dictatorship on the model of [J.B. von] Schweitzer . . . we shall turn the affair over to the . . . - General Council so that you can pass sentence upon the conduct, activities and writings of individuals like Mr Bakunin who are trying to hammer into the heads of the Russian youth infamous negations of the principles of the International.[13]

Misinterpreting Bakunin's successes in Basle, and ignorant of Marx's reaction to the Alliance (which had by then been admitted into the IWMA), the Russian section felt it necessary to apologize for attacking Bakunin. They anticipated a clash with their sponsor, Becker (a member of the Alliance), and they feared that all this might compromise them with Marx. But Karl Marx, of course, could not have been more astonished or delighted. Writing in a 'confidential Communication' to the German Internationalists a couple of weeks after receiving the Russian section's letter, he stressed that he had neither organized nor manipulated the impending attack on Bakunin. On the contrary, the assailants were people who apparently thought of him as Bakunin's friend.[14]

Marx had known since February that the Russian group existed and that it would take an anti-panslav stance.[15] The opposition to Bakunin, however, was an unexpected bonus, particularly in view of the fact that the section's sponsor was a man who had trafficked with Bakunin—Becker. It soon became evident that the members of the Russian section did not seriously believe in the existence of panslavism (and indeed we may certainly agree with them), but they were convinced that Bakunin and Nechaev embodied a serious threat to the Russian revolutionary movement and to the International. Their decision to attack Bakunin was quite independent and was not remotely a capitulation to Marx or anyone else. Personal quarrels did figure in the affair to a certain extent, but it largely turned on matters of principle. Like the members of the Chaikovsky group in Russia, the Russian section disapproved of Nechaev's tactics; and unlike the *Chaikovtsy*, the Russian section insisted from the beginning that Nechaevism was the natural child of Bakuninism.

Hermann Jung presented the candidacy of the Russian section to the General Council on March 22, 1870. Recovering from a cold and an attack of carbuncles, Marx did not attend. Jung summed up the letters from the section, which wanted Marx for its representative on the Council 'because the practical character of the movement was so similar in Germany and Russia.' That extremely dubious proposition elicited no discussion, and the Council unanimously approved the affiliation.[16]

Marx and the Russian Section

One of Europe's most prominent Russophobes saw the humour in the situation. Marx wrote to Engels, 'Drôle de position für mich, als Repräsentant der Jeune Russie zu funktionieren.'[17] In this new capacity he transmitted the General Council's decision to the Geneva group. He called attention to the comment in the section's programme that described the occupation of Poland as a brake on progress both there and in Russia itself:

> You might add that Russia's rape of Poland provides a pernicious support and real reason for the existence of a military regime in Germany, and, as a consequence, on the whole continent. Therefore, in working to break Poland's chains, Russian socialists take on themselves the lofty task of destroying the military regime; that is essential as a precondition for the overall emancipation of the European proletariat.[18]

The thesis that the destruction of the most reactionary regime on the continent would precede the triumph of socialism derived from Marx's understanding of the existing informal league against revolution. He foresaw the reconstitution of the Holy Alliance; and the events that followed the Franco-Prussian War proved him right. (He was right, too, in predicting that socialism would not come to power anywhere in Europe until tsarism fell. When it did, it triumphed only in Russia—and there only briefly—but that only proved the original argument: in 1917 still stronger powers shared tsarist Russia's anti-revolutionary animus.)

Marx praised *The Condition of the Working Class in Russia* of 'N. Flerovsky' (the economist V.V. Bervi). Nicholas Danielson had sent him the book and Marx had learned Russian in order to read it. He told the Russian section that, although it contained a few theoretical shortcomings, the Flerovsky work was a 'real eye-opener for Europe':

> It is the book of a serious observer, a tireless worker, an unbiased critic, a great artist and, above all, of a person intolerant of oppression in all its forms and of all national anthems, and ardently sharing all the sufferings and all the aspirations of the producing class. Such works... and those of your teacher Chernyshevsky do real honour to Russia and prove that your country is also beginning to take part in the movement of our age.[19]

The members of the Russian section were probably embarrassed by these comments, for so far as we know none of them had ever heard of Bervi-Flerovsky. Only in May 1870 did *Narodnoe Delo* mention his book. Then, as if to rectify an oversight, the journal urged its readers to learn the work by heart.[20]

The Russian section wanted to carve out a Marxist position in the International and to counter the Nechaev-Bakunin propaganda barrage. Marx wanted the section to work for the liberation of Poland and the overthrow of tsarism. Becker hoped that it would fight panslavism, bring the 'urban and village workers of all Slavic countries' into fraternal union with the Western proletariat, and 'paralyze the bloodthirsty aspirations of the Russian government to intervene in the discord in the West.'[21] The members of the new section undoubtedly questioned their ability to achieve the goals Marx and Becker set for them, but they had every reason to rejoice in their new legitimacy as representatives of Russia in the International.

The Programme of the Russian Section

In the first of the three parts of its programme, the Russian section declared that tsarist oppression was identical to that in Europe and America, by which it meant that the material distress of the lower classes arose out of political and social institutions. The 'Russian people' had always adhered, the programme claimed, to the 'basic principles' of the International, namely, common ownership of the tools of production and of land. Further, the principle of the 'communality of labour' existed in Russia in the *artel*, a workshop co-operative that Russian populists came to regard as, roughly, the urban equivalent of the peasant commune. According to the programme, the Russian people had the traditions and organizations to form a new society. The International would help them understand the causes of their present misery, to rise up against tsarism and create new society. The section considered it one of its chief tasks to sharpen the class consciousness of the masses.[22]

The second part of the programme indicated how that task would be performed. The section would (1) disseminate 'by all possible rational means' the ideas and principles of the IWMA; (2) establish sections among the Russian working masses; and (3) build firm ties between those masses and their Western counterparts.

The final section outlined the anticipated relations between the working classes of the various Slav lands. Condemning panslavism as 'pernicious' and 'a foul trap,' the Russian section equated it with 'nationalism . . . now evilly misused by the enemies of the people against all socialist and Internationalist propaganda . . . [which] they present to the people as a bugbear that destroys all independence and originality.' The programme condemned all 'aggressive' regimes and denounced the Russian oppression of Poland. (The section may have emphasized this point to please Marx, but Utin had championed the cause of Polish freedom since his days in Land and Liberty.) It appealed to 'our brothers' in all Slav lands to join the Russian section, to propagandize their countrymen and work for the formation of sections in each country.

The Russian section also published its statutes. Devoted to organization, governance, rules and procedures, the statutes defined the relationship of individuals in 'sections inside Russia' to the Geneva group. Further, they made provision for supplying repatriated Geneva members with cards bearing a number instead of a name. The statutes made some attempt to establish financial priorities, regularize publication of *Narodnoe Delo,* and define the position of 'agents-correspondents' from other Slavic lands. They also provided for the creation of a mutual assistance fund that would 'aid our brothers who are struggling in Russia for the Liberation of the People and those of them who are suffering in banishment and exile.'[23]

The programme · and statutes of the Russian section, approved though they were by Becker, Jung, Marx and the General Council of the IWMA, were in many respects politically immature. The levels of economic development and social relationships in Russia did not correspond to those in the West. Though rapidly decaying, feudalism still existed in Russia, and industrial capitalism was showing but the first faint signs of life. The peasant commune and the urban *artel* had no contemporary counterparts in the West. For all that, however, the creation of the section constituted an important event both for the Russian revolutionary movement and for the International itself. The coming of the IWMA to Russia brought new hope at least to a tiny fraction of the intellectual élite on the extreme left and even to a few workers, and the implanting of its banner in new soil . strengthened the International and enhanced its prestige. While no one thought that an expeditionary force captained by Karl Marx would set out from London to overthrow the Tsar and bring justice and tranquillity to the Russian land, the Russians who joined the IWMA did expect that their action would help the revolutionary movement in their country shed its parochial, student character and make common cause with the modern European working-class movement. They were correct—more than a decade ahead of their time.

The First Test: La Chaux-de-Fonds

More than a little audacity was required to establish a new

section of the International in Geneva early in 1870. The local political climate was hostile to the Internationalists and was increasingly critical of foreign radicals. Furthermore, co-operation between Swiss and Russian authorities had reached a new plateau of cordiality; Anton Trusov wrote to Svetozar Marković, the Russian section's Serbian agent-correspondent, 'We know that the Federal Council is hand in glove with Russian espionage.'[24] Nevertheless, the Russian section organized and notices of that fact appeared in the socialist press around Europe.[25]

The section immediately entered the struggle between the General Council and the Bakuninists. The first direct clash since the Basle Congress took place in the Swiss mountain town of La Chaux-de-Fonds, where the Romande Federation (i.e. the Western Swiss sections) held its congress in April 1870. The leading items on the agenda were control of the Federation and its newspaper, L'Egalité, and admission into the organization of Bakunin's Alliance. Twice, the Alliance had attempted to enter the Federation and had been rebuffed. But now, because the General Council inexplicably admitted the Alliance into the IWMA itself, the members of the group demanded that the Federation reconsider.

Nicholas Utin was assigned to combat the Alliance. He wrote to Jung early in April, 'We shall be at the congress in sufficient strength to follow your instructions [not to admit the Alliance] if Bakunin interferes.'[26] He promised that he and his colleagues would 'unmask' Bakunin. The latter knew that a battle of major significance awaited his supporters, to whom he described the situation as a clear fight between 'our mountain sections' and the Geneva International. If he won, Bakunin would recapture control of L'Egalité—from which he had unwisely resigned—and dominate the Federation. If he lost, his new arch-enemy, Utin, would be in a commanding position.[27]

At La Chaux-de-Fonds, the task of defending the Alliance fell to Bakunin's Swiss friend James Guillaume, who did not belong to the organization and knew little about it. Representing the Geneva Central section, Utin attempted to table discussion of the Alliance question. Failing that, he assailed Bakunin and criticized the Alliance for its secrecy. Oddly enough, no one thought to ask why Utin himself had joined the Alliance—the public organization—soon after its formation.[28]

In reply, Guillaume cited J.P. Becker's membership in the Alliance as proof of its legitimacy, but the Utin faction declared that Becker knew nothing of the *secret* Alliance organization that existed side-by-side with the public body. Guillaume made the damaging admission that a secret group did in fact exist and he acknowledged that the founders of the Alliance originally considered its 'comité supérieur' equal with the General Council of the IWMA. He pleaded his lack of knowledge of the secret group and asked that the congress debate only the admission of the public body. He further insisted that, because Bakunin's group had given up its international organization and had joined the parent International, the Romande Federation had to admit it.[29]

Utin now declared himself the 'irreconcilable enemy' of Bakunin, though he said he thought the man was a 'Jesuit' and not a Russian spy. Someone then accused Utin of being an atheist. At any assembly of Internationalists other than one attended by Genevans, that charge would have been akin to calling the Pope a Catholic. J.P. Becker, however, understood Calvin's city: as a parting favour to the Alliance (he had renounced his membership by this time) he had kept it from total depravity by substituting 'materialist' for 'atheist' in its programme.[30]

The oratorical flights exhausted everyone and the delegates voted. Guillaume and the 'mountain sections' triumphed over Utin and the Genevans by a vote of twenty-one to eighteen. Guillaume exclaimed, 'C'est fait; l'Alliance y est.'[31]

Not quite. Utin and the minority refused to accept the verdict, maintaining that they represented twice as many workers as did Guillaume and the majority. That was true; but one of the regulations of the International stated in part that 'every branch, whatever the number of its members, may send a delegate to the [annual] Congress.'[32] The same rule would obviously apply to meetings of regional organizations.

Guillaume and the Bakuninists had the best of the argument, but Utin and his supporters controlled the hall. The minority ejected the majority, declared itself the 'true'

congress, rejected the Alliance's application for admission
and passed its own programme. The expelled anarchists went
to another building, proclaimed themselves the legal representatives of the Federation, reaffirmed admission of the
Alliance and approved a Bakuninist programme.[33]

The General Council had to settle the quarrel. Marx and his
friends argued that the Romande Federation had always
fulfilled its obligations and had adhered to the rules and
regulations. Because the 'nominal' majority at La Chaux-
de-Fonds represented only about half the number of members
as the minority, the Council, ignoring its own established
rules, refused to consider the original vote grounds for
transferring control of the Federation. In June 1870, the
Council unanimously affirmed the right of the original,
anti-Bakuninist Romande Federation to maintain control of
that organization. The Bakunin-Guillaume bloc was welcome
to remain in the IWMA (*sic!*) and call itself by any name it
chose—save Romande Federation.[34]

Though it never admitted it, the General Council had thus
changed the rules of the International, and in a strictly legal
sense the action was indefensible. The rule permitting each
section one vote had passed in open session at the 1866
Geneva Congress and was designed to prevent majority
domination of the minority. As a practical matter in the
spring of 1870, however, the Council could do nothing other
than support the Chaux-de-Fonds minority. Bakunin's insistence upon the independence of sections and the literal
interpretation of the voting rules reflected his doctrine of
political abstention and could only produce melancholy
results. Marx, on the other hand, argued for a centralized,
moderately disciplined International, but he did not—not
yet, anyway—want a rigid political or ideological test as a
precondition for admission; the acceptance of the Alliance
certainly proved that. But one could not expect Marx and the
General Council to be parties to the destruction of the
International. Had the Bakuninist victory at La Chaux-
de-Fonds stood, it is conceivable that the General Council,
then the International itself, would soon have ceased to exist.

The episode at La Chaux-de-Fonds, in which Nicholas
Utin played a key role, marked the beginning of the General

Council's counter-attack against the anarchists. Having been caught by surprise at the Basle Congress, Marx's friends were determined to recapture the initiative. In April 1870, Utin helped launch the tactics that ultimately kept the International out of anarchist hands. And because anarchism could only have a deleterious effect upon the working-class movement, Utin's actions—technically illegal—at the Romande Federation's congress contributed to a victory for social democracy.

Growth of the Russian Section

For some unknown reason, Marx did not comment directly upon the Russian section's plan—about which they had informed him—to publish a separate brochure embodying an attack upon Bakunin. Instead, he asked Becker to inform the group of his approval and his belief that the document should appear before the convening of the 1870 Congress of the IWMA, then still scheduled for September in Mainz. At the Russians' request, Marx sent along his latest evaluation of Bakunin's activities in 1848-9: a 'panslav' to the core, his only 'praiseworthy' exploit had been his participation in the Dresden uprising.[35]

Marx hoped that the Geneva Russians might deal effectively enough with Bakunin to spare him a great deal of trouble. Though he spotted the section's ideological shortcomings at once, he nevertheless appreciated its attempts to establish an alternative for the Russians who might have been tempted into Bakunin's Alliance. And he was soon to be grateful for the section's opposition to Nechaev. Utin and his friends remained attached to the Proudhonist schemes of mutual aid and free credit, but they resolutely condemned the Bakuninist doctrine of political abstention, called for the creation of organized, disciplined labour organizations, and denounced conspiracy. Contrary to Proudhon and Bakunin, the Russian section both advocated and participated in strikes (Utin was a major figure in the 1870 building-trades strikes in Geneva). A *Narodnoe Delo* writer observed that strikes were 'contemporary *partisan* warfare by labour against capital.'[36]

The addition of several new members, adding to the

approximately one dozen original ones, strengthened the
Russian section in the summer of 1870. This was a time when
reliable new blood was especially welcome, for the section
had discovered a spy in its midst. Vladimir Serebrennikov, a
student, went to prison during the disorders in the spring of
1869. In November of that year he escaped and made his way
to Geneva. Proclaiming himself Nechaev's sworn enemy, he
received a warm welcome from the *Narodnoe Delo* group. He
was, however, Nechaev's agent.

Serebrennikov showed Utin and the others what he
claimed were lists of Nechaev's contacts, outlines of his plans
and details of his movements. He begged for an opportunity
to work against the dangerous extremist. Normally, Utin and
his friends were quite cautious: they had refused, for example,
to deal with the Smorgon Academy's Ivan Bochkaryov in
1868 because they considered him a spy. But now, contempt
for Nechaev and Bakunin overcame their hesitation and they
accepted Serebrennikov as a colleague. Fortunately for them,
however, Serebrennikov was a braggart who soon began to
boast in taverns and cafés of his clever deception. The Utin
group learned of this early in the summer of 1870 and severed
all relations with their unscrupulous countryman whom
Nechaev, however, continued to find useful.[37]

A new member of the section who helped erase the painful
memory of the Serebrennikov episode was Elizabeth Tomanovskaya, *née* Kusheleva, a daughter of a wealthy Pskov district
landowner. Born in 1851, educated at home and in a local
girls' school, she had not experienced the vibrant intellectual
life of the cities that radicalized so many women of her
generation. But she read radical literature, some of which the
composer Modest Mussorgsky (a family friend) gave to her.
Chernyshevsky's *What Is To Be Done?* inspired her decision
—at the age of sixteen—to enter into a 'fictitious' marriage to
escape her tyrannical father. An agreeable bridegroom appeared in the form of Colonel M.N. Tomanovsky. Twice
Elizabeth's age and sickly, Tomanovsky allowed his young
bride to do as she pleased.[38]

What pleased her was to leave Russia, though the exact date
remains in dispute. Most Soviet writers speak of her going
abroad at the end of 1868, but there are no records of her

presence in Geneva—she could obviously have been else-where—before the summer of 1870. At that time, she joined both the Russian section and a section of women workers. She organized co-operatives, putting the lessons of *What Is To Be Done?* to the practical test. Strikingly pretty, gifted in languages, only nineteen years old—she charmed the Geneva Internationalists of all nationalities and lifted their spirits in the dark summer of 1870. And as the notorious 'Madame Dmitrieff' she was to do likewise for the Communards of Paris the following year.[39]

Another young Russian woman joined the section about the same time. Anna Korvin-Krukovskaya, daughter of an army general, was born in Moscow in 1843. At the end of the 1850's the family moved to Vitebsk province. Anna and her sister Sophia faced a life of deadly provincial boredom; but in that era, a few young women of the gentry class were beginning to reject such a fate. Anna turned at first to literature and wrote short stories. Fyodor Dostoevsky published two of them and told her,

> You are an artist. That already means a lot, and if beyond that there is talent and perspective, you have no right to neglect it. Just one thing: study and read. Read serious books. Life will do the rest. And it is also necessary to believe. Without that there is nothing.[40]

Though his daughter could hardly have found a more conservative literary mentor, General Korvin-Krukovsky was suspicious of most books other than the Bible. In any event young women had no business writing them. He allegedly told Anna, 'Today you sell your stories, tomorrow yourself.'[41]

Dostoevsky met Anna in 1865 and immediately fell in love. He saw in her his Galatea; under his tutelage she would become Russia's first great woman writer. He proposed marriage (his first wife had died in 1864). Anna was flattered but not seriously tempted, for Dostoevsky had a real and not a 'fictitious' marriage in mind. She declined so gracefully that the writer felt no insult and indeed preserved the kindest memories of her.[42]

Anna and Sophia resolved to go abroad, and that meant that one of them, at least, had to get married, for the father would never permit them to go by themselves. In 1868 V.O. Kovalevsky, later to become a noted paleontologist, agreed to a 'fictitious' marriage with Sophia—who, as Sophia Kova-levskaya, herself became a famous mathematician. General Korvin-Krukovsky then gave Anna permission to go abroad with her sister and her new brother-in-law. The three went to Vienna, where Kovalevsky—true to his bargain—remained while the women continued on to Heidelberg. In May 1869 Anna went alone to Paris against her father's wishes; the latter promptly cut off all financial support. Anna went to work as a bookbinder and began to frequent working-class circles. There she soon met the man who became her common-law husband and who later married her, the Blan-quist revolutionary Charles Victor Jaclard. It was probably Benoît Malon, the well-known socialist, or his *amie*, the writer Mme André Léo (the pseudonym of Léodile Béra), who introduced the couple.[43]

Victor Jaclard had been associating with Russians for several years. One of the Blanquist militants at the 1865 Liège student congress, he may have met the mysterious Russian (Khudiakov?) who attended that meeting. Certainly he knew Bakunin, Utin and several others of the Lac Léman colony because he met them at the 1868 Berne congress of the League of Peace and Freedom, following which he joined the Alliance. Jaclard broke with Blanqui personally in 1869 over the planning of (yet another) *coup d'état* and drifted into the International. Paul Lafargue and Charles Longuet—future sons-in-law of Marx—sponsored his admission into a Paris section. At Lafargue's suggestion, Marx had sent him a copy of *Capital*, and Jaclard entered the IWMA a friend of the Marxists. He quickly made a mark as an organizer and agitator; and when the French government cracked down on such types after the May, 1870, plebiscite, an order went out for Jaclard's arrest. He and Anna Korvin-Krukovskaya fled to Geneva.[44]

We have only fragmentary information on their activities in Switzerland. Anna entered the Russian section, agreed to translate some of Marx's works into Russian, and wrote children's stories for magazines. Jaclard gave mathematics lessons and schemed to return to France. Whether he actually joined the Russian section we do not know, but he almost certainly advised the members on the art and science of revolution. Jaclard was to have a long association with the Russian left and indeed he later lived in Russia—following the Paris Commune—for several years. But his heart was always in France, and the disaster of the Franco-Prussian War gave him the opportunity to go back. In September 1870 he and Anna returned to Paris.[45]

The Russian Section and Russia

Given the previously uneven success of the *Narodnoe Delo* group in making an impression upon radical circles inside Russia, the progress made after the summer of 1870 probably owed something to the newcomers. Almost certainly at the urging of the new members, Catherine Barteneva and Olga Levashyova returned to Russia for brief visits in the autumn. According to fragmentary evidence, they undertook a brazenly active campaign to recruit members for the Russian section. With their more up-to-date knowledge of people and events in Russia, the new women in the section (Tomanovskaya and Korvin-Krukovskaya) would have been in a position to suggest how to proceed with this campaign, and Victor Jaclard would have given the emissaries the benefit of his experience and expertise.

In November, a Third Section agent reported that Catherine Barteneva had persuaded many students to enroll in the Russian section of the International. He had only a few details and but one name; he did not know that he had stumbled onto the 'Malaya Vulfovskaya' (a St Petersburg street) student commune. The vague nature of the report notwithstanding, the authorities launched an investigation into what seemed an ominous development. Behind the International, they reasoned, might lurk the notorious 'European Revolutionary Committee' that had sponsored the Karakozov and Cohen affairs. Beyond this, the fall of the Second Empire and the proclamation of the Republic (September 4, 1870) in France had reawakened the old fears that constantly haunted conservatives all over Europe. If revolution in France were to coincide with a wave of

Internationalist terror, the continent would tremble again.[46]

Early in September, the spy Apollon Mlochowski informed the Viennese police that the Parisian Internationalists supported the new Republic and were sending secret agents to Vienna, Prague, Lwów (Lemberg), Berlin, Frankfurt, Dresden, Munich and 'even to St Petersburg' to rally the 'democratic-socialist party.' He provided a list of activists that would have frightened any king or police chief: Garibaldi, Bakunin, Kossuth, Louis Blanc, Victor Hugo, Ludwik Mieroslawski.[47] This list and this information surely reached the Third Section, for whom Mlochowski also worked. He notified his Russian superiors in January 1871 that Catherine Barteneva and Olga Levashyova were associated with Mark Natanson, a known radical and a student at the St Petersburg Medical-Surgical Academy. Mlochowski advised the Third Section to determine who had visited Mrs Levashyova when she was in the capital the previous autumn (he seemed unaware that Barteneva had also been there); anyone who called upon her, he warned with impeccable police logic, was probably a member of the 'Geneva society' to which she and Barteneva belonged. That society, however, was not the Russian section but a 'group d'initiative et de propagande' formed in November 1870 to revive the local International.[48]

It was of course exceedingly unlikely that anyone in St Petersburg belonged to an obscure political action group in Geneva, but Mlochowski—whose reports to several police agencies helped launch a European-wide campaign against the International—never had any need for factual accuracy: he told his employers what they wanted to hear. In the case of Natanson, whom Olga Levashyova did know, the Third Section was unable to establish a firm connection with the International, but that was only because their investigation was slipshod. Born in 1850 into a family of well-to-do Vilna Jews, Natanson came to the capital to study in 1868. In October of that year he founded the commune on Malaya Vulfovskaya Street. He participated in the 1869 student disorders, and in the internecine quarrels in the student movement he sided with Stepan Ezersky against Nechaev.

When Catherine Barteneva and Olga Levashyova made their way to the Natanson commune in 1870, only remnants remained. Nevertheless, there is considerable evidence that Natanson and his friends, for about a year after the visits of the two women from Geneva, worked with the Russian section of the International. They received and disseminated the section's publications (and also *L'Egalité*, now edited by Nicholas Utin), tried to spread the International's message of socialism, and attempted to recruit members. Isolated as they were, Natanson and his colleagues welcomed the opportunity to co-operate with an émigré group; and the Russian section jumped at the chance to establish a firm presence inside Russia.[49]

Affiliated with the *Chaikovtsy* and other, less well-known groups, Natanson and his associates played an important role in the Russian section's attempt to propagandize the International in Russia. At that time and in that context, however, 'Russia' still meant an audience of intellectuals and students who preached largely to each other. The groups inside Russia had limited contact with the urban workers and the peasantry, and the émigrés of course had virtually none. It was partly in order to remedy that situation that, in the latter part of 1871, Natanson and his friends relegated their co-operation with the Russian section to a secondary position as they set out to transform the *Chaikovtsy* into a 'Great Propaganda Society,' the goals of which were unification of all revolutionary groups in Russia and the conducting of propaganda among the peasant masses.[50]

Thus the most promising initiative of the Russian section was to come to grief in the winter of 1871/2 as the Natanson group joined the populist 'to the people' movement. The 'people' meant the peasantry; the industrial workers to whom the International appealed—indeed for whom it was created —were few in number in Russia and their needs, even their very existence, remained, at this stage, beyond the ken of most Russian radicals. The 'to the people' movement was a backward step, a reversion to the illusions of Herzen, Pisarev, Bakunin and even Chernyshevsky. Once again, the revolutionaries tried and failed to incite the peasantry to revolution.

The Russian section was ahead of its time in sending the message of the International to Russia. The necessary cadres and constituency were simply not yet there, at least not in coherent form. Nevertheless, the section made the required initial moves, and its labours helped to make Marx's name and theories as well known in the 1870's and 1880's as those of Fourier had been in the 1840's and 1850's. A few seeds fell into isolated and protected soil; roots began to grow.

NOTES

1. Bakunin, 'Intrigi gospodina Utina,' p. 411.
2. Bakunin, *Izbrannye sochineniia*, vol. 5, pp. 142-3..
3. Bakunin, *Pis'ma*, p. 242 (see also pp. 228-46). The General Council had scolded both *L'Egalité* and *Progrès* for attacking the Council itself and the journal of the Zürich Internationalists, *Die Tagwacht*, and this triggered the resignation of the Bakunists from *L'Egalité*. See *L'Egalité*, Oct. 1, 1869, and Jan. 15, 1870; *DFI*, vol. 3, pp. 198, 201, 354-63. *Narodnoe Delo* no. 7-10, November, 1869, p. 111) hinted that *L'Egalité's* coverage of Russian developments would soon be improved—i.e. Bakunin would leave.
4. *Narodnoe Delo* no. 7-10, p. 117.
5. *Der Vorbote*, no. 1, January, 1870, p. 12. The Russian section claimed adherents among the Czechs, Poles and Serbs, but Becker's reference to the Habsburg Slavs nevertheless remains puzzling.
6. Koz'min, *Russkaia sektsiia*, pp. 189-90, errs in claiming that the Utin group knew in March 1870 that the General Council was hostile toward Bakunin.
7. Z. Ralli published Bakunin's letter in *Minuvshie gody*, vol. 10, 1908, pp. 153-7. Max Nettlau misinterpreted it in 'Bakunin und die russische revolutionäre Bewegung in den Jahren 1868-1873,' *Archiv für die Geschichte des Sozialismus und der Arbeiterbewegung*, vol. 5, p. 411. B.P. Koz'min *(Russkaia sektsiia*, p. 189) and Franco Venturi *(Roots of Revolution*, pp. 434, 443) have made the same mistake.
8. Bakunin, *Pis'ma*, pp. 255, 260.
9. IISG, *Becker*, D II 534. The Russian section published Becker's work as a brochure later in 1870; it originally appeared in *Der Vorbote*, December, 1869, pp. 177-84. This was perhaps the International's most important statement on the peasant question. For its relationship to the Russian situation see Alan Kimball, 'The First International and the Russian *Obshchina*,' *Slavic Review*, vol. 32, no. 3, Sept., 1973, especially pp. 493-4. See also Koz'min *Russkaia sektsiia*, pp. 190n-191n., and *Freymond*, vol. 3, notes 360, 889.
10. Jaeckh, *Die Internationale*, pp. 231ff.; IISG, *Marx-Engels Correspondence*, D 238.
11 IISG, *Jung*, 864a.
12. *Werke*, vol. 32, p. 466; IISG, *Jung*, 864b.
13. *MERR*, pp. 168-70.

14. *Werke*, vol. 16, p. 420.
15. *Ibid.*, vol. 32, p. 444.
16. *DFI*, vol. 3, pp. 219-20.
17. *Werke*, vol. 32, p. 466.
18. *DFI*, vol. 3, pp. 410-11. The official reply was first published in *Narodnoe Delo*, no. 1, April 15, 1870, p. 4.
19. *DFI*, vol. 3, p. 411; see also *Werke*, vol. 32, p. 377, 637, 656. Bervi-Flerovsky's work appeared in St Petersburg in 1869. For Marx's reservations about it, see O. Abramovich's introduction to the 1938 (Moscow) edition, pp. xiv-v. Though he mentioned him in his letter to the Russian ,section, Marx knew little about Chernyshevsky until Lopatin came to London in the summer of 1870; see *Werke*, vol. 32, p. 521, and Koz'min, *Russkaia sektsiia*, p. 212. See also the article by V. Diuvel' (Wolf Düwel), 'Chernyshevskii v nemetskoi rabochei pechati (1868-1889),' *LN*, vol. 67, pp. 163-205. Incidentally, Marx learned Russian in order to read the works of Chernyshevsky and Bervi-Flerovsky.
20. *Narodnoe Delo*, no. 3, May 31, 1870, p. 2.
21. *Ibid.*, no. 1, April 15, 1870, p. 4.
22. *Ibid.*, pp. 3-4. The group simultaneously published its documents as a brochure, appending the rules and administrative regulations of the IWMA: 'Mezhdunarodnoe Tovarishchestvo Rabochikh,' Geneva, 1870. On the section see also N.K. Karataev, ed., *Ekonomicheskaia platforma Russkoi sektsii I Internatsionala*, Moscow, 1959; I.P. Shpadaruk, *Russkaia sektsiia I Internatsionala i eë sotsiologicheskie vozzreniia*, Minsk, 1970; L.S. Bocharova, 'Russkaia sektsiia I Internatsionala i eë sotsial'no-ekonomicheskaia platforma,' unpublished kand. diss., Moscow State University, 1955. A famous *artel* was the one of seamstresses in Chernyshevsky's *What Is To Be Done?* (New York, 1961). A recent study of peasant *artels* in the 19th century is P.G. Ryndziunskii, *Krest'ianskaia promyshlennost' v poreformennoi Rossii (60-80-e gody XIX v.)*, Moscow, 1966.
23. The section would use its funds for propaganda in Russia; support for strikes in Russia; sending delegates to IWMA meetings; dues to the General Council.
24. *Archives Bakounine*, vol. 4, pp. 359-60.
25. Anton Trusov's Mar. 23, 1870, note appeared in *L'Egalité* on Mar. 26, in *La Marseillaise* on Apr. 12, in *Der Volksstaat* on May 14, and in *Der Vorbote* for Mar., 1870, pp. 39-40. The Austrian police took note of this; see *HHStA*, IB 1870, no. 719, daily report of the Vienna police directorate for May 16, 1870. The *Journal de Genève* complained on Jan. 27, 1870, that the General Council was plotting still another strike in Geneva; see also on this *HHStA*, PSMA, Département II, No. 250, communication of Feb. 15, 1870.
26. IISG, *Jung*, 864b, 889. See also *L'Egalité*, Apr. 2, 1870.
27. Polonskii, *Materialy dlia biografii M.A. Bakunina*, vol. 3, p. 570.
28. Bert Andréas and Miklós Molnár, eds., 'L'Alliance de la démocratie socialiste: procès-verbaux de la section de Genève (15 janvier

1869—3 décembre 1870),' in Jacques Freymond, ed., *Etudes et documents sur la Première Internationale en Suisse*, Geneva, 1964, p. 221 note 80. Victor and Catherine Bartenev were founding members of the public Alliance; see *ibid.*, p. 205, where they use the names Alexeiev and Alexeieva. Nicholas Zhukovsky, Victor Jaclard and J.P. Becker were also founding members. At a Sept. 17, 1869, meeting of the *secret* Alliance, Bakunin warned against admitting Utin, Trusov and their friends; see *ibid.*, p. 168.

29.	*L'Egalité*, April 30, 1870.

30.	Andréas and Molnár, 'L'Alliance,' p. 186; Carr, *Bakunin*, p. 430.

31.	*L'Egalité*, April 30, 1870.

32.	IISG, *Jung*, 564, 'Seance du Congrès Romand'; *DFI*, vol. 2, p. 269; *Werke*, vol. 32, pp. 474, 677.

33.	*Guillaume*, vol. 2, pp. 5-7; Carr, *Bakunin*, p. 430.

34.	*DFI*, vol. 3, pp. 256, 368.

35.	*Werke*, vol. 33, pp. 129-30. A distorted version of this letter is in *Guillaume*, vol. 2, p. 77.

36.	*Narodnoe Delo*, no. 5, July 31, 1870, pp. 2-3.

37.	*Deiateli*, vol. 1, part 2, p. 370; Koz'min, *Russkaia sektsiia*, p. 220; Meijer, *Knowledge and Revolution*, pp. 62-4; *AEG*, Etrangers, Dh 22, 23, no. 47437; Dh 40, 128, no. 47437.

38.	I.S. Knizhnik-Vetrov, *Russkie deiatel'nitsy Pervogo Internatsionala i Parizhskoi Kommuny: E.L. Dmitrieva, A.V. Zhaklar, E. G. Barteneva*, Moscow-Leningrad, 1964, pp. 16-26.

39.	*Ibid.*, pp. 27-57; Bocharova, 'Russkaia sektsiia,' pp. 167-8; IISG, *Jung*, 865; Koz'min, *Russkaia sektsiia*, pp. 110-1.

40.	Knizhnik-Vetrov, *Russkie deiatel'nitsy*, p. 146.

41.	*Ibid.*, p. 147; S.D. Kuniskii, *Russkoe obshchestvo i Parizhskaia Kommuna*, Moscow, 1962, pp. 108-9.

42.	Knizhnik-Vetrov, *Russkie deiatel'nitsy*, pp. 148-52. On Dostoevsky in this period see V. Ia. Kirpotin, *Dostoevskii v shestidesiatye gody*, Moscow, 1966, ch. 6.

43.	Knizhnik-Vetrov, *Russkie deiatel'nitsy*, pp. 147-57; Kuniskii, *Russkoe obshchestvo i Parizhskaia Kommuna*, pp. 108-9; Edith Thomas, *The Women Incendiaries*, New York, 1966. pp. 89-90.

44.	Gustave Geffroy, *L'Enfermé*, Paris, 1926, pp. 48-52; M. Dommanget, *Blanqui et l'opposition révolutionnaire à la fin du Second Empire*, Paris, 1960, p. 216; *Werke*, vol. 32, pp. 475, 544-5; *DFI*, vol. 3, pp. 118, 473-4 note 335; France, Ministère de la Guerre, Etat-Major de l'Armée, *Archives Historiques*, dr. 'Charles-Victor Jaclard,' Tribunal de 1re instance du Dép. de la Seine, Aug. 25, 1871; Charles Seignobos, *Le déclin de l'Empire et l'établissement de la 3e République*, Paris, 1921, p. 96; Knizhnik-Vetrov, *Russkie deiatel'nitsy*, p. 170.

45.	Knizhnik-Vetrov, *Russkie deiatel'nitsy*, pp. 171-6.

46.	*TsGAOR*, f. III otd., sekr. arkhiv, opis' no. 1, ed. khr. no. 512, 1. 2. See also B.S. Itenberg, *Pervyi Internatsional i revoliutsionnaia Rossiia*, Moscow, 1964, pp. 56, 203 note 32.

47.	*HHStA*, PSMA, 1870, nos. 1390, 1395. Mlochowski used the name

'Isidore Schmidt' when working for the Austrians; see *ibid.*, IB 1875, no. 238.

48. *TsGAOR*, f. III otd., sekr. arkhiv, opis' no. 1, ed. khr. no. 517, 'Agenturnye doneseniia o nabliudenii za uchastnikami narodnicheskogo kruzhka, organizovannogo instituta Natansonom M., i o sviaziakh kruzhka s russkoi sektsiei Internatsionala,' 11. 2-3; *ibid.*, f. III otd., 3 eksp., d. no. 163, 1871, 'Ob ot'ezhaiushchikh litsakh za granitsu i vozvrashchaiushchikhsia obratno,' 11. 5-9. On the 'groupe d'initiative' see IISG, *Jung*, 895, and IISG, *Marx-Engels Correspondence*, D 3890.

49. See the first dossier cited in the previous footnote, esp. 11. 2-3, 10, 14-15; Koz'min, *Russkaia sektsiia*, pp. 224-8; Venturi, *Roots of Revolution*, pp. 356-7; *Deiateli*, vol. 2, part 3, pp. 1002-6.

50. N.A. Troitskii, *Bol'shoe obshchestvo propagandy*, Saratov, 1963; R.V. Filippov, *Ideologiia Bol'shogo obshchestva propagandy (1869-1874)*, Petrozavodsk, 1963; M.A. Miller, 'Ideological Conflicts in Russian Populism: The Revolutionary Manifestoes of the Chaikovsky Circle, 1869-1874,' *Slavic Review*, vol. 29, no. 1, March, 1970, pp. 1-21.

CHAPTER SIX

Shifting Revolutionary Currents

A wave of strikes swept over Europe in the first half of 1870, demonstrating a remarkable uniformity in labour-capital relations on the continent. That uniformity was in large measure the product of Europe's growing economic interdependence, and in that phenomenon lay also the *raison d'être* of the International, which figured in many of the 1870 strikes and bore the blame for most of them. The strike fever affected even remote, autocratic Russia, where the IWMA played no role. A strike and lock-out late in May 1870 partially shut down the huge 'Neva' cotton mills of Stieglitz and Company in St Petersburg. The dispute started when several score employees protested against the unfair computation of their wages and their wretched working conditions; eventually nearly half the 2,000 workers were involved. The Russian press spoke of the 'unprecedented' situation, and a high governmental official referred to the 'absolutely new phenomenon' of a large-scale work stoppage. So novel was the event that the strikers went to prison for only a few days, and an appellate court reversed their convictions. Tsarist Russia had not, however, changed its spots: the tsar ordered the Ministry of the Interior to exile many of the strikers to distant provinces.[1]

Coming at a time when the Nechaev affair had disorganized and depleted the ranks of the revolutionaries, the strike did not have a significant impact upon the Russian radicals. They simply failed to grasp its importance. They, the government and the factory owners still thought of the worker as a kind of city peasant, a man who thought in peasant categories and would respond to the same provocations and inducements as had always stirred the Russian peasantry. The Russian worker, however, was losing his identification with the countryside more rapidly than anyone realized. He was not fully at home in the cities, yet he had no incentive to return to the village. He was increasingly alienated from both his labour and his environment at a time when great historical forces were increasing both his numbers and his misery. A proletariat was taking form in Russia.

If even the historically passive Russian workers were calling into question the blessings of the industrial revolution, the situation in the West was certain to be still more tense. In France, the gigantic Schneider enterprise at Le Creusot (Saône-et-Loire), where over 10,000 workers made locomotives, rails, engines and armaments, experienced a serious labour dispute in mid-January 1870. Several workers lost their jobs in a disagreement over an aid fund, and most of-the employees left their workbenches in protest. Management then locked all entrances to the factories and shops. Elsewhere, a work stoppage in some of the Silesian mines was already several weeks old when Le Creusot went on strike. Sporadic, frequently violent disorders plagued the Borinage and other Belgian mining districts. Labour unrest, led by the Bakuninist-dominated International, racked Italy until the government made hundreds of arrests in June. Spain, politically unstable under military government and beset by widespread unemployment, suffered serious working-class violence in April, especially in Barcelona, and again the Bakuninists made progress in organizing the workers. Viennese printers struck in March; troops and strikers clashed in Prague and elsewhere in Bohemia in April and May; Belgian textile workers walked out of the mills in April; Hamburg carpenters struck in May. In Geneva, the tilers rebelled against low wages and a sixteen-hour working day; they struck in April and other crafts joined them. This labour solidarity was the result, in part, of the *patronat's* policy of dismissing workers who joined the International. By the end of the spring Geneva was in the throes of a general strike. European conservatives accused the International of fomenting this dispute and indeed most of the others.[2]

The Russian Section and the Strike Movement

From its sanctuary in Geneva, *Narodnoe Delo* commented only briefly upon the St Petersburg strike (actually two separate strikes).[3] Having only the information it could glean from the conservative Western press, the journal had to be content with describing the legal disabilities that shackled the Russian workers; it also claimed that the oppression of the workers would strengthen the International in Russia.

The Russian section could plant the flag of the IWMA in Russia only by clandestine and uncertain means, but it could give unqualified support to the great labour organization in the West. That included assisting in strikes in which the International figured. Henri Rochefort's *La Marseillaise* opened a public subscription for the Le Creusot strikers, and *Figaro* then accused the workers of receiving outside subsidies. The conservative press in general hinted darkly at a vast republican conspiracy led by the International; and the government closed down *La Marseillaise*.

The Russian section sent 100 francs to the strike fund and a letter that Rochefort published just before his journal was shut down. Signed by Anton Trusov, the letter declared that labour and the intellectuals, acting in concert on an international basis, had to deal resolutely with the 'atrocities and crimes of the international coalition of capital and chassepot . . . . In their unhappy country, as in exile, your Russian brothers follow with warm sympathy your victorious movement toward social liberation and the destruction of the whole hateful contemporary order.' Trusov went on to note that the Russian people, no less than the French workers to the capitalists, were in thrall to the 'executioner of Poland' who had 'robbed the Russian people by his false freedom and who was now enticing all other Slavs, beckoning to them with the panslavism that is so disastrous to the West.' (Invariably, an ostentatious disavowal of panslavist sympathies preceded the section's assurances that it was 'hoisting the banner of the International in Russia.')[4]

At the end of March the Geneva correspondent of the *Neue Zürcher Zeitung* wrote,

> The number of Russian émigrés of the so-called nihilist party who live in our city is very large. The newspaper 'Kolokol,' founded by Herzen, now appears again under the editorship of a committee of Russian men of the movement . . . . so active is the 'International' that it sends its propaganda not only all over Switzerland and the neighbouring French and Italian regions but also to faraway countries. Geneva is at present—it would be folly not to acknowledge it—one of the capitals of the European socialist movement.[5]

The resurrection—or rather the parodying—of *Kolokol* was Nechaev's handiwork and we shall speak of that presently. We note now that Nicholas Utin emerged as a leader of the Geneva strike commission established by the local International to co-ordinate the work stoppages and combat the lock-outs. Consciously striving to emulate Alexander Serno-Solovyovich's prestigious role in the 1868 construction industry strike, Utin tried to create a united front among the workers. He assumed control, for all practical purposes, of *L'Egalité* and during the strikes edited both the newspaper and a weekly supplement. He participated in the interminable daily meetings in the Temple Unique (a former Masonic hall that was the IWMA's headquarters), helped negotiate between the *patronat* and labour, directed propaganda, and continued to edit *Narodnoe Delo*. His Russian section colleagues joined him in these endeavours.[6]

The Swiss recognized, of course, that foreigners were among the chief agitators of the International in Geneva, and the spring of 1870 saw another of those periodic campaigns (which have continued into the 1970's) against foreigners in Switzerland. The campaign took the form of newspaper attacks, threats of expulsion, co-operation with foreign police agencies and *visites domiciliaires*. It reached a peak on June 5, when the city awakened to find posters everywhere urging the rejection of the workers' demands, which were branded the work of 'foreign agitators' in the International. The *patronat's* broad-

sheets gave the workers four days to abandon their demands,
admit their 'guilt' and return to work. In the event of refusal,
every employer in Geneva would lock his doors. The employers also demanded the dissolution of the International
and the expulsion of foreigners who disturbed Swiss peace
and tranquillity.[7]

These extreme measures did not materialize. In the tense
European summer of 1870, new and more vital concerns
arose, and the strike movement fizzled out. But in Geneva,
the local International and the foreign radicals (especially
Russians, Germans and Frenchmen) had received notice that
the business community, backed by religious leaders of both
major denominations and the cantonal government, was
intent upon destroying the organization and intimidating its
members.[8]

The New Nechaev

Fearing that the successes of the Russian section might leave
them behind, Nechaev and Bakunin tried, in the spring and
summer of 1870, to recapture the revolutionary momentum
they had attained in the summer of 1869. Occasionally
working together but more often separately, they launched a
new campaign. In February Nechaev told Natalie Herzen of
his 'society's' wish to create a 'centre' in Geneva.[9] He could
not carry out that plan, however, because he had to flee to
London. But he soon returned, and for a time he co-operated
with Bakunin in the attempt to strengthen the anarchist
organizations in the Jura, in Italy and in Spain. To achieve
respectability in the eyes of Western socialists, the two men
flooded the leftist press with letters. Bakunin went so far as to
declare in *Der Volksstaat* that 'Russia was in large part
civilized by Germans.' Needing to atone for his foolish
charges aginst Bakunin on the eve of the Basle Congress,
Liebknecht felt obliged to publish this letter and Bakunin's
notes on the Russian revolutionary movement. Karl Marx
and Sigismund Borkheim, however, wanted no part of a
reconciliation with the Russian anarchist.[10]

In March, Borkeim sharply attacked Nechaev in a letter to
Der Volksstaat. Signing himself 'A Social Democrat from

Russia,' Nechaev defended himself in the same journal a short time later. In April, 'Three Party Comrades' (members of the Russian section) joined the budding polemic and attacked both Nechaev and Borkheim. The farce continued into the summer. Borkheim and Nechaev (neither of whom used his name in print) traded wild charges. The 'Three Party Comrades,' discovering Borkheim's identity (and knowing him to be Marx's friend), worried lest their own identity become known to Marx. For his part, Borkheim thought the 'Three' were Nechaev and a couple of friends and suggested that they go to Hell. Utin, Trusov and Bartenev wrote to Marx in July asking him to thank Borkheim for this enlightening commentary.[11]

Friedrich Engels saw this charade for what it was:

> Russian remains Russian. What kind of stupid nonsense is this, half a dozen Russians squabbling among themselves as though world supremacy depended upon the outcome. And the accusations against Bakunin really do not come out: the whole thing is merely a lamentation about minor plots and prattle [Klüngelei] in Switzerland. In any case they [the Russian section] seem to be honestly ours, in so far as that is possible for Russians; I would, however, be cautious with them. In the meantime it is good to know all the gossip, for it belongs to the diplomacy of the proletariat.[12]

Part of the Nechaev-Bakunin offensive of 1870 involved the revival of Herzen's famous *Kolokol*. Plans for the resurrection emerged as soon as the original suspended publication in 1867, but nothing came of them. *Kolokol* was nothing without Herzen, and he had lost the capacity for sustained enthusiasm. His death in January 1870, however, opened the way for those who wished to capitalize upon his fame. Bakunin proposed a new *Kolokol* as a 'bureau for the regular dissemination of news from Russia.' He, Ogaryov and a couple of others would direct it; Nechaev would supply news from the homeland. Bakunin had learned a little more about 'Boy' and he did not want him at the centre of things. For his part, Nechaev did not include Bakunin at all in his own plans for the revival of Herzen's journal. And the youthful, forceful Nechaev, armed with the Bakhmetev fund and tales of his 'committee' and 'society' inside Russia, easily prevailed.[13]

Nechaev told Natalie Herzen (who protested at the use of the name *Kolokol* and refused to serve as nominal editor) that the political line of the revived journal would not be 'red,' as Bakunin and Ogaryov had assumed, but 'variegated' or even 'colourless' in order to attract as broad a spectrum of support as possible.[14] Nechaev wanted to adopt a conciliatory line in the new publication. His *Kolokol* carried no exhortations to popular rebellion, no demands for rivers of landlord blood. There was instead a summons to unity, a plea for all the forces of opposition—from liberals to radicals—to work for the overthrow of absolutism:

> The resurrected *Kolokol* will be primarily—one may say exclusively—the organ of Russian practical action. To have the right to participate in its work only two conditions must be met: (1) a conviction that the existing order is disastrous for Russia; (2) a firm commitment to work against that order.[15]

The new journal could not very well insist upon ideological purity because it had no ideology. Most Russian revolutionaries—ideologues *par excellence*—could not comprehend this position.

Already cursing himself for his role in helping to create Nechaev, Bakunin wrote a plaintive letter that appeared in the second issue:

> Having read attentively the first issue ... I remain confused. What do you want? What is your banner? What theoretical principles do you profess, and what is your ultimate goal? In a word, what kind of system do you wish for Russia ... Who are you, socialists or champions of the exploitation of the people's labour? Friends or enemies of the state? Federalists or centralizers?

Bakunin worried about Nechaev's call for a coalition against tsarism. He had himself proposed precisely that in two recent works, but he urged the new *Kolokol* to be cautious:

> Every coalition is in theory immoral and impossible. A coalition in practice is also extremely dangerous, but it is sometimes necessary and salutary, specifically in those instances when it is limited, temporary, and has a broadly defined goal.[16]

Nechaev replied in the same issue. The overthrow of tsarism, he argued, must override differences—even contradictions—among the oppositionists. Only those (such as Bakunin, he strongly implied) cursed by 'petty self-esteem' would refuse to work for the revolution because of policy disagreements. Those who merely sat around spinning theories did so out of weakness and indecision. Theory and details could wait; anyone who disagreed was 'not a serious person.' These arguments did not constitute a program, but then Nechaev himself did not know how to go about fighting tsarism. In many respects, *Kolokol* merely stalled while the new editor tried to get his bearings. To a reader who demanded a halt to temporizing and the seizing of 'our rights from Alexander II by force,' Nechaev replied,

> The peculiar radicalism of principles which people concerned with theory are pleading for seems to us an untimely luxury. Everything must be subordinated to the struggle against imperial absolutism ... We repeat: the struggle with absolutism and victory over it—this is the first and most important step for all of us. It follows that we shall not talk about victory until we begin the struggle.[17]

This was, manifestly sheer nonsense. The intellectual content of the Nechaevist *Kolokol* was mediocre at best, the 'practical' side simply incomprehensible. In April and May the journal featured jejeune commentary upon the impossibility of establishing a constitutional monarchy in Russia. There were vicious attacks upon Herzen and others, gratuitous insults in abundance, and much gibberish about revolution. The new journal was as anti-intellectual as the first *The People's Summary Justice* (Narodnaya Rasprava), in which Nechaev had written, 'We perceive only the negative, immense plan to total destruction. We directly renounce the elaboration of the future conditions of life as incompatible with our work; and therefore we consider fruitless all theoretical work.'[18]

Nechaev never forgot the snubs he endured when—a country bumpkin—he entered the world of St Petersburg radicalism. In the third issue of his *Kolokol* he wrote that the greatest harm to the cause came from those who theorized excessively about it. The 'golden dreams' of émigré theorists about 'fairy-tale lands' were meaningless. Theory was useless. Years of hairsplitting disputation had not so much as bruised tsarism. Action counted above all. Nechaev's was in short a positivist stance that embodied increasingly heavy doses of Blanquism.[19]

With the selectively sharpened insights of the self-taught political fanatic, Nechaev discerned the futility of the Bakunin-Proudhon policy of political abstention. But he also, in the spring of 1870, no longer believed (as Bakunin most certainly still did) in a 'spontaneous uprising.' The Russian peasant, Nechaev realized, would fight for what was his—and for what he thought ought to be his—when goaded beyond endurance, but his zeal for battle would diminish with every step away from his homestead, and his awe of the tsar would remain. Nechaev did not minimize the importance—indeed the necessity—of mass peasant violence in the overthrow of tsarism, but he perceived that, in order to transform the unsuccessful jacqueries of the past into a victorious revolution, a revolutionary elite would have to guide and sustain the mass violence. An undisciplined peasant rabble could create havoc on a grand scale but could never seize political power (a Nechaevian goal which Bakunin expressly rejected); the revolutionary elite alone could accomplish that. And the elite would obviously administer political power after seizing it; there would be no room for the unlettered Russian peasantry in government.

Therefore, Nechaev asked in his *Kolokol*, why not turn to some of the liberal gentry and urge them to join the revolution and thus earn a share in governing the country after tsarism's fall? This too brought Nechaev close to Blanqui's teachings. Having lost faith in Bakunin's popular revolution, Nechaev had begun to see the possibilities of Blanqui's political revolution. He believed that a leader like himself could inspire the revolution that would create a communist society. That was his goal, but because he really did not know exactly what he meant by 'communism' he refused to discuss it. Needless to say, his potential allies were not impressed. The *Kolokol* episode represented an attempt to woo the Russian liberals, the last social group untouched by the 1869 propaganda campaign. Failure was almost inevitable. Few people took seriously the efforts of the notorious young zealot to present himself as a unifying figure in the opposition movement.[20]

Lopatin and the Fall of Nechaev

Nechaev had taken care to remain anonymous in the new *Kolokol*. He sent most of his correspondence and manuscripts to Vladmimir Serebrennikov in London for re-posting, but nevertheless the search for him in western Switzerland continued. The unremitting pressure from the authorities deeply disturbed some of the émigrés, who called a meeting in Geneva early in May 1870 to discuss their alternatives. Several Geneva Russians attended, as did a few of their countrymen who were studying in Zürich, and Herman Lopatin—recently arrived from the homeland—was also present. Lev Mechnikov, Garibaldi's former adjutant, presided. The discussion opened with an enquiry into the danger to the émigré community that the Russo-Swiss co-operation in the Nechaev search posed. The fugitive's friends (Ogaryov, Nicholas Zhukovsky and the Zürich students) wanted to denounce that collaboration publicly. Semyon Zhemanov of *Narodnoe Delo* argued that such a denunciation would have no practical effect. Zhemanov also attacked Nechaev's misuse of the Bakhmetev fund and his desecration of the name of *Kolokol*.[21]

Herman Lopatin held back at first, limiting himself to a few general comments on the nature of political asylum. He quickly saw, however, that everything hinged on Nechaev's authenticity. If the man were indeed determined to be a bona fide revolutionary rather than a common murderer, the émigrés would naturally have to try to save him. The meeting stalled on that question. Lopatin then spoke, and the others listened. He proved that Nechaev's 'Committee' in Russia did not exist, at least not in the form Nechaev claimed; that Nechaev had played a very minor—if controversial—role in the student movement of 1868-9; that the police had never arrested him, and therefore he could not have made his miraculous escapes; that he remained chiefly in Moscow in the autumn of 1869 and had not created 'fives' all over Russia; and that the murder of Ivanov had been an act of personal vengeance. Nechaev could not escape his past.

Some of the émigrés had regarded Nechaev as a man who had in fact done what they all *should* have done, that is, fight the enemy in the field. His blunt, brutal ways fascinated them in the same way Rasputin was later to fascinate Russian high society: the man seemed indeed to be from the 'people' with all the people's earthy strengths and faults. After Lopatin's lengthy speech, however, the fascination with Nechaev ebbed dramatically. The 'lost' man of the famous 'Catechism' seemed, Natalie Herzen wrote, more a 'base swindler' than a revolutionary idealist. The *Kolokol* affair and Lopatin's startling revelations stunned the credulous and convinced the waverers. Trapped, Nechaev turned upon his former friends, attempting to slander Bakunin and to rob the Herzens of their fortune and even their honour. The effort naturally backfired; even the most gullible individuals were outraged. The final blow came when Nechaev tried to persuade the son of Ogaryov's mistress to form a bandit gang to rob tourists. Now abandoned by everyone, the discredited young conspirator slunk away to London.[22]

Lopatin and Marx

Herman Lopatin had few illusions about the prospects of unifying the émigrés, whose endless squabbling disgusted him. He found a depressing mediocrity in the Geneva colony, which lacked a leader of real stature. He might have played that role himself save for his utter lack of selfish ambition. Born into a Nizhny Novgorod gentry family in 1845, he entered St Petersburg University when he was seventeen. He came to the attention of the police in 1865 because of his association—not affiliation—with members of the Ishutin circles and the following year he was arrested after Karakozov shot at the Tsar. He soon proved that he had never participated in any revolutionary activities and he was released in time to defend his dissertation.

Although he sympathized with them, Lopatin had refused to join the revolutionary circles because he disliked their preoccupation with theory, their ignorance of the real life and needs of Russia. Like Nechaev and Blanqui (and for that matter Tkachev), he was a man of action; and in this connection we should remember that the members of the Ishutin circles *condemned* Karakozov's attack on Alexander. In 1867 Lopatin went to Italy. His hopes of joining Garibaldi collapsed on the day he arrived: in the Battle of Mentana, papal forces won a smashing triumph and captured the guerilla hero. Lopatin went to Nice, where he had an unsatisfactory—for reasons that are not clear—interview with Herzen. Returning to St Petersburg at the end of the year, he joined the Ruble Society only to fall into police hands, along with the other members, in February 1868. After eight months in prison, he went to his father's home in Stavropol under informal house arrest. He became the unofficial librarian of the provincial governor and from that post disseminated revolutionary literature, including the first issues of *Narodnoe Delo*. In December 1869 the police arrested him again when they discovered a letter outlining his plans to escape abroad; somehow they construed this letter—damaging enough on its face—as proof of his involvement in the Nechaev affair. Within a month, however, Lopatin did escape, and he made his way to St Petersburg.[23]

In the capital, Maria Negreskul, daughter of Peter Lavrov, told Lopatin of her father's plight. The noted philosopher and socialist had been under semi-arrest since the Karakozov affair and at the time was in exile in Vologda province. Maria told Lopatin that her father wanted to go abroad to see Herzen and to attend to urgent personal affairs. Without hesitating Lopatin gave Lavrov a bogus passport he had obtained for himself. He reasoned that the famous author of the *Historical Letters* desperately needed to escape and that his flight would better serve the cause of the revolution than his own. Lavrov left Russia in February 1870 and arrived in Paris two weeks later, only to learn that Herzen had died on January 21. He sent the passport back to Russia; Lopatin used it to cross the frontier in April.[24]

Joining Lavrov in Paris, Lopatin quickly appraised the situation among the émigrés. He went to Geneva in May ostensibly to make peace among the several groups there, but

in reality he had probably already decided to expose
Nechaev. He was angry—as scores of revolutionaries were
—because of the irresponsible propaganda campaign of 1869
and offended by the juvenile nonsense published under the
hallowed rubric of *Kolokol.*

His later friendship with Marx developed in spite of
Lopatin's negative reaction to Marx's friends in Geneva.
Bakunin thought that Lopatin was in league with Utin, but
this was not the case. Lopatin visited the *Narodnoe Delo* offices
several times and saw members of the staff privately, but he
remained cool toward the Utin circle. His exposure of
Nechaev certainly did not herald his alignment with
Nchaev's enemies. He refused to give Utin the letter Nechaev
had written threatening Liubavin over the Bakunin translation of Capital and he scorned Utin's suggestion that he help
'unmask' Bakunin as he had destroyed Nechaev.[25]

Lopatin left Geneva abruptly at the end of May and went to
Paris, where he joined one of the sections of the International.
That was an act that, in view of the political developments in
France, took some courage, and it is noteworthy also that
Lopatin joined a Paris section rather than the Utin group in
Geneva. He met the local socialists through Paul Lafargue
('my medical Creole,' Marx called the man who married his
daughter Laura in 1868) and the Alsatian Charles Keller.
Keller was working on a French translation (never completed) of *Capital.* Because his friends Danielson and Liubavin
were attempting to produce a Russian translation, Lopatin
surely discussed this work with Keller. In June 1870 he went
to England to see Karl Marx.[26]

For some reason—Marx thought perhaps he liked to swim
—Lopatin took a room in Brighton. He went up to London
for the first time on July 3, concerned lest he be unable to
converse in a language Marx knew on a level that would hold
his interest. His fears were groundless. The two men spoke a
kind of Indo-European dominated by French and thoroughly
enjoyed each other's company. Lopatin was the first Russian
other than Bakunin with whom Marx had had any real
personal contact since the 1840's; even his old hostility
toward the Slavs—all Slavs—did not prevent him from liking
his young visitor. From Lopatin Marx learned the true

story of the Nechaev affair, the personal histories of Bervi-Flerovsky and Chernyshevsky, and the sad truth that Sigismud Borkheim (who had translated entire books for him) knew very little Russian. The only thing Marx did not like about Lopatin, he wrote to Engels, was his attitude toward the Polish question: 'Here he talks like an Englishman—say a Chartist of the old school—about Ireland.' But not even this shortcoming dissuaded Marx from the conviction that Lopatin was the 'only "solid" Russian whom I have known.' He told Engels that he would 'soon knock national prejudice out of ... [Lopatin's] bones.' And in mid-December Lopatin, back in Russia, wrote that he was 'beginning to share' the view of Marx and Engels that the only way to destroy tsarism was through war.[27]

In an expansive mood Marx kept his visitor almost the entire day. Lopatin wrote to Lavrov that he had received a very cordial welcome; Jenny Marx insisted that he dine with them whenever he came to London. In 1918 Lopatin recalled his delight at the absence in Marx of any 'professorial manner' and at Marx's extraordinary ability to go immediately to the heart of any subject. Beyond that, Marx's high regard for Chernyshevsky—which can only have increased as he listened to Lopatin—had impressed him favourably.[28]

At Marx's suggestion Lopatin moved to London, where he supported himself with a clerical job and by doing translations for the Russian press. When a project to translate Louis Blanc's works collapsed, Lopatin found himself with some free time. He then reluctantly agreed to a task that had been proposed to him more than once, the translation of *Capital* into Russian. Marx himself convinced him to undertake the work, which Lopatin insisted on doing without fee in order not to compromise himself with the Bakuninists. The latter still hoped that one of their number would do the translation, and therefore Lopatin rejected the thousand rubles that his St Petersburg friends offered.[29]

The man of action set about the tedious labour with characteristic energy. He found the first two chapters so abstruse as to present an obstacle to potential readers in Russia; Marx advised him to begin with the third chapter while the first two were under revision. The work proceeded with considerable despatch; by late November Lopatin had completed nearly a third of the book.[30]

Marx introduced Lopatin into London socialist circles, and in September of 1870 Auguste Serraillier, a French émigré, proposed Lopatin's election to the General Council of the IWMA. Marx seconded the motion, which was passed unanimously two weeks later. Lopatin thus became the first Russian to participate in the work of the International at this level. He attended ten consecutive weekly meetings, and in his one recorded speech discussed the attempt of the French government to crush the International.[31]

Soviet historians argue that Lopatin 'aided Marx in the struggle against Bakuninism' during his tenure on the Council.[32] Undoubtedly anything Lopatin did for Marx worked to Bakunin's disadvantage, but it is not true that he was an active opponent of his countryman. For one thing, the struggle had not yet reached the active, public stage. For another, Marx never made any reference to Lopatin's having helped him against Bakunin. Further, the records yield only one instance in which Lopatin criticized Bakunin in Marx's presence. There may of course have been other, private instances of such criticism, but the evidence to justify the exaggerated claims of Soviet scholars is lacking.[33]

Lopatin felt that discussion of purely Russian affairs and quarrels in the presence of foreigners was in poor political taste. There were certain things about Russia, he believed, that outsiders simply could not understand. (Engels later recalled that Lopatin strongly disapproved of Nicholas Utin's participation in the politicking that led to Bakunin's expulsion from the IWMA.[34]) Lopatin told Lavrov in the summer of 1870, after he knew Marx, that he thought the socialist movement had room for a variety of schools and that no one faction had a monopoly on the correct political line. He found the Marx-Bakunin split extremely unpleasant and harmful but saw no hope of successful mediation. Lopatin disagreed with Bakunin on many issues, but he did not join the campaign against him.[35]

Late in November of 1870 Lopatin received a cryptic message summoning him to Russia. He left at once, not even taking leave of the Marxes. He wrote two weeks later from St

Petersburg that an affair of the gravest importance had required his unceremonious departure. That 'affair' was yet another scheme to liberate Chernyshevsky, whom Lopatin hoped to take to the West and install as the leader of the revolutionary émigrés. Lopatin had discussed this plan in Geneva with the members of the Russian section, who enthusiastically endorsed it, and (to his later regret) with Michael Elpidin.[36]

P.A. Rovinsky, who had helped Nicholas Utin and other revolutionaries flee to the West in the 1860's, conceived the new plan for Chernyshevsky's escape. A noted ethnographer, Rovinsky had been a member of Land and Liberty and had performed many missions for the revolutionaries. At the end of 1870, the Russian Geographical Society commissioned him to undertake an expedition to Siberia and China; he readily accepted, because the journey would take him 'near' (in the broad Siberian sense) to Chernyshevsky. Summoning Lopatin from London, Rovinsky went ahead to Irkutsk, where he gathered information of Chernyshevsky's whereabouts, the strength of the guard, and other details.

Arriving in the capital, Lopatin gave the unfinished manuscript of his translation of Marx's masterpiece to Danielson and awaited word from Rovinsky. When that arrived, he set out at once and reached Irkutsk in the middle of January, 1871. He and Rovinsky pondered their mission, and as they were trying to come up with a plan Lopatin was arrested: a telegram from Geneva had warned the Third Section about the scheme. Michael Elpidin had revealed everything to a spy. (Lopatin generously ascribed this to indiscretion, but Elpidin's subsequent record showed him capable of deliberate treachery.) Lopatin escaped from prison after serving thirty months. Rovinsky was fortunately untouched by the affair. Chernyshevsky remained locked away in the distant settlement of Aleksandrovsky Zavod.[37]

Herman Lopatin's activities in 1870 considerably strengthened the Russian revolutionary movement. He aided the escape of Peter Lavrov, who soon became the leader of a wide and important émigré circle. He exposed Nechaev and ended that threat to the stability of the movement. Thanks to Lopatin, Marx obtained a much clearer view of Russian radicalism. The work of translating *Capital* was well under way; Lopatin completed a good share of the work and turned it over to Danielson, who completed it a little over a year later. These were all considerable accomplishments, the more so because Lopatin never sought power or influence in the movement. But that coin had another side: the Russian revolutionaries still lacked a leader.

Enter Lavrov

The sterile émigré quarrels that distressed Lopatin were, as Peter Lavrov later wrote, a 'natural pathological phenomenon in every emigration torn away from its homeland.' The émigrés schemed endlessly to return to Russia and fulfill their revolutionary dreams; but time and events inevitably altered the dreams themselves, and 'practical' work seemed ever more futile.

One émigré who did no idle scheming was Lavrov. Born near Pskov in 1823, he was the son of a prominent army officer and landlord; Alexander I stayed at the family estate on his last journey south in 1825. Peter's father, a friend of the notorious Count Arakcheev (who ordered all the cats on his estates hanged because he loved the singing of the nightingales), subjected him to firm discipline, tutoring in mathematics and foreign languages, and abuse for his love of poetry. At fourteen Lavrov entered the Mikhailovsky Artillery School. He progressed in his studies and through the ranks, served in the Crimean War, and by the end of the 1850's held the rank of colonel and was teaching mathematics in military academies.

Political maturity came slowly to Lavrov, who was eleven years younger than Herzen, five years older than Chernyshevsky. He served on the St Petersburg city council and seems not to have questioned the tsarist system until the disaster in the Crimea. After the war, he and millions of his countrymen re-examined the old assumptions. Like nearly everyone in Russia, Lavrov welcomed the accession of Alexander II; sooner than most he became disillusioned. He wrote to Herzen in 1856 that he feared the coming emancipation might actually worsen the condition of the peasants by leaving them at the mercy of the bureaucrats and 'kulaks' (rich peasants).[38] His old complacency gone, Lavrov moved toward philosophical radicalism. In a series of articles that appeared in 1858-9, and in his famous *Historical Letters* a decade later, he sought to explain why German idealist philosophy, and especially Hegel's system, had not fulfilled the hopes of its Russian adherents. He also tried to put into accurate focus the Russian left's materialism and to work out a theory of progress and history. His philosophical views, which became a pillar of the populism of the 1870's and 1880's, influenced few of the Russians who joined the International prior to 1872. But after that year, Lavrov became a major leader of a generation that was tired of sterile nihilism, only peripherally attracted to anarchism, and still not certain how to interpret those distant echoes of Marxism.

Chernyshevsky and Dmitry Pisarev attacked Lavrov for his eclecticism, his alleged failure to master Feuerbach and Comte, his criticism of a kind of Hegelianism not preached in Russia since the 1840's and his lukewarm regard for the materialist philosophy. The assault miscarried. Lavrov became an important figure in radical circles in the 1860's and later went on to a position of respected leadership.[39] In the early 1860's he was denied the chair of philosophy at St Petersburg University because of his association with radicals. Prohibited also from delivering public lectures, Lavrov devoted the next few years to various literary activities. The police arrested him in the post-Karakozov roundup. In October of 1866 a military court found him guilty of having insulted Nicholas I and Alexander II, of consorting with 'persons known to the government for their criminal proclivities,' of disseminating harmful ideas in the press, and of other offenses. The court stripped him of his rank and banished him to 'one of the interior provinces, under police surveillance.'

In February of 1867 Lavrov came under guard to the hamlet of Totma in Vologda province. He continued to write; the *Historical Letters* appeared in a progressive St Petersburg weekly under a transparent pseudonym.[40] In August 1868 he had to move some distance away to the village of Kadnikov, apparently because the authorities disapproved of his relations with other exiles in Totma. Among the latter was Anna Czaplicka, *née* Modzelewska, a Polish woman exiled for revolutionary activities. She and Lavrov became friends, then lovers. They entered into a common-law marriage that the local gendarmerie did not recognize (Lavrov's first wife had died in 1866).

Anna Czaplicka escaped to the West in 1869, we know not how. Lavrov made repeated attempts to follow her (this was the 'personal affair' his daughter spoke of to Lopatin). He and his mother appealed to a former governor of St Petersburg, Prince A.A. Suvorov, who had helped more than one leftist in distress (including Nicholas Utin). This time Suvorov could do nothing; all Lavrov's petitions and pleas encountered refusal. Surreptitious flight was impossible because—as his daughter said—the myopic Lavrov could not distinguish a police uniform at three paces. Life in exile, onerous under any circumstances, became all but unbearable without Anna Czaplicka. Beyond that, Lavrov longed to see Herzen, who had told friends he wanted to meet the author of the *Historical Letters* and perhaps undertake some joint work.[41] Frustrated at every turn, Lavrov must have despaired of the future. But then Herman Lopatin learned of his predicament, and he spent the next thirty years of his exile in Paris and London.[42]

The choice of Paris as a permanent base was a little surprising. Public opinion and reasons of state dictated that France shelter the Polish refugees of various rebellions, but Louis Bonaparte had no intention of turning the country into a haven for foreign malcontents. France had many domestic varieties of that species, and foreign revolutionaries who came to the attention of the French police ran a grave risk of expulsion or extradition.

It was really Anna Cazplicka who made Lavrov's decision. She had been in the French capital for a year, had made some friends among the local Poles, and had established a modest business making artificial flowers. And so Lavrov moved in with her to enjoy the last truly happy years of his life.[43] He had at least one good contact of his own in Paris. Paul Broca, the founder of modern anthropology, had some knowledge of Lavrov's scientific works; he befriended the Russian savant and introduced him into the intellectual and academic communities. Further, a few of Herzen's old friends—Russians and Frenchmen—provided agreeable company. But Lavrov had to be cautious, for he had no passport. Calling himself 'Sidorov' in the company of strangers, he blended quietly into the local Russo-Polish colony.[44]

Lavrov valued obscurity, but he probably also craved a little excitement after a lifetime in the 'dark kingdom.' He must have relished the Paris that throbbed, in the spring of 1870, with that peculiar political tension that the 1789-1815 generation had permanently grafted onto the city's soul. It was all to culminate in the Paris Commune, and Lavrov would participate in the great *bouleversement*.

But that came the following year, and in 1870 he lived quietly with his Anna, worried about their precarious financial situation (to the relief of which he initially could contribute nothing), and carried on an extensive correspondence. He avoided political activity. Bakunin wrote to him in July asking his collaboration on an atheistic, 'collectivist,' anti-Marxist review. Though he was not seriously tempted, Lavrov asked Lopatin's advice. The latter replied that the potential collaborators were ' "puny" . . . coryphaei like Bakunin, Ogaryov, Mechnikov and Company who, as *coryphaei*, are not worth a brass farthing!' Lopatin had earlier made it clear that he thought the proposal preposterous, and he urged Lavrov to decline the invitation. Lavrov was spared a decision when the project, like so many of Bakunin's ventures, failed to materialize.[45]

Bakunin in Limbo

Bakunin wanted to enlist Lavrov's collaboration on his proposed journal, but he did not know what to make of Lopatin. Confronted by a genuine revolutionary, Bakunin—who had mistakenly seen Nechaev in that role—found his views in disarray. He now regretted having tossed away the right to translate *Capital*, and Nicholas Zhukovsky's announced desire to take over that project confused him. The new *Kolokol* humiliated him. Bakunin broke with Nechaev and went to Locarno to lick his wounds.[46]

Ensconced on the lake, he wrote to Ogaryov, 'Hey, brother! Things are good here! It's quiet, peaceful, you can think as much as you want and do whatever you want. There is none of Utin's filth, Mechnikov's eloquence, Zh[emanov]'s profundity. E[lpidin]'s wisdom, Zh[ukovsky]'s hot air.'[47] He had earlier blamed 'my compatriot, the Russian yid Utin,' for the deterioration, as he saw it, of the International in Geneva. The local organization had joined the reactionaries, Bakunin claimed, in seeking the bourgeois-radical path of peaceful reform. That meant, of course, that the Geneva Internationalists had rejected Bakunin's admonition to abstain from politics and were engaging in strikes and contesting for political office.[48]

After the General Council upheld the Chaux-de-Fonds minority, the initiative in the Geneva International belonged to Utin and Bakunin's other opponents. Bakunin could only watch helplessly from Locarno as the Romande Federation prepared to 'discipline' him and his friends. The victorious minority decided to punish the Bakuninists for attempting to seize control of the Federation. On August 13, 1870, the Geneva Central section expelled Bakunin, Zhukovsky, Charles Perron and Henry Sutherland (the son of Ogaryov's mistress) for their alleged attempt to split and take over the Romande Federation. Utin sponsored the successful motion.[49]

This was by no means the end of the Bakuninists in Switzerland. They remained members of the Geneva Alliance section, which was still a legitimate branch of the parent IWMA though not of the Romande Federation; this curious anomaly was to play an important role at the International's Hague Congress in 1872. But the precedent of La Chaux-de-Fonds, however, wherein Utin and a minority had prevailed over the Bakuninist majority and had won the support of the General Council, spelled danger for Bakunin and his friends. For them, as for every other faction among the Russian émigrés and within the International, a great deal would depend upon their conduct in the crisis that exploded in the summer of 1870.

NOTES

1. R.E. Zelnik, *Labour and Society in Tsarist Russia,* Stanford, 1971, pp. 340-69; *Rabochee dvizhenie v Rossii v XIX veke,* vol. 2, pt. 1, *1861-74,* Moscow, 1950, pp. 238-43; *L'Egalité,* June 18, 1870; *Le Nord,* June 19, 1870; *Die Tagwacht,* July 30, Aug. 20, 1870 (Eugene Utin, Nicholas's brother, probably wrote these latter two articles, which were signed with initials he frequently used, 'A.B.' [see I.F. Masanov, *Slovar' psevdonimov russkikh pisatelei, uchenykh i obshchestvennykh deiatelei,* vol. 1, Moscow, 1956, p. 33]).

2. The strikes mentioned here were large-scale affairs involving hundreds and in several cases thousands of workers. Innumerable minor strikes and work stoppages occurred in the period January-June, 1870, especially in France, Belgium and some of the German states.

3. *Narodnoe Delo,* no. 4, Apr. 30, 1870, p. 1.

4. *La Marseillaise,* Apr. 26, 1870; *Narodnoe Delo,* no. 2, May 7, 1870, p. 4.

5. *Neue Zürcher Zeitung,* no. 163, Mar. 30, 1870.

6. IISG, *Marx-Engels Correspondence,* D 3889 (in Russian translation in *MERR,* pp. 172-80). See also *La Suisse Radicale,* Feb. 22, 1872; *Werke,* vol. 33, p. 17; *DFI,* vol. 3, pp. 251ff., 369-71; Erich Gruner, *Die Arbeiter in der Schweiz im 19. Jahrhundert,* Berne, 1968, p. 625; *Narodnoe Delo,* no. 4, June 30, 1870, pp. 2-4.

7. *L'Egalité,* June 11, 1870; *Narodnoe Delo,* no. 5, July 31, 1870, pp. 3-4.

8. *AEG,* Registre du Conseil d'Etat, 1er sem., 1870, R.C. 425, 544-5; *ibid.,* O.D. No. 116; *La Suisse Radicale,* June 10, 1870; *Narodnoe Delo,* no. 4, June 30, 1870.

9. See Natalie's diary in *CMRS,* vol. 10, no. 1, pp. 103-5.

10. *Der Volksstaat,* Apr. 16, 20, 1870; *La Marseillaise,* Apr. 24, 1870; see also *APP,* B/A 944, *pièces* 4-5.

11. *MERR,* pp. 172-80. The polemic took place in the pages of *Der Volksstaat* between March and June of 1870. At the end of March, Nechaev—not using his own name—advertised in several Geneva newspapers that the new *Kolokol* would publish a Russian translation of the *Communist Manifesto.* Marx, who had not known of these plans, requested six copies, and Nechaev promised to send them. The advertisements appeared in *La Suisse Radicale* beginning on Mar. 20, 1870. Marx's letter to *Kolokol* has not survived; Nechaev's April 26, 1870, reply is in IISG, *Marx-Engels correspondence,* D V 84.

12. *Werke,* vol. 33, p. 17. Marx had earlier criticized the Geneva Russians. Utin had written (*Narodnoe Delo,* no. 2, May 7, 1870, pp. 1-3) that communal landownership, the 'sole great heritage of the Russian people,' was consistent with the principles of the International, which shared the Russian goals of 'land and liberty.' Marx wrote on his copy, 'Asinus!' and noted that 'Russian communal property can get along with Russian barbarism, but not with bourgeois civilization.' See Koz'min, *Russkaia sektsiia,* pp. 252-3.

13.   Bakunin, *Pis'ma,* pp. 257-8; Carr, *Bakunin,* p. 406; see also Michael Confino's introduction to Natalie Herzen's diary in *CMRS,* vol. 10 no. 1, p. 69.

14.   See Natalie Herzen's diary just cited, 9 above, pp. 123ff., 137. Few people knew who controlled the new journal; the Russian section told Marx that Bakunin was the editor (*MERR,* p. 177).

15.   *Kolokol* (Geneva), no. 1, April 2, 1870, p. 1 (quoted also in Venturi, *Roots of Revolution,* pp. 384-5).

16.   *Kolokol,* no. 2, April 9, 1870, pp. 4-5 (Bakunin's letter is reproduced in *Archives Bakounine,* vol. 4, pp. 85-7.

17.   *Kolokol,* no. 3, April, 16, 1870, pp. 22-3.

18.   Quoted in Koz'min, *P.N. Tkachev,* p. 180; see also Koz'min, *Iz istorii,* pp. 566-7.

19.   B.P. Koz'min has argued, erroneously in my view, that such thinking proved Nechaev had not shaken off Bakunin's influence; see *P.N. Tkachev,* p. 182. Nechaev was much closer to Pisarev and Blanqui than to Bakunin.

20.   We know little about Nechaev's collaborators. Ogaryov wrote a few articles, as did Nicholas Zhukovsky and V.A. Zaitsev. The latter also propagandized ideas from *Capital* in Russia; see IISG, *Jung,* 246; *Deiateli,* vol. 1, part 2, pp. 135-6; Reuel', *Russkaia ekon. mysl',* pp. 221-2.

21.   This meeting recalled a similar one in Geneva in December 1864 and January 1865 at which the 'young emigration' failed to reach an accord with Herzen. On the 1870 gathering see Meijer, *Knowledge and Revolution,* pp. 62-4 (which contains some errors based upon Semyon Serebrennikov's 'Zapiska'); Trusov's letter to Svetozar Marković in *Archives Bakounine,* vol. 4, pp. 359-60; Bakunin, *Pis'ma,* 1906 edition, pp. 379-81; R. Sh. Tagirov, 'Iz istorii Russkoi sektsii Mezhdunarodnogo Tovarishchestva Rabochikh (Russkaia sektsiia i evropeiskoe revoliutsionnoe dvizhenie),' *Uchenye zapiski Kazanskogo gosudarstvennogo instituta,* vyp. 2, pt. 2, 1956, p. 93n.

22.   *CMRS,* vol. 7, no. 4, pp. 625-97 (esp. pp. 683ff.); *ibid.,* vol. 8, no. 3, pp. 469-73; *ibid.,* vol. 10, no. 1, pp. 147-149; Carr, *Romantic Exiles,* pp. 306-7; *MERR,* p. 175; Koz'min, *Iz istorii,* p. 571; Iu. M. Rapoport, *Iz istorii sviazei russkikh revoliutsionerov s osnovopolozhnikami nauchnogo sotsializma (K. Marks i G. Lopatin),* Moscow, 1960, pp. 13ff. On Bakunin's break with Nechaev see *Archives Bakounine,* vol. 4, pp. 103-57.

23.   *Kolokol,* no. 2, April 9, 1870, p. 15; *La Suisse Radicale,* May 12, 1870. Franco Venturi (*Roots of Revolution,* pp. 355-6) errs in stating that Lopatin went abroad immediately after his escape.

24.   Ivan Knizhnik-Vetrov, 'P.L. Lavrov ot pervykh publitsisticheskikh vystuplenii do izdaniia 'Vpered' (1857—mart 1872),' in P.L. Lavrov, *Izbrannye sochineniia na sotsial'no-politicheskie temy v vos'mi tomakh,* vol. 1, Moscow, 1934, pp. 50-1; N.S. Rusanov (pseudonym of N.E. Kudrin), *Sotsialisty zapada i Rossii,* St Petersburg, 1908, pp. 228-32; L.F. Panteleev, *Vospominaniia,* Leningrad, 1948, p. 550; N. Samorukov, 'Obshchestvenno-politicheskaia deiatel'nost' G.A. Lopatina,' *Voprosy*

Istorii, 1953, no. 3, p. 34; Venturi, *Roots of Revolution*, pp. 451-2.

25. IISG, *Lavrov*, no. 5, July 8, [1870]; *CMRS*, vol. 8, no. 1, pp. 87-9; *ibid.*, vol. 8, no. 3, Michael Confino, 'Autour de "L'affaire Nečaev",' pp. 457-8, 477; Rapoport, *Iz istorii sviazei*, pp. 26-9. Late in 1873 Engels told Marx that the 'shadow of their first chilly contact' still clouded relations between Lopatin and Utin; see *Werke*, vol. 33, p. 93.

26. 'Pis'ma P.L. Lavrova k E.A. Shtakenshneider,' *Golos Minuvshego*, 1916, no. 7-8, pp. 111-112; Knizhnik-Vetrov, 'P.L. Lavrov,' p. 54; Confino, 'Autour de "L"Affaire Nečaev",' pp. 456-7, 467, 481; Lavrov, *Protsess 21-go s prilozheniem biograficheskoi zametki o G.A. Lopatine*, Geneva, 1888, p. xviii; Institute of Marxism-Leninism of the Central Committee of the CPSU, *Russkie sovremenniki o K. Markse i F. Engel'se*, Moscow, 1869, p. 48. Keller translated only one chapter; Joseph Roy completed the work. See *Werke*, vol. 32, pp. 416, 635-6, 699-700, 727 note 46, 782 note 455.

27. *Werke*, vol. 32, pp. 520-2; *ibid.*, vol. 33, p. 28; *Russkie sovremenniki*, p. 49; *MERR*, p. 186.

28. *Russkie sovremenniki*, pp. 45-9, 129-31.

29. *Ibid.*, pp. 139-40. See also Lopatin's letter to Bakunin in *CMRS*, vol. 8, no. 3, p. 477, and Rapoport, *Iz istorii sviazei*, pp. 31ff.

30. TsGALI, f. no. 1329, Opis' no. 1, ed., khr., no. 4, 'Lopatin, G.A.,' no *listy*, where Lopatin makes it clear that he, not Danielson, negotiated with Marx concerning the translation. See also *Werke*, vol. 32, p. 522; *ibid.*, vol. 33, p. 28; *MERR*, p. 172; *Russkie sovremenniki*, pp. 49, 139-40. See also Lopatin's introduction to *Pis'ma Marksa i Engel'sa k Nikolaiu -onu*, St Petersburg, 1908, p. i.

31. DFI, vol. 4, pp. 49, 61, 66, 88-9, 341.

32. *SIE*, vol. 8, p. 786.

33. *Werke*, vol. 33, p. 28.

34. *Ibid.*, p. 93.

35. *Russkie sovremenniki*, p. 133.

36. *MERR*, pp. 184-6, 238; Rapoport, *Iz istorii sviazei*, p. 46; *LN*, vol. 63, pp. 710-11.

37. *Russkie sovremenniki*, pp. 45-7, 49; Lavrov, *Protsess 21-go*, pp. xxi-ii; Koz'min, *Russkaia sektsiia*, pp. 228-30; N.M. Chernyshevskaia-Bystrova, *Letopis' zhizni i deiatel'nosti N.G. Chernyshevskogo*, Moscow-Leningrad, 1933, pp. 138, 141.

38. Lavrov, *Izbrannye sochineniia*, vol. 1, pp. 108-17; *Herzen*, vol. 13, pp. 367, 590, 606-8.

39. B.P. Koz'min, *Ot 'deviatnadtsatogo fevralia' k 'pervomu marta'*, Moscow, 1933, pp. 112, 115n.; Lavrov, *Filosofiia i sotsiologiia: izbrannye proizvedeniia*, 2 vols., Moscow, 1965, vol. 2, pp. 620-1. Nicholas Utin's father helped support Lavrov in the 1860's.

40. On the various editions of the *Letters* see James Scanlan's definitive English translation, Berkeley and Los Angeles, 1967, pp. 352-3.

41. *Herzen*, vol. 29. pp. 460-5; *ibid.*, vol. 30, pt. 1, pp. 105-6, 109.

42. There is an enormous literature on Lavrov. A good recent study in English is Philip Pomper, *Peter Lavrov and the Russian Revolutionary*

Movement, Chicago and London, 1972, which has an extensive bibliography. On Anna Czaplicka see R.M. Kantor's notes in the symposium, *P.L. Lavrov. Sbornik statei,* Petrograd, 1922, and P. Vitiazev's notes in *Materialy dlia biografii P.L. Lavrova,* Petrograd, 1921, pp. 20-1. I am grateful to Mr Boris Sapir of Amsterdam for helping me locate these and other sources.

43. M.P. Sazhin (*Vospominaniia, 1860-1880-kh gg.,* Moscow, 1925, p. 33) prudishly claimed that Lavrov and Czaplicka lived in separate apartments.

44. 'Pis'ma P.L. Lavrova k E.A. Shtakenshneider iz Parizha v 1870-1873 g.,' *Golos Minuvshego,* 1916, no. 7-8 pp. 107-8, 120.

45. Boris Sapir, ed., *'Vpered!' 1873-1877: Materialy iz arkhiva Valeriana Nikolaevicha Smirnova,* vol. 2, *Dokumenty,* Dordrecht, 1970, pp. 28-32; IISG, *Lavrov,* no. 8, Lavrov to Lopatin, July 19, [1870], and No. 22, Lavrov to Lopatin, Sept. 12, [1870]; *Russkie sovremenniki,* pp. 131-2; *LN,* vol. 63, pp. 710-11.

46. See Bakunin's June 2, 1870, letter to Nechaev in *CMRS,* vol. 7, no. 4, pp. 679, 681, 689, 691, 693; see further Lopatin to Bakunin (May 26, [1870] in *ibid.,* vol. 8, no. 3, pp. 456, 477, and Bakunin to Lopatin (June 9, 1870 in *ibid.,* pp. 487ff.

47. Bakunin, *Pis'ma,* 1906 edition, p. 386. This letter is erroneously dated by the editor, Dragomanov; the correct date is May 30, 1870. See also *LN,* vol. 62, p. 775.

48. Koz'min, *Russkaia sektsiia,* pp. 290-1.

49. *DFI,* vol. 4, p. 50; IISG, *Jung,* 549-57; *Guillaume,* vol. 2, pp. 75-7.

CHAPTER SEVEN

The Slav Emigrés and the Crisis of 1870

Until the first week in July of 1870, the General Council of the International and for that matter all Europe went about normal business. But Louis Bonaparte of France, with advisers of the calibre of the Duc de Gramont, Marshal Le Boeuf and the Empress Eugénie, had little difficulty in finding the right time, place and excuse to blunder into war. French reaction to the famous Ems Despatch brought war dangerously near. The French and German Internationalists protested against the preparations for war and affirmed their solidarity with each other, but in events of such magnitude they were powerless. Louis Bonaparte confused his own destiny with that of France, and the still greater tragedy was that much of France agreed with him. Bismarck, on the other hand, identified Prussia's destiny with that of Germany; his case was sounder, if the consequences no less disastrous.[1]

Armies were already on the move when the General Council met on July 19 and commissioned Marx to draw up an address on the war. Within four days a document of great polemical power duly came forth from Marx's pen. In it there appeared the prophetic lines, 'Whatever may be the incidents of Louis Bonaparte's war with Prussia, the death knell of the Second Empire has already sounded at Paris. It will end, as it began, by a parody.'[2] France had initiated the war, he wrote, but the German working class nevertheless had to keep a vigilant eye upon Prussia lest Bismarck turn a defensive war into a 'war against the French people.' Finally, Marx declared, 'In the background of this suicidal strife looms the dark figure of Russia.' He found Russian troop movements and railway construction in Bessarabia ominous (Lopatin informed him of these events) and warned that Prussia might have contingency plans to make use of 'Cossacks.' Russian intervention would cost Prussia whatever sympathy might otherwise be her due in a 'war of defence against Bonapartist aggression.' Marx and other observers recalled the recent meetings in Berlin and Ems between the king of Prussia and the Russian tsar, and they waited anxiously to see whether the war would force the revelation of the alliance that had surely, they felt, been concluded. A prompt Russian declaration of neutrality quieted few fears.[3]

Since the 1840's Karl Marx had been convinced that every Russian was at heart a panslav. He was surprised, therefore, to find *Narodnoe Delo,* the journal of his Russian friends in Geneva, hoping for a Russian defeat should Alexander II intervene in the Franco-Prussian War. Such an attitude was, however, quite consistent with the course of Russian radicalism over the preceding decade. Despairing of their own ability to challenge the tsarist regime, many Russian revolutionaries concluded that their country's salvation lay in military defeat. As the Crimean War had emancipated the serfs, so might a future war emancipate the country from tsarism. The journal of the Russian section held this view, and in its role of Marx's champion it went further, seeing industrialists and stock exchanges behind the war between France and Prussia. It insisted that the middle class favoured war, the working class peace. Once mankind was freed from the scourge of capitalist conflicts, the journal declared, 'we will proceed from war to Revolution.'[4]

In September 1870 *Narodnoe Delo* carried a translation of the General Council's (Marx's) 'First Address' on the war. In its commentary, the journal agreed with Marx that a German victory was to be preferred over a Bonapartist triumph, but only a victory of the dimensions necessary to defend the German states from attack. The support of the IWMA for the

Germans would end abruptly if Prussia and her allies entered into an alliance with Russia.[5]

The war threw the Geneva International into confusion. The spring strikes (in which members of the Russian section participated) melted away in July as the workers, concerned for their families, returned to their jobs. Many foreign workers went off to join one of the armies. Foreign socialists, unable to see how the war might affect Swiss neutrality, felt all the anxieties of people caught away from home in times of great upheaval. The Russians were no exception: after September, *Narodnoe Delo* ceased to appear.

The Franco-Prussian War confronted the IWMA with its severest test. The Brussels Congress resolution calling for a general strike against war was clearly, if not quite the 'Belgian imbecility' Marx called it, no more than a pious wish.[6] An organization dedicated to class solidarity and peace among nations watched helplessly as its French and German members responded enthusiastically to the calls to arms. However one chose to describe this phenomenon, the workingmen of France and Prussia rushed to the defence of a system that had, according to the International, exploited them unmercifully. Needless to say, the IWMA would not emerge unscathed.

The Polish Emigrés and the War

The tsar promptly issued an ukase forbidding his subjects from fighting on either side. He especially feared the possibility of émigré Poles aiding the French. There were few people, however, who believed that his order would deter the many Poles who were anxious to join the fray. And because the majority of these Poles were Francophiles, the ukase lent support to the popular belief that Alexander II favoured Prussia.[7] Russian diplomats had been warning the French about the Polish émigrés since the Partitions. So frequently had they cried 'Wolf!' that the cautions had ceased to have any effect. After 1863, however, a different kind of Polish refugee had sought asylum in the West. That uprising, unlike the earlier ones, was not an exclusively gentry affair, and the new refugees represented in part the middle and even the

lower classes. These individuals, many of them political
radicals, constituted a serious problem for France. The
attempt of Berezowski (a Pole) upon the tsar's life in Paris in
1867, and the subsequent refusal of the French court to
sentence him to death, had deeply embarrassed the government of Louis Bonaparte. Polish counterfeiters, both common
criminals and a few otherwise honest revolutionaries, brazenly pursued their operations on French soil and strained
Franco-Russian relations in the period before the war.[8]

Few Poles cared to risk their skins for the Second Empire,
but many joined the forces of the new Republic after the
Sedan disaster. One prominent émigré who tried to help was
Jaroslaw Dombrowski, who had flitted around the fringes of
radical exile circles since his arrival in the West in 1865.
Some Poles did not trust him because of his good relations
with Russians; his enemies claimed that the governor-general
of St Petersburg, General Trepov, was among his friends (this
was not true). The Russian embassy tried to implicate
Dombrowski in the Berezowski affair. That failed, and the the
Third Section, with the aid of the finance ministry agent
Gabriel Kamensky and the spy Apollon Mlochowski, tried to
convince the French authorities that Dombrowski was a
member of a counterfeiting ring. Dombrowski was arrested on
that charge in September 1869. He won acquittal the
following summer, but several of his co-defendants received
prison terms.[9]

Released on the eve of the war, Dombrowski went to
London. He contacted the Russian revolutionary Vladimir
Ozerov, who had rescued him from a Moscow prison in 1865.
Ozerov introduced him to Herman Lopatin, who thought he
might be useful to the revolutionary movement because of his
proficiency in fabricating documents; this suggests that
Dombrowski's acquittal in 1870 was perhaps no triumph of
French justice. But by the end of August Lopatin was cursing
Ozerov for having hung a Polish 'enfant terrible' in the form
of Dombrowski around his neck.[10]

The Polish émigrés showed their contempt for the government that had sheltered them, volunteering by the hundreds
for military service after the rump *Corps Législatif* proclaimed
the Republic on September 4. Dombrowski, then in London,

offered the new president (General Trochu) some reasons for making use of the Poles: 'The Polish emigration offers France excellent material for the organization of partisan units. Good horsemen, accustomed to wars of surprise and ambush, most of them knowing German, the Poles are ready to shed their blood for the French Republic.'[11]

The Government of National Defence, however, was already planning to seek Russian mediation, and Adolphe Thiers was preparing to leave on a mission to London, Vienna and St Petersburg. Dominated by conservatives, the new government naturally placed a higher value on good relations with Russia than on the assistance of a few hundred Polish cavalry. It refused to grant permission for the formation of a Polish Legion. In the fluid situation of the day, however, plans to form such a unit went forward. Bronislaw Wolowski, an émigré of the 1830-1831 generation who had contacts with influential politicians, went to Lyon and put together a volunteer unit composed of Poles. He had hoped that Dombrowski would command them, but when the government rejected that proposal Wolowski turned to the eccentric Tytus O'Byrn Grzymala. The Wolowski force saw limited action in the autumn, then the French government transferred it to one of the Alpine passes for guard duty.[12]

Many Polish émigrés fought under French command. More than two hundred of them enlisted in the Foreign Legion at Tours. Elsewhere, 120 Poles died in the battle of Orléans. Ksawery Branicki (who had helped finance Bakunin's abortive attempt to aid the rebels of 1863) raised half a million francs among the Poles for the defence of the Republic.[13]

Denied permission to go to Lyon, Dombrowski fretted in Paris. But then Garibaldi—released from an Italian prison— came to France for what proved to be his last campaign. He telegraphed Léon Gambetta (who had secured a command for him over conservative objections), 'Envoyez-moi l'intelligent Dombrowski, général Polonais, par n'importe quel moyen.' Gambetta would gladly have complied, but Trochu and others blocked him. The angry Dombrowski then began visiting the radical clubs in Paris, criticizing the government's defence plans and outlining his own schemes (some of which the Paris Commune was to adopt). He defied the authorities by repeatedly crossing the battle lines without a valid pass. Finally, on Trochu's order, the police arrested him and charged him with spying for the Prussians. Only Gambetta's intervention saved him from prison or perhaps even the firing squad. All this difficulty and disagreement with the Republicans, of course, helped prepare the way for Dombrowski to assume an important position under the Commune.[14]

Count Jósef Hauke ('Bosak') had better success in his search for a command. Scion of a distinguished Polish family, he had trained for a career in the military and had participated in some of the final battles of the Caucasian Wars. A Polish patriot, he left the Russian army and fought valiantly on the rebel side in 1863. After the collapse, he went first to Geneva, then to Italy, where he met Garibaldi (as did most émigré leftists) in May of 1865. The following year he attempted unsuccessfully to raise a regiment of Polish volunteers to aid the Italians against Austria. After that war he returned to Geneva, participated in the labour movement and joined the International. When the Franco-Prussian War broke out, Hauke, a member of the League of Peace and Freedom, met with the officers of that organization in Basle and issued appeals for an immediate cease-fire and the summoning of an international convention to form a 'United States of Europe.' Needless to say, none of this had the slightest impact. Many members of a society dedicated to peace turned to war, Hauke among them.[15]

Hauke joined Garibaldi, who took command of the Armée des Vosges. This was a motley assortment of 12,000 irregulars, soldiers of fortune, idealists-intellectuals, opportunists, tramps and assorted riffraff. It occupied the southern positions formerly held by the shattered units of Le Boeuf, Bazaine and MacMahon. Garibaldi appointed Hauke commander of the first brigade. When this force could bring its cavalry irregulars (chiefly Poles) and sharpshooters to bear, it won an occasional skirmish. But the Armée des Vosges was untrained, poorly armed and badly supplied. It received little support from a population demoralized by the incredibly swift defeat of the regular army and the collapse of the Bonapartist government. Communication with Paris did not exist; with

Lyon it was uncertain. Not even Garibaldi could save France. He could only fight delaying actions, and in one such engagement Jósef Hauke, trying to deflect a Prussian advance on Dijon, perished near Val-de-Suzon on January 21, 1871.[16]

Lavrov, Jaclard and the New Republic

On September 5, 1870, an editorial laconically observed that 'Paris et la France se sont réveillés ce matin en pleine république.'[17] The proclamation of the Republic the preceding day was France's response to Sedan. All over Europe the left rejoiced that France had regained her honour; the right feared that she was embarking upon yet another uncertain and dangerous adventure.

The only prominent Russian radical in Paris at the time was Peter Lavrov. He had been wary of the government of the Second Empire, but that government was no more. On September 4 he went with the rest of Paris to the Place de la Concorde and the *Corps Législatif* and later wrote to a friend about his experiences:

> with the others I cried 'Vive la République!' and I saw them tear down the eagles of the Empire. Now I am going to offer my services to the republican government, and in a few days, with another Russian, one of my former students, I shall probably put on a brassard and a hat with a cross . . . and set off as a medical orderly for what used to be the Bois de Boulogne.[18]

As the ring around Paris grew tighter, however, Lavrov's situation grew precarious. He could not prove his loyalty to the new regime by volunteering; to Lopatin's suggestion that he serve in the artillery he replied that his experience came only from books and that he would be useless in the field. In mid-September he complained that no one in the city could vouch for his identity.[19] The return of Anna Korvin-Krukovskaya and Victor Jaclard to Paris, coupled with Lavrov's entry into the International, relieved the situation. Lavrov had not, so far as we know, previously met Anna and Victor, but he came into contact with them now through the IWMA; he joined the Ternes section in the Batignolles district, where Jaclard had long been prominent politically.[20]

Lavrov confined his increasing doubts about the conservative trend of the Republic to private correspondence. Jaclard —an entirely different political type in any case—was not under the same restraints. Elected one of Clemenceau's deputy mayors in the 18th *arrondissement*, he used his new platform to criticize the Government of National Defence, accusing it of maintaining the social and economic system of the old Empire. Rejoining some of his former Blanquist associates (who had allied with socialists of various persuasions and with left-wing republicans), Jaclard plotted to exploit the crisis to bring about fundamental changes in French society. When a revolutionary putsch late in October came to a miserable end, he and other conspirators went to prison.[21]

Bakunin in Lyon

On their way from Geneva to Paris, Jaclard and Anna Korvin-Krukovskaya had stopped briefly in Lyon, where a 'committee of public safety' ruled. Jaclard advised the local International concerning its political line, then went on to Paris. He did not return to Lyon as he had hoped; provincial leadership rested with the provincials . . . and with Michael Bakunin.

Bakunin, who had collaborated with Jaclard in 1868, had taken in his stride the relatively minor setback of expulsion from the Geneva Central section of the IWMA. That was Utin's work; Bakunin's shame and disgust over Nechaev's treachery overshadowed his anger at Utin, whom he considered a mere annoyance easy to eliminate when the occasion demanded. As usual there were many distractions, and not for the first time he decided to found a journal. He wrote to Lavrov, Ogaryov and others asking their collaboration and persuaded 'Colonel Postnikov' (K.-A.I. Roman, whom he refused to believe a spy, a mass of evidence notwithstanding) to go to Russia to bring back news of the revolutionary movement; this was the mission originally intended for the intrepid Nechaev.

Now the war opened new revolutionary vistas. Bakunin wrote to Ogaryov early in August,

> You are only a Russian, while I am an internationalist, and because of this the events that are taking place have caused a veritable fever to rise in me.... I have worked out a complete plan; O[zer]ov will give it to you, or, better yet, he will read to you a letter I have written to a Frenchman.[22]

This was a typically transparent reference to 'Lettres à un français sur la crise actuelle, Septembre 1870,' his latest scheme for fomenting revolution. In September Bakunin went to Lyon to put the plan into action.

The Lyon escapade is fairly well known, but historians—even E.H. Carr, the best of the lot—have neglected part of it. Claiming that 'mes amis les socialistes révolutionnaires' had sent for him, Bakunin hurried from Locarno to Neuchâtel, where he left with James Guillaume the manuscript of 'Lettres à un français.' In this work, he called upon France to turn to 'social-revolutionary anarchism' to save herself from the Prussians. Guillaume wisely eliminated this suggestion from the version he published.

Gathering up Vladimir Ozerov and Walenty Lankiewicz (a young Pole), Bakunin made his way to Lyon. By the time he arrived in the middle of September, the situation had stabilized. The 'committee of public safety' had given way to an elected municipal council, with which the local Internationalists and the members of Bakunin's Alliance were co-operating. Chastizing the latter for betraying the revolution, Bakunin promptly formed them into a 'Committee for the Salvation of France.' He drew up two revolutionary programmes, one for Lyon and one for all France. Both called for the creation of either a series of 'Committees for the Salvation of France' or (he could not make up his mind) 'Revolutionary Communes.' The Lyon programme has been published,[23] but the one for France has received little attention. At the head of the latter was 'République Française. Commune Révolutionnaire de . . . ' And in the upper left-hand corner was 'DESTRUCTION'. It was vintage Bakunin.[24]

The programme claimed that the 'communes révolutionnaires' of Paris, Lyon, Marseille and other cities, having overthrown the Bonapartist regime, had federated to seize power and had decreed the following:

Art. 2.   All property sequestered in the name of the Republic.

Art. 3   All debts annulled.

Art. 4.   The right of inheritance abolished.

Art. 5.   All law codes, statues and regulations of the former government nullified.

Art. 6.   Taxes abolished.

Art. 7.   All public officials dismissed.

Art. 8.   All members of the armed forces, save those in the colonies, furloughed.

Art. 9.   All churches disestablished, all clergymen dismissed.

Art. 10   All monasteries, convents, etc. dissolved.

Art. 12. The penalty of death decreed in advance for all who oppose the actions of the revolutionary communes or who try to re-establish institutions that have been abolished.

Art. 14. The revolutionary communes . . . will consider all petitions bearing the signatures of 100 citizens, so long as such petitions do not contravene revolutionary, egalitarian principles.

Art. 15. To facilitate these decrees, the communes will establish a permanent revolutionary military force, composed of male volunteers serving a maximum of six months.[25]

Bakunin and the Lyon Alliancists tried to convince the citizenry that this programme, coupled with the one designed specifically for Lyon, embodied deliverance from the present travail, and future well-being was assured. At that time there was just enough confusion, uncertainty and general delirium to make it all seem faintly possible. Demonstrations and meetings took place; enthusiasm mounted; and at the end of September Bakunin tried to seize power in Lyon.

The ensuing débâcle had one advantage over most of his previous revolutionary failures: no one was hurt. The revolution simply failed to materialize. Even when the local unit of the National Guard (sent by the municipal council to disarm the rebels) handed over its weapons and placed itself at their disposal, the Bakuninists merely stood around wondering what to do. Bakunin had the presence of mind to order the arrest of the municipal council but he could not find anyone to carry out the order. Violent slogans notwithstanding (the Lyon programme concluded, 'TO ARMS!!!'), no one wanted to shoot. The uprising collapsed before it began. The city police arrested Bakunin, whom Ozerov—a master at this sort of thing—then rescued. On the evening following the putsch, Bakunin eluded the police and, after a brief celebration at the station complete with wine, left by train for Marseilles, where he hid in a friend's apartment. He could not resist attempting to seize control of the commune the Marseilles workers had established, but once again he failed. Three weeks later he returned to Locarno, his revolutions in ashes.[26]

Never one to admit responsibility for defeat, Bakunin blamed Paul Cluseret and Albert Richard (a French Bakuninist) for the Lyon fiasco, just as he had blamed a Polish comrade (Józef Card) for the failure of the 1863 expedition, Cluseret, a St-Cyr graduate, had fought with Garibaldi and in the American Civil War under McClellan. At the end of the 1860's he returned to France to participate in opposition politics. He came to Lyon in September 1870 and Bakunin appointed him commander of the anarchist forces. At the moment when he should have been carrying out orders to arrest the municipal council, Cluseret was negotiating with them. Whether he actually intended (as Bakunin claimed) to join them remains unclear; but he certainly wished them no harm. After the collapse he too went to Marseilles, then on to Geneva. There he quickly became a member of Nicholas Utin's circle.[27]

In February 1871, the French consul in Geneva reported to the newly formed Thiers government that Utin, Cluseret and others were plotting another uprising in Lyon. The conspirators had discussed the operation in secret meetings in Utin's apartment, meetings attended by one of the consul's agents. To a desperate French government this report represented only a minor problem. It was moreover short-lived; the consul reported a month later that the Lyonnais movement had collapsed. Disloyal French agents had warned the plotters that they were under surveillance. Cluseret left for Berne, where Utin joined him for a brief time. There was some suspicion in French circles that they had gone there to get instructions from the Prussian minister.[28]

Nechaev and Serebrennikov

Two other Slav revolutionaries, Sergei Nechaev and Vladimir Serebrennikov, used the great crisis of 1870 to try to settle personal accounts. Nechaev had fled to London in the middle of July. Police agents, however, were still looking for him in Switzerland, where he could no longer rely on sympathizers to give him shelter. Before he left the country he acquired, by threat and outright theft, some personal papers of several émigrés which would, were the contents made known, prove embarrassing and compromising.[29] While he debated how to use the purloined documents to best advantage, Nechaev learned that Bakunin and Ogaryov were planning to publish a new journal. Angered by the audacity of men whom he had so easily hoodwinked in Geneva, he resolved to teach them yet another lesson. In September 1870 Nechaev and Serebrennikov published their own *Obshchina* (The Commune —the name Bakunin had planned to use) in London, stealing for it some of Bakunin's ideas in 'Lettres à un français.'

France seemed ripe for regeneration in the summer of 1870, and the 'communal idea' swept the country as Frenchmen, mindful that the highly centralized bureaucratic state had brought them to their present misery, rebelled against powerful, corrupt combinations. Bakunin rode this wave and drew up his programmes; Nechaev and Serebrennikov, having no coherent ideas of their own, followed in his wake. Their *Obshchina* constituted an attempt to outflank him, to punish him for having dared break with Nechaev. Appearing only once, the eight-page newspaper boldly carried the names and addresses of the editors. The leading article purported to be an analysis of the present European crisis. Insipid comments on that subject gave way to an attack upon the International, with which Nechaev identified all his enemies. He assailed the leaders of the organization as speechifiers, phrasemakers, charlatans. Nechaev (it can be assumed that he wrote nearly all the material) claimed that the Internationalists had formed factions, that all socialists hated each other, and that there would soon arise a 'more serious and stronger' organization. This may have been a reference to the secret organization of Bakunin's Alliance, control of which Nechaev and Serebrennikov unquestionably hoped to seize. Finally, Nechaev claimed that the leaders of the IWMA were privileged individuals who did not understand the problems of the proletariat.[30]

The Nechaev-Serebrennikov *Obshchina* attacked Herzen and his generation as 'the last, concluding manifestation of liberal gentryism,' and accused Herzen of having been 'the first to throw a stone at Karakozov.' The new generation had nothing in common with the editor of the original *Kolokol;* it wanted a 'popular revolution' and its goal was 'the COMMUNE.' Prophetic lines. An article entitled 'Our General Programme' proclaimed that 'the fundamental principle is: equality above all.' When the 'social party' seized power, everything would become the property of society, and the people would organize into 'worker *artels.*' Those who refused to enter would lose the right to share in social property; their choice was thus work or death. Each *artel* would elect an 'evaluator,' the person most competent in the work of the group, as a labour boss. Bureaus elected in each *artel* (the French-language supplement translated this word as 'commune') would supervise dormitories, dining halls, schools, hospitals, libraries and all public utilities and services. There would be no judicial or religious institutions. Relations between the sexes would be free.

Only in the last (twenty-second) paragraph did the authors note that they intended this programme specifically for Russia, where a few capable young people would, they declared, emerge from the masses to translate it into action and build the new society. The task would naturally be difficult, but those few revolutionaries, coming mainly from the poorest classes and acting secretly, would accomplish it. They would not seek the support of the liberals, as the Nechaevist *Kolokol* had urged. They would instead build an alliance between the revolutionaries and the masses.

The similarity between this programme and the Bakuninist ones of 1870 is obvious. Nechaev and Serebrennikov stole many of the old anarchist's ideas and improvised a few proposals of their own. The result was a mishmash of anarchism and student utopianism. But there ran through it, as through all Nechaev's schemes, the thread of violence and conspiracy that was his legacy to the Russian revolution.

The last page of *Obshchina* carried an open letter to Bakunin and Ogaryov. Nechaev demanded from them the 'remainder' of the Bakhmetev fund, 'a part of which I received while A. Herzen was alive.' They were to give the money to Natalie Herzen, the 'treasurer' of *Obshchina* (she held no such position). Nechaev declared that, even though he had broken with them, he still considered the two older men the 'finest representatives of a generation that is, unfortunately, leaving the historical scene without a trace.' He did not forsee a clash with them; but he was sure that 'you will never again be practical [i.e. active] figures in the Russian revolution.' Bakunin received a copy of this astonishing publication shortly after he arrived in Lyon.[31]

About half the 1,800 copies had a French-language supplement. The two editors apparently took these to the Continent in October, but they did not distribute them (or the Russian edition) as widely as Nechaev's record would lead one to expect. Few copies found their way into circulation, and it was not until June 1871 that the Russian government informed London of its suspicion that Nechaev was publishing a revolutionary newspaper there. The Home Office, feeling little threatened (even after the Paris Commune), made a few desultory enquiries and learned nothing significant. Nechaev and his colleague had long since vanished.[32]

There was more interest in France. Sensitive to the term 'commune' in any language, *Le Monde* published Nechaev's 'very interesting' programme on Bastille Day, 1871.[33]

NOTES

1. William L. Langer, 'Red Rag and Gallic Bull: The French Decision for War, 1870,' in *Europa and Uebersee. Festschrift für Egmont Zechlin,* Hamburg, 1961, pp. 135-54. The leading article in *L'Egalité* on July 27, 1870, on the French decision to go to war was probably written by Nicholas Utin.
2. *DFI,* vol. 4, pp. 323-9. Marx signed this 'First Address of the General Council of the International Working Men's Association on the Franco-Prussian War' only as corresponding secretary for Germany.

3. S. S. Tatischev, *Imperator Aleksandr II. Ego zhizn' i tsarstvavanie,* 2 vols., St Petersburg, 1903, vol. 2 pp. 68-9; France, *AMAE,* vol. 244, CP, June-Dec. 1870, 136, Fleury in St Petersburg to MAE, July 23, 1870; Belgium, *AMAE,* CPL, *Russie,* vol. 10, 1868-70, no. 132, Mulle in St Petersburg to MAE, Aug. 12, 1870 (indicating that the tsar had summoned the Austrian minister, Count Chotek, to complain about his government's attitude in the conflict). See also *Le Nord,* May 16, July 23, 1870.

4. *Narodnoe Delo,* no. 5, July 31, 1870, pp. 1-2.

5. *Ibid.,* no. 6-7, Aug.-Sept., 1870, pp. 1-12.

6. The original proposal (from the German delegation) wanted to stigmatize any Franco-Prussian war as a 'civil war profiting Russia above all.' Marx could have supported that with pleasure, but the addition of the Belgian codicil calling for a general strike against war seemed to him preposterous. See *Werke,* vol. 32, p. 151.

7. Belgium, *AMAE,* CPL, Russie vol. 10, No. 131, Mulle in St Petersburg to MAE, Aug. 12, 1870.

8. *Le Constitutionnel* (Paris), Sept. 12, 1871, reviewing 'de Belina's' (i.e. Apollon Mlochowski's) *Les Polonais et la Commune de Paris.* See also *Neue Zürcher Zeitung,* no. 238, May 11, 1870; *Le Nord,* May 7, July 28, 1870.

9. *PSB,* vol. 5, pp. 8-10; *APP,* E/A 103:1; *ibid.,* B/A 1,039, especially *pièces* 67-76; *Herzen, vol. 30, pt. 1, pp. 253, 439n.; Der Volksstaat,* Feb. 26, 1870; Bakunin, *Pis'ma,* p. 240; Krystyna Wyczańska, *Polacy w Komunie Paryskiej 1871 R.,* 2nd edition, Warsaw, 1971, p. 48. On Dombrowski's trial see *Journal de Genève,* April 28, 1870; *Le Nord,* April 24, July 15, 16, 1870; IISG, *Lavrov,* Lavrov to Lopatin, No. 6, July 15 [1870]; *ibid.,* no. 12, July 27, [1870] *ibid.,* no. 14, Aug. 5, [1870].

10. *APP,* B/A 1,039, *pièce* 70: *Russkie sovremenniki,* pp. 138-9.

11. *APP,* B/A 1,039, *pièces* 12-13. This is a draft; someone probably corrected Dombrowski's droll French before the final version went to Trochu. See *PSB,* vol. 5, p. 9.

12. Wyczańska, *Polacy w Komunie,* pp. 71-5.

13. *Ibid.,* pp. 75-9; E.A. Zhelubovskaia *et al, Istoriia Parizhskoi Kommuny 1871 goda,* Moscow. 1971, pp. 616-7; Michael Howard, *The Franco-Prussian War,* New York, 1962, pp. 252-3, 296-7. The Germans repatriated Polish prisoners to France, not Russia—thus outraging St Petersburg. See *Journal Officiel de la République Française sous la Commune* (reprinted Paris, 1871; cited hereafter as *Journal Officiel*), Mar. 24, 1871.

14. Jaroslaw Dombrowski, *Trochu comme organisateur et général en chef,* Lyon, 1871. K. Wyczańska (*Polacy w Komunie,* p. 70) errs in stating the Dombrowski's work appeared in part in 'Bakunin's' *La Cloche* (i.e. Nechaev's *Kolokol*). See further *PSB,* vol. 5, pp. 9-10; *APP,* B/A 1,039, *pièces* 70-2.

15. *PSB,* vol. 9, pt. 2, pp. 305-7; Wyczańska, *Polacy w Kommunie,* pp. 30, 32-3, 43-4; *Journal de Genève,* July 30, 1870, *La Suisse Radicale,* July 31, Aug. 1, 2, 4, 14, 1870; *Figaro,* Sept. 10, 1870; *DFI,* vol. 4, p. 43. See

also the summary of the League's history in *Journal des Débats* (Paris), Sept. 11, 1873.

16. Jules Claretie, *Histoire de la Révolution de 1870-1871*, Paris, 1872, pp. 507, 512, 515; *Journal de Genève*, Jan. 27, 1871; *La Suisse Radicale*, Jan. 27 29, Feb. 1, 1871. Hauke and Utin were members of the same Masonic lodge in Geneva and Utin spoke at the funeral; see *La Suisse Radicale*, Feb. 13, 14, 15, 16, March 1, 1871.

17. *Le Nord*, Sept. 6, 1870 (written the previous day).

18. 'Pis'ma P.L. Lavrova k E.A. Shtakenshneider,' p. 114; IISG, *Lavrov*, no. 22, Lavrov to Lopatin, Sept. 12, [1870]. The other Russian was probably V.F. Luginin. The Bois had become an open-air hospital.

19. IISG, *Lavrov*, Lavrov to Lopatin, no. 18, Aug. 18. [1870]; *ibid.*, no. 23, Sept. 16, [1870].

20. Knizhnik-Vetrov, 'P.L. Lavrov,' pp. 59-60; Lavrov, 'Biografiia-ispoved",' *Filosofiia i sotsiologiia*, vol. 2, p. 624; *APP*, B/A 1,123, *pièces*, 2, 22, 33.

21. Neil Stewart, *Blanqui*, London, 1939, pp. 270-81; Geffroy, *L'Enfermé*, vol. 2, pp. 88-108.

22. Bakunin, *Pis'ma*, p. 300; Kantor, *V pogone*, pp. 85-8; Carr, *Bakunin*, p. 413.

23. *Guillaume*, vol 2, pp. 94-5; Carr, *Bakunin*, p. 419. See also Albert Richard, 'Bakounine et l'Internationale à Lyon,' *Revue de Paris*, no. 5, Sept.-Oct., 1896, pp. 140-60.

24. The programme is in Bakunin, *Pis'ma*, pp. 307-9.

25. There followed a paragraph specifying the measures 'that precede and prepare the revolution.'

26. *DFI*, vol. 4, p. 68; *Le Nord*, Oct. 1, 3, 5, 13, 1870.

27. *Journal Officiel*, May 22, 1871.

28. France, *AMAE*, Suisse 1870-1871, CP, Genève, vol. 9, 180-1, Dubruel to Bordeaux, Feb. 24, 1871; *ibid.*, 270-2, 'Notes sur la Neutralisation du Nord de la Savoie . . .'; *APP*, B/A 1,015, Cluseret, Gustave Paul, 1870-4, *pièces* 117, 121, 127. That either Utin or Cluseret worked for Prussia to secure the neutralization of the Haute Savoie (or the occupation of that region by Switzerland, as Art. 92 of the General Treaty of the Congress of Vienna had provided) seems unlikely, but Bismarck was certainly *au courant* regarding developments in Lyon; see Tsentrarkhiv, *Tsarskaia diplomatiia i Parizhskaia Kommuna 1871 goda*, Moscow-Leningrad, 1933, p. 74.

29. Carr, *Bakunin*, pp. 407-8.

30. *Obshchina (La Commune. Die Commune)*, Organ russkikh sotsialistov, pod redaktsiei S. Nechaeva i V. Serebrennikova, no. 1, Sept. 1, 1870 (reproduced in *Archives Bakounine*, vol. 4, pp. 435-42).

31. Bakunin, *Pis'ma*, p. 305; Kantor, *V pogone*, pp. 101-2. Franco Venturi (*Roots of Revolution*, pp. 384, 776n.) mistakenly identifies Semyon Ivanovich and Vladimir Serebryakov as Nechaev's collaborators.

32. Tatishchev, 'Sotsial'no-revoliutsionnoe dvizhenie,' pp. 1233-6; Great Britain, F.O. 65 (Russia), 821, no. 137, Buchanan in St Petersburg to London, June 28, 1871; *ibid.*, Liddell in the Home

Office to Hammond in the Foreign Office, no. 4301, undated; *ibid.*, 822, no. 187, Buchanan to London, Aug. 23, 1871.

33.   *Le Monde,* July 14, 1871. The newspaper mentioned Serebrennikov's name but not Nechaev's; perhaps only one name appeared in the French-language supplement, which I have not seen.

CHAPTER EIGHT

The Slavs and the Paris Commune

The Government of National Defence had a singularly inappropriate name: there was little left to defend. Metz capitulated on October 27; four days later, a Blanquist insurrection erupted in Paris. The National Guard occupied the Hôtel de Ville and Parisians marched through the streets shouting 'Pas d'armistice! La Commune! La levée en masse!' Edmond de Goncourt observed in his diary on October 31, 'We may write down for this date: *Finis Franciae.*'[1]

The insurrectionists, however, proved incapable of seizing and holding power. The National Guard had no idea what to do, orders and counter-orders flew about wildly, and the uprising collapsed in less than twenty-four hours. Several prominent Blanquists and Internationalists (including Victor Jaclard) went to prison. The Government of National Defence struggled on, though to little purpose. As Jaroslaw Dombrowski charged, General Trochu's famous defence 'plan' consisted of praying for a miracle. Gambetta roamed the provinces (having escaped in a balloon) and made fine speeches that contributed little to alleviating the misery of the capital.

The composition and political mentality of the government, coupled of course with the disastrous military situation, made capitulation seem the wisest alternative. Jules Favre, the foreign minister, began negotiations on January 23, 1871, and five days later he signed the armistice. Having shed her blood, France now lost territory, treasure and honour. The Prussians allowed the defeated country less than two weeks to elect a new National Assembly to ratify this harsh peace; an exhausted France returned an overwhelmingly conservative body. Adolphe Thiers, among whose qualifications was his implacable hatred of the left, formed a new government. On March 1, Prussian troops marched down the Champs-Elysées.

Frenchmen lashed out at each other in the search for scapegoats, and the familiar cry of 'Commune!' rang out. Many in Paris (the poor, the working-class, the intellectuals and the students) considered the crises of the 19th century the results of the failure to complete the Great Revolution. The city frequently called for the resurrection of the Commune of 1792-4 that had, in leftist eyes, saved the Revolution. As the demands for a Commune mounted, the Thiers government excerbated the situation by moving the National Assembly to the monarchist stronghold of Bordeaux; it also abolished the pay of the National Guard. The latter action was a blow to the Parisian poor, thousands of whom depended upon the daily stipend. Upon the signing of the preliminary peace treaty, the National Assembly moved north to Versailles, an even greater symbol of the monarchy. And at the same time the Thiers regime abolished the moratorium on rents and the payment of commercial notes, thus adding the lower middle class to the ranks of its enemies.

Thiers struck the fatal sparks when he ordered, first, the seizure of the cannons of Belleville and Montmartre (which the working-class population had bought by popular subscription), and secondly, the arrest of the Central Committee of the National Guard. The lynching of Generals Clément Thomas and Claude-Martin Lecomte followed. Thiers panicked and withdrew his forces to Versailles, leaving Paris in a state of insurrection. The Central Committee of the National Guard seized power and began to organize elections. The mayors of the *arrondissements,* including Georges Clemenceau of the 18th, tried unsuccessfully to reach an accommodation with Thiers. The latter, having capitulated to the Prussians, could only urge his example upon the petitioners. The mayors rejected that advice and returned to the capital. Elections

took place on March 26 without incident; and on the
following day the Paris Commune was officially born.

A government of proletarians did relatively little for that
class. The Internationalists and their allies, however, rarely
had a majority on the Conseil communal and beyond that
they had only seventy-two days in which to work out a
programme. Many observers have remarked the insurrection's serious errors: failure to seize the Bank of France,
failure to arrest the Thiers government on March 18-20,
failure to march on Versailles, failure to nationalize all
property. The Commune did decree a ten-hour working day,
abolish night work in the bakeries, limit the salaries of public
officials to 6,000 francs (about the wages of a skilled worker)
and nationalize the shops and businesses of people who fled
the city or publicly opposed the Commune. The moratorium
on rents and commercial notes was reinstated. Despite the
Commune's shortcomings, the people of Paris believed that
they had at last, as the noted diarist wrote, 'a government
with balls.'[2]

The great working-class uprising caught European socialists by surprise. Labour in general and the International in
particular had not recovered from the shock of the war when
the Commune burst into being. The General Council appealed to all sections for financial aid for the revolutionary
government, commissioned Marx's famous 'The Civil War in
France,' and despatched several agents (including a Russian
woman) to Paris. There was not much else that could be
done. Greetings, congratulations and expressions of solidarity
poured in from all sides. Nicholas Utin wrote one for the
Geneva International:

> Receive, therefore, pioneers of the social and international
> Revolution, the fraternal recognition that we send you and the
> firm and sincere assurance of the workers that, despite all the
> distance that separates us geographically, we are all at your side,
> and we shall devote all our efforts to ensure that the reaction will
> not triumph before the disappearance of the last of us. Long
> live the Paris Commune! Long live the revolution of the pro-
> letarians![3]

Men and women who sympathized with the Commune

were slow to act in its defence. By the time they had resolved to do something, the moment had passed. Backed by Bismarck's assurance of all necessary support, Thiers moved against Paris in May, conveniently ignoring his own assertion that any government that dared bombard the capital would surely fall.[4] The insurrectionists could not defend Baron Haussmann's wide new avenues in the prosperous western arrondissements; falling back upon their own working-class districts they fought bravely against overwhelming odds. The Versailles forces ground on, supported by the many citizens who had opposed the Commune from the beginning. Some of the revolutionary government's leaders, including Jaroslaw Dombrowski (the last military commandant), fell on the barricades. And with them fell the Commune.

There ensued a savage taking of vengeance. The Communards had shot hostages (including the Archbishop of Paris), burned public buildings and destroyed Thiers's home. The Republican government held them to account for these acts. Firing squads shot hundreds of men, women and even children at the 'mur des fédérés' in Père Lachaise cemetery; thousands of others met the same fate elsewhere in the city and in prison camps. Soldiers mistreated and tortured uncounted numbers of prisoners before shipping them off to the New Caledonia penal colony.[5]

An enduring myth that came out of the Commune held that the International Working Men's Association begat and sustained the insurrection. There was a kernel of truth here. Engels observed in 1874 that the International's greatest success,

> The Commune...so far as its intellectual inspiration was concerned, was unmistakably a child of the International, although the International had not stirred a finger to bring it into being—for the International is with good reason made responsible for its creation.[6]

The Paris Commune wrote a new chapter in the history of the international working-class and socialist movements. The first proletarian revolution in history, the Commune contributed enormously to the mythology and martyrology of those movements. The myth of the Commune grew to gigantic proportions and exercised—indeed continues to do so—a great influence upon revolutionaries around the world.

'Madam Dmitrieff'

No foreigner (and for that matter no Frenchman) was forced to serve the Commune, but hundreds who found themselves in Paris that spring of 1871 freely chose to do so. Among those who became Communards, several Russians and Poles occupied positions of importance and scores of others served the insurrection in lesser capacities. The most famous Russian participant was Elizabeth Tomanovskaya. As we have seen, she came to Geneva in the summer of 1870, joined the Russian section of the International, and established herself as a favourite of the local socialists and workers. In December she left for London on a twofold mission: to report to the General Council on Developments in the Geneva IWMA, and to inform Marx of the work of the Russian section (which he represented on the Council).[7]

Marx, Engels and Hermann Jung welcomed Tomanovskaya warmly. Intelligent, attractive and stylishly frail, she was the first Russian woman Marx ever knew well. She became a family favourite. Some anti-Semites among Marx's anarchist opponents later claimed that Tomanovskaya was both Jewish and a 'fanatical admirer of Marx, whom she calls, synagogue-style, the *Modern Moses.'*[8] Neither Jewess nor Marxist, she was simply Marx's friend and informant on Russian affairs. The two discussed the Russian peasant commune, a subject that intensely interested all Russian socialists and one in which Marx expressed a lively concern in the 1870's and 1880's. Tomanovskaya told Marx she thought the commune would die: the peasants were constantly trying to convert communal holdings into private property, and the government itself preserved the commune only as a coercive agency and fiscal institution. Tomanovskaya's views on the commune's potential role in a socialist society are unknown; her one letter to Marx on the subject simply advises him to read Baron von Haxthausen (a Prussian authority on the commune) and *Narodnoe Delo* . . . and we have seen what Marx thought of *Narodnoe Delo's* analysis.[9]

Upon the proclamation of the Commune, Elizabeth Tomanovskaya asked the General Council to send her to Paris as its delegate. Her request was granted. She had probably been in touch earlier with the socialist leader Benoît Malon,[10] and now in Paris she met his *amie*, the writer Mme André Léo. With the latter she joined the Comité des femmes. Mme. André Léo found her organizational home there; she did not care to push the struggle for women's rights and socialism beyond the modest limits the timid Comité proposed. But Elizabeth Tomanovskaya, now known as 'Madame Dmitrieff,' found the organization ineffective. Early in April she created the Union des femmes pour la défense de Paris et les soins aux blessés, the mission of which was to 'defend the cause of the people, the Revolution and the Commune . . . to give assistance to the government's commissions, and to serve at ambulance stations, canteens and on the barricades.' She sought working-class women as members; the executive committee of the Union had four workers and three women (including herself) who had no fixed profession.[11]

Elizabeth Tomanovskaya toured Paris day and night, encouraging seamstresses here, chatting with bandage-makers there, befriending laundresses, finding medical aid and respectable employment for ex-prostitutes, ministering to the wounded, helping to bury the dead. A police report later described her:

> Twenty-eight years old [she was twenty]; 1m 66cm; hair and eyebrows chestnut; grey-blue eyes; well-shaped nose; average mouth; round chin; slightly pale; active disposition; usually dressed in black and always elegant in manner.[12]

Her Union des femmes was remarkably successful. She wrote to Hermann Jung that the nightly meetings attracted between three and four thousand women. That may have been an exaggeration, but on the other hand we should note that the Thiers government later claimed that 'Mme Dmitrieff' and her organization bore responsibility for most of the insurrectionary acts committed by women in the Commune. Be that as it may, the Union des femmes was easily the most prominent and important of the many women's organizations in the uprising.[13]

Under great emotional stress toward the end of April, Tomanovskaya upbraided Jung and the General Council for 'remaining there in idleness at a time when Paris is on the edge of destruction.' She thought that the IWMA should at least attempt to rally the French provinces to aid the Commune. Paris was holding out well, she wrote, but everyone knew that the Versailles forces were regrouping and would soon launch an attack. Although Jaroslaw Dombrowski was valiantly attempting to reorganize the Commune's military forces, Tomanovskaya was pessimistic. She wrote that 'I see everything in dark colours.' But she also observed that,

> If the Commune is victorious, our political organization will be transformed into a social one, and we will create sections of the International. This idea has had great success, as has in general the internationalist propaganda I have been conducting with a view to demonstrating that all countries, including Germany, are on the eve of a social revolution.[14]

This was not to be the last time that Russian revolutionaries pinned their hopes on an upheaval in Germany.

Tomanovskaya's combination of hope and despair marked most of the correspondence that came out of Paris by balloon, pigeon and secret courier. In general the outlook was not promising. Tomanovskaya wrote, 'I have prepared myself to die on the barricades in the next few days.'

About May 20, 'Madame Dmitrieff' issued a stern order to the Union des femmes in the 11th arrondissment, one of the few areas still in Communard hands: 'Muster all the women and the committee itself and come immediately to GO TO THE BARRICADES.'[15] She herself went at the head of the detachment. Shortly after the fall of the Commune at the end of May, a Russian diplomat filed a report on her activities:

> This dangerous woman, a Russian subject, has long been active in the socialist movement. She was much more interested in the acts of the Commune than in the wounded, and she took an active part in the manifestations mounted by her colleagues at the Hôtel de Ville. She came to organize a Central women's committee in the 10th [sic] arrondissement, and it could have been foreseen that she would play a notable role in the final period of

the insurrection. And indeed, on May 23, during the attack of the army in this quarter, Elisabeth Dmitriew was seen behind the barricades, encouraging the federals in their resistance, distributing ammunition, and firing, while leading a gang of Mégères. It is certain that she contributed actively in words and deeds to the fires that desolated Paris . . . . What has become of this Fury? Did they execute her summarily, without establishing her identity? Did they move her to Versailles, or to some seaport under some false name she dreamed up?[16]

Another possibility was too terrible for the diplomat to contemplate: along with an astonishing number of her fellow Communard leaders, Elizabeth Tomanovskaya escaped. On June 1, 1871, Hermann Jung received a telegram from Geneva informing him of her safe arrival there. Five weeks later, the French government filed charges of inciting to revolution against 'a woman named Elise, who lives with Utin, a Russian,' in Geneva. The great witch-hunt had begun.[17]

Anna and Victor Jaclard

Anna Korvin-Krukovskaya played a lesser role in the great insurrection. She and Victor Jaclard arrived in Paris in September 1870, a week after the fall of the Second Empire. Jaclard plunged into political activity and served briefly as the elected commander of the 158th battalion of the National Guard. Imprisoned after the abortive Blanquist uprising of late October, he was not released until early January. While he was in prison, Anna—who had now begun to use his name—worked for the Vigilance Committee of the 18th arrondissement, where her chief concern was raising money for the Guard. Later she was active in the movement for women's education.[18]

Released from prison, Jaclard went to his home town of Metz to campaign for a seat in the National Assembly. Anna remained in Paris, but on February 13 she received permission to cross through the Prussian lines and travel to Strasbourg 'on family business.' Her sister and brother-in-law, the Kovalevskys, had come to Alsace in January. Something interfered with their plans to travel on to Versailles and Anna went to help them. She did not immediately succeed, but the Kovalevskys persevered in their efforts to visit France; for that, Victor Jaclard later had reason to be grateful.[19] Jaclard lost the Metz election, after which he returned to Paris and participated in the events of March 18 that ignited the insurrection. He was elected to command the Montmartre battalion which later became the XVIIe Légion fédérée. Though not wholly reconciled with Blanqui, Jaclard remained a partisan of direct action. On the evening of March 18 he urged the National Guard and the mayors of the working-class *arrondissements* to march immediately on Versailles and seize power from the National Assembly. Failure to follow this course of action has been cited by many as a major cause of the collapse of the Commune, but such an assault was simply not possible on March 18. Later, when the Communards could have attacked, the Versailles forces had regrouped.[20]

In the Parisian elections of March 26, Victor Jaclard received only 503 votes in the 18th *arrondissement*. Blanqui, then in prison in Versailles, led the list with 14,953; the six other successful candidates all received over 13,000 votes. Jaclard's poor showing was no doubt the wages of quarrelling with Blanqui.[21] After the defeat, he returned to his military duties. Anna Jaclard began to collaborate with Mme André Léo on *La Sociale*, a newspaper that followed a quasi-Proudhonist line. Her name did not appear in the journal, however, and we cannot determine the extent of her contributions. She worked at Jaclard's side on the Vigilance Committee and served on the Hospital and Ambulance Committee. Her work on the Women's Club of Montmartre earned her *Figaro's* scorn as a 'fougueuse clubiste'. Anna's first concern, however, was for women's education. She and Mme André Léo directed the Commune's policy in this field, but that policy received little implementation. The insurrectionary government appointed the two women and some others to a special commission—on May 21.[22] Anna had little if any contact with Elizabeth Tomanovskaya's Union des femmes. A certain tension existed between the clubs and the more formal organizations such as the Union. The latter, it should be noted, affected an arrogance that offended some contemporaries.[23]

Several prominent Communards (Louise Michel, Maxime Vuillaume and others) later praised Anna Jaclard and Elizabeth Tomanovskaya for their bravery during the last desperate days and hours of the insurrection. The women fought on the barricades and did not falter or flinch in the face of certain defeat. Whether their devotion to the cause actually did lead—as a court-martial later charged—Anna and Victor Jaclard to burn and pillage the Hôtel Crillon remains uncertain.[24] For some unknown reason, Jaclard quarrelled with his staff and resigned from his battalion on May 10. A few days later he became inspector-general of fortifications. During 'Bloody Week' (the last of the Commune) he fought at Benoît Malon's side.[25]

Jaclard fell into the hands of the Versailles forces. He and Anna had become separated during the fighting and neither knew the other's fate. The ranking Russian diplomat at Versailles thought that Anna too was in custody:

> This Mégère . . . has been transferred to Versailles, where [she and Jaclard] await their trial. It is probable that she will go to console herself in her impending widowhood to New Caledonia, where the 'pétroleuses' are destined to populate the penal colony. God save Europe from the return of their children.[26]

But Anna—no doubt to the eternal dismay of the diplomat who spoke so smugly of her 'impending widowhood'—had escaped. How she did so remains a mystery; the number of leading Communards who eluded both the Prussians and the Versailles forces suggests that the task was not insurmountably difficult. Victor Jaclard was simply unlucky. In the first week of June, the government transferred him to a prison camp at Versailles, severely diminishing his prospects of escape.[27]

In one important respect, however, Jaclard was unique among all the Communard prisoners. On the first day of the insurrection he had married Anna Korvin-Krukovskaya in a civil ceremony performed by Benoît Malon (deputy major of the 17th *arrondissement* and a member of the Conseil Communal). Thus Jaclard, a Blanquist, Internationalist and Communard, became the son-in-law of a Russian major-general. He probably told his captors at once of his status, thus saving himself from execution. Government troops asked no questions in that period, and the anti-Commune public applauded each salvo from the firing squads.[28]

Learning of Jaclard's arrest, the Kovalevskys (still in Strasbourg) redoubled their efforts to reach the capital. After a couple of months they succeeded, and old General Korvin-Krukovsky, concerned about his daughter, was not far behind. The general met Thiers, who told him that the situation was grave: the public demanded punishment of the Communards, and Jaclard was a well-known conspirator and official of the insurrectionary government. But the very next day, October 1, 1871, Jaclard escaped while being transferred to another prison. Thiers obviously connived in his flight, for he had given General Korvin-Krukovsky the precise details of the transfer.[29]

Peter Lavrov

Although he was in Paris throughout the war, the siege and much of the Commune, Peter Lavrov did not play a significant role in any of these events. Rather, he became a chronicler of the insurrection and one of the architects of the great myth. From the beginning he suffered like everyone else in Paris, having little heat and a diet of dog and occasionally cat. He considered himself luckier than most because he was not squeamish.[30] The chaotic political situation offered enormous opportunities to a unified, purposeful party, and Lavrov thought the International might be that party. In January of 1871 he wrote a proclamation which he called 'A l'Oeuvre!' Only recently discovered and published in Moscow, this was a remarkable document:

> To work, workers! To work, brothers of the International! to work!
> Your work is the reign of truth and justice.
> Your work is the fraternity of all the workers of humanity.
> Your work is the uncompromising struggle against all society's parasites, against all the exploiters of the labour of others.
> Your work is the regeneration of the world by labour. [31]

The 'uncompromising struggle' was nothing less than the class struggle, 'an idea that has occupied my thoughts since I entered the International.' Lavrov called for an 'egalitarian revolution' and declared that 'no matter how many ruins are heaped up, the republic of workers must be founded.' He appealed to the workers of the world to unite in the International, to put aside the nationalism that served only kings and capital and build a 'universal, fraternal republic of workers . . . the only just State, the only true State, the only State that belongs to the future.'

The surprisingly peaceful establishment of the Commune astonished Lavrov and led him to modify his earlier view that violence was required to bring the new order into existence. He welcomed the Commune in two articles in the Brussels *L'Internationale,* and in an unpublished 'Letter to the Citizens of Paris' he wrote that he believed the 'struggle' would be peaceful, with education and moral right the workers' weapons.[32]

Especially heartening to Lavrov was the Commune's origin in the people. Just before the uprising he wrote that 'All the big names in France, all the well-known party leaders, all the orators and journalists . . . on the local scene—none are worth a brass farthing.'[33] Who now had power, in the Commune? 'Oui, madame, des simples ouvriers.' (This recalls Victor Hugo's 'Mais ce sont des inconnus!'[34]) Even the prominent old radicals—excepting Delescluze—had disappeared. Workers and Internationalists were in power. The government functioned normally, effectively and without using coercion; the streets were safe. The Commune was the vanguard of a movement that would destroy the bourgeois system.

But Lavrov had some private doubts. He feared that the 'unknown dictators' and simple workers who had carried out the seizure of power would retire to their workbenches and shops after the elections, leaving power to 'bureaucrats, chatterboxes and cowards.' He hoped he was wrong: 'it seems to me that one can sympathize more with this republic, and wish it more success, than with any preceding form [of government]' At the end of March he wrote, 'I am very sympathetic toward this party [i.e. the Commune], and my only connections here (incidentally very insignificant) are in this circle.'[35] He later complained that the Commune had not permitted him to work as 'energetically and usefully' as he desired, and he pointed to the fact that socialist circles in Brussels, to which city he went in May, had immediately accepted him as a comrade. He also admitted some jealousy of 'Mme Dmitrieff's' active role in the Commune.[36]

Lavrov had ties only to the socialists, who formed but a part of the leadership. Later in 1871 he sharply criticized the old Jacobins, who were 'living in the traditions of the late 18th century.' He singled out Pyat and Delescluze for their failure to understand the proletarian, socialist character of the uprising, i.e. that trend with which he himself particularly sympathized. The socialist minority, Lavrov observed, should have banded together to dismiss those 'harmful comrades' who 'neutralized the genuine, healthy worker faction.' The Jacobins, with the old republican distrust of the military, had refused to grant sufficient authority to the defence forces until the last days of the insurrection. Lavrov argued that the 'phrase-makers of radicalism' such as Gambetta, Louis Blanc and Ledru-Rollin had also hindered the proletarian cause.[37]

What of the future? Shortly after leaving Paris early in May, Lavrov wrote that a 'federation of independent communes' (the ultimate extension of the Paris Commune) must be 'made a reality.'[38] One cannot determine precisely what he meant, but the conclusion of some Soviet scholars that this was a populist concept is questionable. It is impossible to mistake Lavrov's sympathy for the Commune, a government of proletarians, and it is clear that he regarded the failure of the countryside to support the Commune as a major reason for its collapse. Thus his 'federation of communes' was probably just that, an association of urban *and* rural communes.

Accompanied by Anna Czaplicka, Lavrov went to Brussels and London early in May to seek aid for the Commune. Eugène Varlin (who had sponsored his entry into the IWMA) gave him letters of introduction to the prominent Belgian socialists César De Paepe and Désiré Brismée, and he and Anna also met Eugène Hins, who had a Russian wife.[39] Lavrov was happy to be out of Paris, where the only useful weapons, carbines, were 'not at all in keeping with my character.' He had to go where he could use his pen in the service of the revolution. A Russian acquaintance saw him in London shortly after his arrival; remembering his phlegmatic, reserved manner, she was astonished to find him now an ardent revolutionary.[40]

Lavrov reported on the Commune to the Belgians before going on to London with Anna Czaplicka. The two arrived in the British capital after the collapse of the uprising. Marx and Jung invited Lavrov to recount his experiences to the General Council, and he did so during the three July meetings he attended. He failed, however, to obtain the kind of support for the defeated insurrectionists that he thought the IWMA should render. He criticized the General Council, but at that late date there was little to be done but shelter the Communards who had escaped, and the International certainly did that. Although he was displeased with the organization, Lavrov admired its leaders, and his acquaintance with Marx—with whom he had earlier corresponded—ripened into mutual respect, if not friendship.[41]

At the end of July, Lavrov and Anna Czaplicka returned to Paris. This involved certain serious risks, but presumably Anna insisted and Lavrov acquiesced. In the event, the authorities did not molest them.

In 1875, Lavrov published a lengthy article praising the Parisian insurrection and calling it the first proletarian revolution. Four years later he expanded his views into a book that even the Bolsheviks, for all their branding of Lavrov as a populist, admired greatly.[42] Recalling the fatal tension between the Jacobinist republicans and the socialists, Lavrov returned, in these studies, to the militant stand of the unpublished 'A l'Oeuvre!' He realized now, half a decade later, that he had paid too much attention to the purely political side of the insurrection and had ignored the need for a massive social and economic revolution. The latter, he wrote, would have to shed all middle-class scruples and fetishes: the Commune had made the mistake of fighting the middle class on the latter's own terms and assumptions. Nothing else could explain, for example, the superstitious reluctance to seize the Bank of France. Likewise, the

Commune had been reluctant to use force and had allowed every democratic 'chatterbox' to present his ideas. Even the form of the Commune had probably been a mistake. The industrial proletariat required political organizations responsive to class interests rather than to those of estates, professions or the broad civil categories of medieval times. In short, revolution must be revolution, not merely a reshuffling of old ideas, forms, practices and myths.

The evolution of Lavrov's views on the Commune took place against the background of his quarrel—later in the decade and in the 1880's—with Peter Tkachev and other Russian Blanquists. Discussing the Parisian uprising, Lavrov sought to prove the futility of revolutionary impetuosity and stressed the need for thorough preparation. He decried Tkachev's reliance upon the 'spontaneity' of the masses as a Jacobin-anarchist illusion. Analyzing the Commune as the first attempt to create a dictatorship of the proletariat, he came close to Marx's view of the insurrection, and he certainly agreed with Engels's famous comment, 'Well and good, gentlemen, do you want to know what this dictatorship looks like? Look at the Paris Commune. That was the Dictatorship of the Proletariat.'[43]

Peter Lavrov's history of the Commune became one of the most popular and important pieces of Russian revolutionary literature. More than any other work save Marx's own 'The Civil War in France,' his book helped make the myth of the Commune part of the revolutionary tradition of the Russian left. The ex-professor of mathematics was indeed useless with a carbine in his hands, but he served the Paris Commune as did few others.[44]

Other Russians in the Commune

Several less well-known Russians were in Paris during the uprising, but some familiar figures were conspicuous by their absence. Bakunin wrote from Locarno early in April asking a Geneva friend why Nicholas Zhukovsky and Nicholas Utin were not going to Paris, but he himself made no such effort. In the same letter he predicted the prompt collapse of the Commune. Approaching his fifty-seventh birthday, Bakunin was exhausted and dispirited after his recent failures in Lyon and Marseilles. Not until July did he publicly defend the Paris insurrection, and then his comments were merely in the form of an aside in an attack on Mazzini.[45] Only much later did he devote a longer work to the event. In an article entitled 'The Paris Commune and the Concept of Statehood,' he proclaimed himself a 'fanatical devotee of liberty . . . but not of that purely formal liberty that the State concedes, measures and regulates.' No, Michael Bakunin was a

> partisan of the Paris Commune, which, being suppressed, drowned in blood by the butchers of the monarchic and clerical reaction, became something more vital, more powerful in the imagination and in the heart of the European proletariat. I am especially a partisan of the Paris Commune because it was a bold, clearly expressed negation of the State.[46]

At least, that was the way he saw it. He attacked Delescluze and the Jacobins for their 'statist' revolutionism and praised the socialists for renouncing the creation of a dictatorship. Better to lose the revolution, he always argued, than win by adopting the enemy's institutions.[47]

No one from the Russian section in Geneva joined their former colleagues Tomanovskaya and the Jaclards in Paris. Utin wrote a whiney letter to Marx saying that he had thought about going to Paris but could not make up his mind; and these remarks signalled the beginning of the end of his career in the revolutionary movement. He continued, to be sure, to work in the Geneva International, and he did much to help the Communard refugees. But he allowed the great opportunity for 'practical' work to slip away.[48]

Sergei Nechaev, whom one would expect to find on the barricades, conveniently absented himself from Paris on the eve of the Commune. He had come to France from London in the autumn of 1870 and had taken a room in the Latin Quarter. For the first time in his life he had a love affair, and—astonishingly—he wrote articles for the Russian press (using a pseudonym). For some reason he left around the middle of February, 1871, telling the French authorities that he intended to go to Serbia (he was still using the Serbian passport) to visit relatives. It would seem unlikely that he left because he was in financial distress, for he probably still had some of the Bakhmetev money, and in any event he continued to travel around Europe. Nechaev spent the period of the Commune in Brussels. What he did there other than compile long lists of the addresses of local socialists we do not know. Late in June he appeared at the French consulate in Neuchâtel to have his passport validated for travel back to France. Any evaluation of Nechaev's position in the Russian revolutionary pantheon must take into account his strange behaviour in the spring of 1871.[49]

M.P. Sazhin ('Armand Ross'), a friend of Nechaev and Bakunin, travelled from Zürich to Paris in April 1871 with Walenty Lankiewicz, the young Pole who had been with Bakunin in Lyon. The two tried to present to the Commune a project hatched by some of the Russian émigrés in Switzerland: Vladimir Ozerov and others proposed that the Commune give a million francs to form partisan detachments in the provinces. This sum would equip one hundred thousand men, who would then pin down the Versailles forces with guerrilla warfare, at the same time launching a massive propaganda barrage against the Thiers regime.[50]

Whether the Conseil Communal actually received this improbable proposal is unknown. In memoirs written half a century later, Sazhin reproduced entire conversations of the 1860's but described the Commune only briefly and superficially; this suggests that his own role was not a glorious one. During 'Bloody Week' he left Lavrov's apartment, which he had occupied when his countryman went to Brussels, for the home of a respectable Russian journalist. He returned to Zürich in June. Lankiewicz apparently died in the fighting.[51]

Another Russian Communard was Valerian Potapenko, the son of a petty Warsaw province official. The family moved to Belgium in 1862; after quarrelling with his father, Valerian went to Paris in 1868 and worked at odd jobs. In 1870 he joined the National Guard and rose swiftly to the rank of captain. He pledged his loyalty to the Commune in 1871 and served on Jaroslaw Dombrowski's staff. When the uprising collapsed he went to Germany. Believing that his long absence would shield him from trouble, he returned to the Russian empire, only to be arrested as soon as he crossed the frontier. He was tried and convicted on charges of insurrectionism in Paris (*sic*) and went to Siberia.[52]

Still another Russian Communard, Nicholas Shevelyov, was a friend of Ogaryov and he knew Herzen and Bakunin. We know little of his activities during the Commune; he told a Russian court in October of 1872 that he had been 'commanded by my party to go to Paris.' That sounds a little far fetched, but our information is extremely scanty. Shevelyov told the same court that he had been arrested during 'Bloody Week' and sentenced to death, but escaped when another man bearing the same name was shot by a firing squad.[53] Nicholas Shevelyov escaped from France and unsuccessfully sought political asylum in, of all places, San Marino. He then asked the Russian government's permission to return home. His request was granted and he was arrested as soon as he crossed the frontier. At his trial in St Petersburg on charges of having participated in the Commune, Shevelyov learned that he had also—according to the prosecutor—taken part in the Karakozov affair. He bravely taunted the court, defended his role in the Commune, and accepted his prison sentence with equanimity. (We know nothing about his namesake who perished before a Versailles firing squad.)[54]

Several Russian journalists were in Paris when the Commune was proclaimed, but apparently only one, G.N. Vyrubov (in whose apartment Sazhin hid), remained in the city through the spring of 1871. The others stayed in Versailles, Bordeaux or some other 'safe' location. Their reportage was generally critical of the Commune, but P.D. Boborykin managed to slip some guardedly favourable comments past the censor, and Eugene Utin (Nicholas's brother) wrote very sympathetically of the uprising—from the safety of Germany.[55]

The Poles in the Commune

Official French sources reported in 1875 that twenty-three Russians and 110 Poles had incurred criminal responsibility in the Commune.[56] The first figure was probably exaggerated, the second an understatement: there were at least 250 Polish Communards, and one modern researcher (who includes

Poles born outside Poland) places the figure at 443.[57] But no matter what the exact figure, Poles were the most prominent foreigners in the insurrection and bore much of the abuse heaped upon the 'outside agitators' who flocked to Paris. Apollon Mlochowski expressed the bitterness the conservatives felt toward his countrymen:

> O philanthropists and Polonophiles! What do you think today of these 'brave Poles' who have spilled French blood, burned the city that accorded them hospitality and spat in the largesse that you have showered upon them for so many years? What say today *Siècle, Opinion National* and other Parisian journals, insulters of Muravyov ['Hangman'] and his summary justice? Who is going to recommence today the diplomatic campaign of 1863?[58]

When the April encounters with the Versailles forces demonstrated the folly of entrusting the defence of the Commune to men whose bravery exceeded their military capacities, the revolutionary government turned to Jaroslaw Dombrowski and appointed him military commandant. Dombrowski had attracted attention through his role in the 1863 Rebellion, his escape from Russia, his trial and acquittal on counterfeiting charges in 1870, and his espousal of socialist causes. Hundreds of Poles and other East Europeans flocked to his new headquarters and offered their services to the colourful general. The Poles were brave men who knew how to fight under guerrilla conditions and even in the open field, but they were out of their element in a siege. Dombrowski tried to teach them, and the French forces, how to defend the city. He replaced incompetent commanders—of whom there were more than a few—and began to train new ones, resupplied the forward positions, instilled discipline and order. He had no plan for victory. He merely hoped that Paris could resist long enough to break the will of Frenchmen to continue fighting each other.

In the final ordeal, some French Communards forgot that the Poles had unselfishly given themselves to the cause. Ugly rumours blamed Dombrowski for the desperate situation, and some emotionally distraught rebels whispered that some of the Poles were Prussian or Versailles agents. The stories stained Dombrowski's reputation only temporarily. While touring the barricades on May 22, he fell, wounded by rifle fire. The Prussians, who held all the forts east of the Seine, denied him a pass to St Denis, where he might have obtained medical aid. He died the next day, bitterly lamenting the fact that some of his French comrades thought he had betrayed them.[59]

The victorious forces of order naturally were disinclined to look upon the Poles as their own agents inside the camp of the Communards. Speaking for conservative opinion, *Figaro* declared, 'It is formally demanded that all members of the Commune, all journalists who basely made a pact with the triumphant uprising, all the two-faced Poles and flighty Wallachians be shot before the assembled people.'[60] But most Poles who escaped death on the barricades managed to flee. Some—there are no exact figures— fell into government hands and were either executed or sent in chains to New Caledonia. Once again Polish sacrifices came to no immediate positive end. But Polish honour, in the eyes of the European left, shone more brightly than ever.

Reaction in Russia to the Commune

Russian influence west of the Elbe plummeted after the Prussian victory. The unified German Reich no longer needed a 'protector on the Neva.' Moreover, the tsar could not even pursue his natural inclinations and send aid to the anti-Commune French forces because Germany would not allow it. Thus the Paris Commune, coming so soon after the fall of France, stimulated still another re-examination of Russian foreign policy. That policy was already in confusion following the rapid Prussian triumph and the proclamation of the Republic in France. In the official Russian view, any government that could not deal with revolution did not deserve to survive. It was only later that Alexander and his ministers learned that the new Republic, first under Trochu and then under Thiers, was as reactionary as Russian interests could possibly wish.

Journalistic opinion in Russia about the Commune followed easily predictable lines. The official and conservative press, which devoted enormous space to the Commune, was naturally virulently hostile. The liberal press, which likewise gave the uprising extensive coverage, hardly approved of events in Paris but it was at once more objective and more platitudinous. The leftist press no longer existed.[61]

The Commune had its defenders in Russia, but they generally resorted to 'Aesopian' language or kept silent. A dramatic response came from a former member of the Smorgon Academy, Nicholas Goncharov, who published four leaflets called *Viselitsa* (The Gibbet) at a hand-operated press. Goncharov declared upon learning of the uprising, 'The universal revolution has already begun . . . whether Paris is strangled or not . . . the endless, bloody revolution is upon us.' He welcomed the revolution 'into the muzhik's hut,' whence it would issue forth to overthrow the 'savage Tatar rule of the tsar.' Goncharov signed his first leaflet, 'A Communist.' Three more one-page leaflets followed at ten-day intervals. The second called for the assassination of the reactionary Moscow journalist, Michael Katkov. The third looked forward to the 'victory of our bloody Russian revolution,' following which 'thousands of communes will cover the Russian land.' The fourth and final *Viselitsa* predicted the end of the Paris Commune. Goncharov lamented the atrocities of 'Bloody Week' and summoned 'honest men . . . to arms! to arms!' in response to the agonized city's cries for help.[62]

According to the official indictment, Goncharov printed only twenty copies of each leaflet, and only about half of those were legible. He distributed them by mail and by hand, placing them, in some instances, on the doorsteps of strangers. The recipients were dumbfounded, not to say frightened, for the police normally held that, if anyone received a revolutionary proclamation, he had obviously solicited the material (this logic had prevailed in the Nechaev-Bakunin escapade of 1869).

Goncharov came under suspicion and slipped away to Vilna, where the police arrested him in the middle of June. He appeared in court the following February, defended by Eugene Utin (a lawyer as well as a journalist). Utin attempted to convince the court that his client was emotionally unstable because of his unhappy marriage. Unimpressed, the judges sent Goncharov to Siberia. There was, however, some sympathy in official quarters for the terrible and complex tragedy that followed Utin's distasteful courtoom tactics: the authorities reduced Goncharov's sentence from penal servitude to banishment from the major cities of European Russia.[63]

In the spring of 1871, all Europe seemed to see the work of the Commune and the International in every disorder. On the eve of Easter and Passover the annual pogrom erupted in Odessa, where for four days mobs burned and looted the Jewish ghetto while the police and the military commander of Novorossiisk province, P.E. Kotzebue (called 'Shorty' because of his small stature), simply looked on. The French ambassador in St Petersburg telegraphed Versailles that the Odessa Jews had proclaimed some sort of 'commune,' and although the report was utterly false it found its way into the press. The officially-condoned rioting had no more profound basis than anti-Semitism; the hapless Jews of Odessa had troubles enough without seeking to emulate the Paris Commune. After four days the mayor, Bukharin, ordered the mobs to desist. By that time they were tired anyway, and Odessa returned to normal.[64]

The Russian government watched the Odessa riots subside, disciplined Goncharov, and kept a tight rein on writers and intellectuals. Shortly after the beginning of the Paris insurrection, the head of the Third Section and chief of gendarmes, Count P.A. Shuvalov, ordered the redoubling of surveillance over all individuals who might be inclined to 'seditious agitation' out of sympathy with the 'recent troubles in Europe.' At the end of April the government closed Helsinki University, ostensibly because of student disturbances over local grievances. Such a drastic response to an insignificant affair, however, clearly reflected the régime's nervousness.[65]

The tsarist régime also responded to the Paris Commune with the law of May 19, 1871 (Old Style), dealing with political crimes. The law gave the police more authority in the investigation and prosecution of such offences. The new statute entrusted the Third Section with the investigation of all crimes against the state and gave it the right (which the courts and the Senate already possessed) to define such crimes. Further upon agreement between the Third Section and the prosecutor, the government could decide such cases administratively, without public trial. Surprisingly, this legislation proved ineffective. A new law of June 7, 1872 (Old Style), assigned the adjudication of treason to the Governing Senate but specified that the tsar could, at his discretion, turn such cases over to the Supreme Criminal Court.[66] Another June, 1872, law sought to halt dissemination in the press of subversive propaganda. The government withdrew the examption from preliminary censorship of books and periodicals of a certain length and increased the penalties for 'press crimes.'[67] Also in the spring of 1872, and also in response to the Commune, the tsarist government rectified an earlier oversight: the censor finally discerned a connection between the *Communist Manifesto* and revolution, and that work was now banned in Russia.[68]

NOTES

1. Edmond and Jules de Goncourt, *Journal: Mémoires de la vie littéraire, 1864-1878*, vol. 3, Paris, 1956, p. 657. See also Geffroy, *L'Enfermé*, vol. 2, pp. 96-100. Part of the Goncourt diaries appears in English as *Paris Under Siege, 1870-1871*, edited and translated by G.J. Becker, Ithaca, New York, 1969.

2. Goncourt, *Journal*, vol. 3, p. 782.

3. *Journal Officiel*, May 7, 1871, pp. 497-8; also in *L'Egalité*, May 7, 1871.

4. Thiers got around this by declaring he was not 'bombarding' but rather 'cannonading' the city. See Marx's 'The Civil War in France' in *DFI*, vol. 4, pp. 361, 395. See also Thiers's *Histoire de la révolution du 4 septembre et de l'insurrection du 18 mars*, Paris, 1875, pp. 142-4, cited in A.I. Molok, *Germanskaia interventsiia protiv Parizhskoi Kommuny*, Leningrad, 1939, pp. 8, 28n. See further Germany, Auswärtiges Amt, *Die Grosse Politik der Europäischen Kabinette, 1871-1914*, vol. 1, *Der Frankfurter Friede und seine Nachwirkung, 1871-1887*, Berlin, 1927, p. 12, no. 3, Fabrice to Bismarck, April 15, 1871, and pp. 13-14, no. 4, Bismarck to Fabrice, April 18, 1871. See also *Tsarskaia diplomatiia i Parizhskaia Kommuna*, p. 77.

5. One Communard noted that, in the days of Vercingétorix, the Parisians burned their town to prevent it from falling intact into Caesar's hands; see Benoît Malon, *La troisième défaite du prolétariat français*, Neuchâtel, 1871, p. 281.

6. *Werke*, vol. 33, p. 642.

7. IISG, *Jung*, 895; *ibid.*, *Marx-Engels Correspondence*, D 3890.

8. *Mémoire présenté par la Fédération jurassienne*, Sonvilier, 1873, pp. 199-200; *Guillaume*, vol. 2, pp. 157-8.

9. IISG, *Marx-Engels Correspondence*, D 4320. Marx had long known von

Haxthausen's work; see *Das Kapital*, Hamburg, 1867, p. 763, and *Werke*, vol. 19, p. 107.

10. Knizhnik-Vetrov, *Russkie deiatel'nitsy*, pp. 75-6. The Russian section had corresponded with Malon since the Le Creusot strike.

11. *Ibid.*, p. 77n; Thomas,*The Women Incendiaries*, pp. 40-1, 70-87.

12. *APP*, B/A 483, 'Insurgés Contumax,' 186 (calling her 'Dmitrion'). See also France, *Archives Nationales*, BB24 856, no. 2, 382.

13. *MERR*, pp. 189-90; Sazhin, *Vospominaniia*, pp. 77-8. A French police spy reported that Elizabeth bragged of setting fire to the Louvre (*APP*, B/A 431, *pièce* 152), but another report held that 'aucun crime ou délit de droit commun n'a été relevé à sa charge par d'antécédents judiciaires' (*Archives Nationales*, BB24 856, no. 2, 382).

14. *MERR*, pp. 189-90.

15. Claretie, *Histoire de la Révolution*, p. 703.

16. *TsGAOR*, f. III otd., 3 eksp., ed. khr. no. 50-2/1871, 'O revoliutsion-nom Internatsionalnom obshchestve. Prodolzhenie k 1871 godu,' 11. 75-7. See also Prosper Lissagaray, *History of the Commune of 1871*, London, 1886, p. 359.

17. France, Ministère de la Guerre, Etat-Major de l'Armée, *Archives Historiques*, Conseil de Guerre Permanent de la 1 re Division Militaire, Versailles, no. 685; Switzerland, *Bundesarchiv*, GeschäftsControlle und Register der schweizerischen Justiz- und PolizeiDepartment, 1871, no. 382, July 12, 1871. See also IISG, *Marx-Engels Correspondence*, 2587. Jenny Marx (daughter) wrote to her parents from Bordeaux early in June, 'Poor Mrs Tomanovskaya, I fear we have lost her forever,' See *Voprosy Istorii KPSS*, 1971, no. 5, p. 97. There were unsubstantiated rumours that Tomanovskaya was Nicholas Utin's mistress; see France, Assemblée Nationale, *Enquête parlementaire sur l'Insurrection du 18 mars 1871*, vol. 1, Versailles, 1872, p. 289; IISG, *Jung*, 899; E.S. Mason, *The Paris Commune*, New York, 1930, p. 291.

18. *APP*, B/A 1,123, *pièces* 41, 42.

19. *Ibid.*, *pièce* 52; see also *pièces* 33, 34, 43. Jaclard received 59,570 votes in Metz. On the eve of the March elections in Paris, when he was again a candidate, he said that 'J'appartiens au parti de l'insurrection et non à celui des candidatures.' See *ibid.*, *pièce* 28.

20. Jean Maitron, ed., *Dictionnaire biographique du mouvement ouvrier français*, 2nd series, vol. 6, Paris, 1969, pp. 360-2.

21. *Journal Officiel*, Mar. 31, 1871, p. 107. Clemenceau likewise fared badly, receiving only 752 votes.

22. J. Lemonnyer, *Les journaux de Paris pendant la Commune. Revue bibliographique complète de la presse parisienne du 19 mars au 27 mai*, Paris, 1871, p. 72. Lemonnyer does not list Anna Jaclard among *La Sociale's* collaborators, but police records and other evidence prove that she was on the staff.

23. *APP*, B/A 1,123, *pièces* 7, 302, 303, *Journal Officiel*, May 22, 1871, p. 631; Thomas, *The Women Incendiaries*, pp. 88-103; *Cri du Peuple* (Paris), April 26, 1871; *TsGAOR*, 'O revoliutsionnom Internatsionalnom

obshchestve. Prodolzhenie k 1871 godu,' 11. 75-7.

24.　Louise Michel, *La Commune,* Paris, 1898, p. 222; Maxime Vuillaume, *Mes cahiers rouges au temps de la Commune,* republished Paris, 1971, p. 392.

25.　Nicholas Zhukovsky and Michael Elpidin wrote to *La Suisse Radicale* (Jan. 22, 1872) protesting, along with others of Jaclard's friends, at the accusations levied against him by Alphonse Vergès. The latter claimed (*Le coin du voile: trahison et défection au sein de la Commune,* Geneva, 1872) that Jaclard deserted his post under fire. See further Lemonnyer, *Les Journaux,* p. 29; Malon, *La troisième défaite,* p. 214; Maitron, *Dictionnaire Biographique,* 2nd series, vol. 6, pp. 360-2.

26.　*TsGAOR,* O revoliutsionnom Internatsionalnom obshchestve. Prodolzhenie k 1871 godu,' 11. 75-7.

27.　A writer for *La Liberté,* possibly Apollon Mlochowski, described Jaclard: 'Pale beneath his képi decorated with . . . officer's stripes, with curly hair and gloomily curled beard, Colonel Jaclard, called the Lara of the Batignolles, liked to walk the street theatrically clothed in a dark old cloak into which he had tucked his sword. He would pass by, more melancholy than Hamlet, talking to himself. In conversation he affected a profound contempt for life, but that did not prevent him from fleeing enthusiastically at the slightest danger.' Quoted in *Le Nord,* June 7, 1871.

28.　*APP,* B/A 1,123, *pièces* 272-5. The Tribunal Civil of the Seine annulled the marriage in 1873 on the grounds that no legally constituted authority had performed it.

29.　*Ibid., pièces* 56-9, 63-4, 66, 71-3, 75-6; Anna Carlotta Leffler, *Sonya Kovalevsky,* London, 1895, pp. 30-2; Knizhnik-Vetrov, *Russkie deiatel-'nitsy,* pp. 190-203. August Okolowicz, a Polish Communard, escaped with Jaclard. Some Soviet historians claim that the Kovalevskys, and Catherine Barteneva, were Communards; this is incorrect. See Z.S. Efimova, 'Parizhskaia Kommuna i organ russkoi revoliutsionnoi demokratii 'Iskra',' *Istoricheskie zapiski,* vol. 59, pp. 311-12.

30.　*Golos Minuvshego,* 1916, no. 7-8, pp. 118-9; Pomper, *Lavrov,* pp. 119-25.

31.　B.S. Itenberg, ed., 'Parizhskaia Kommuna i P.L. Lavrov (Novye dokumenty),' *Istoriia SSSR,* 1971, no. 2, pp. 79-90.

32.　*Ibid.,* op. 102-4; *L'Internationale,* Mar. 26, April 2, 1871 (on these articles see Venturi, *Roots of Revolution,* pp. 453-4, and Meijer, *Knowledge and Revolution,* pp. 113-4).

33.　*Golos Minuvshego,* 1916, no. 7-8, p. 117.

34.　*L'Express* (Paris), no. 1,038, May 31 - June 6, 1971, p. 76.

35.　*Golos Minuvshego,* 1916, no. 7-8, pp. 121-4.

36.　*Ibid.,* p. 125. The Paris *L'Indépendant* claimed on Feb. 18, 1882, that Lavrov had played a 'very active' role in the Commune, participating in the defence of one of the forts, and that he and Raoul Rigault had been arrested together. See *APP,* B/A 1,144, 'Lawroff ou Lawrow, Pierre,' no *pièce* numbers.

37.　*Golos Minuvshego,* 1916, no. 7-8, pp. 134-5.

38.　*Ibid.,* p. 125.

39. Herman Lopatin, 'K rasskazam o P.L. Lavrove,' in Sazhin, *Vospomin-aniia*, p. 122. Hins was in Paris in June 1870 - February 1871; there he met and later married a woman we know only as Maria Iastke-vich.

40. Panteleev, *Vospominaniia*, p. 550n. The woman was Nadezhda Suslova (*femme* Erisman), the first Russian woman medical doctor. Her sister Apollinariia ('Polina') was Dostoevsky's mistress in the early 1860's. On Lavrov's departure from Paris see N.S. Rusanov (Kudrin), 'P.L. Lavrov (Ocherk ego zhizni i deiatel'nosti),' *Byloe*, February 1907, no. 2/14, pp. 264-6, and Sh.M. Levin, *Obshchestvennoe dvizhenie v Rossii v 60-70-e gody XIX veka*, Moscow, 1958, pp. 331-3.

41. *Werke*, vol. 33, p. 185; *Karl Marx Chronik*, pp. 309, 450; *DFI*, vol. 4, pp. 226, 231, 235.

42. B.S. Itenberg, *Rossiia i Parizhskaia Kommuna*, Moscow, 1971, p. 130. Lavrov's 1875 article, first published in *Vpered!*, is in his *Izbrannye sochineniia*, vol. 4, pp. 22-7. His book, *18 marta 1871 goda*, first appeared in Geneva in 1880. There are four Soviet editions, 1919 (two editions), 1922, 1925, all Petrograd-Leningrad.

43. *Werke*, vol. 22, p. 199. On Lavrov's polemic with Tkachev see Koz'min, *Ot 'deviatnadtsatogo fevralia'*, pp. 107-52. On Lavrov and the Commune see Pomper's study and Venturi, *Roots of Revolution*, pp. 454-6, and Itenberg, *Rossiia i Parizhskaia Kommuna*, pp. 109-39.

44. Lavrov differed with Marx on one crucial point, the form of the Commune. Marx argued that those who saw it as the revival of a medieval form of government were mistaken. See Koz'min, *Russkaia sektsiia*, pp. 324-5.

45. Bakunin, *Pis'ma*, p. 317; Bakunin, *Izbrannye sochineniia*, vol. 5, pp. 59-70; Carr, *Bakunin*, pp. 434-5.

46. Bakunin, *Izbrannye sochieneniia*, vol. 4, pp. 250-52.

47. *Ibid.*, pp. 254-7. See further Klaus Meschkat, *Die Pariser Kommune von 1871 im Spiegel der sowjetischen Geschichtsschreibung*, Berlin, 1965, pp. 41-50.

48. *MERR*, p. 188; Marc Vuilleumier, 'L'International à Genève et la Commune de Paris (1871),' in *Mélanges offerts à M. Paul-E. Martin*, Geneva, 1961, pp. 625-43.

49. Zürich, *Staatsarchiv*, 'Auslieferung des Sergius Netshajeff,' *pièces* 19, 56-44, 56-52. At *pièce* 56-7 there is a May, 1872, letter from the editor of the *Birzhevye Vedomosti* (Stock Exchange Gazette [!]) in St Petersburg to 'M. Et'en,' i.e. Etienne—Stepan Grazhdanov—the name Nechaev was using. This partially confirms the report in Sazhin, *Vospominaniia*, p. 66, of Nechaev's journalistic activities.

50. *LN*, vol. 62, pp. 457-60; *MERR*, pp. 266-7.

51. Sazhin, *Vospominaniia*, pp. 75-80; Zhelubovskaia, *Istoriia Parizhskoi Kommuny*, pp. 610-11; *LN*, vol. 62, p. 462. In 1874 Lavrov warned Hermann Jung that Sazhin was an intriguer; see IISG, *Jung*, 750. Reports of Lankiewicz's death are in Wycańska, *Polacy w Komunie*, pp. 282-3, and *Guillaume*, vol. 2, p. 156n.

52. *TsGAOR*, f. III otd., 3 eksp., ed. khr. No. 78, chast' 3/1871, 'Ob

usilenii nadzora na granitsakh Imperii dlia nevpuska lits prinadlez-
hashchikhsia k Parizhskoi Kommune i o zaderzhaňii ikh v sluchae
poiavleniia,' 11. 75-6; *ibid.*, chast' 4, 11. 189-214; *Deiateli*, vol. 2, pt. 3,
pp. 1253-4; Zhelubovskaia, *Istoriia Parizhskoi Kommuny,* pp. 611-12;
Wyczańska, *Polacy w Komunie*, po. 299-300; B.S. Itenberg, 'Russkie
revolutsionery-Uchastniki Parizhskoi Kommuny,' in AN SSSR,
Institut istorii, *Parizhskaia Kommuna 1871 g.*, vol. 2, Moscow, 1961, pp.
346-8.

53.   *Golos* (St Petersburg), Oct. 16, 1872 (Old Style).
54.   *Ibid.* See also *Deiateli*, vol. 2, pt. 4, pp. 2003-4, and *Le Nord*, Mar 16,
1872. The French police found copies of *Narodnoe Delo* on Shevelyov;
see Itenberg, 'Rasprostranenie izdanii' p. 45. On the shooting of
another Shevelyov, see *TsGAOR*, 'Ob ustroistve v Moskve osoboi
sekretnoi agentury,' 11. 143-4. This dossier contains a report (1. 152)
that Konstantin Kirillovich Shorov ('if this is not a pseudonym'), a
Communard, intended to go to Russia. We have no information on
any 'Shorov' and the report was surely false.

55.   On Russian press accounts see Itenberg, *Rossiia i Parizhskaia Kommuna*, pp. 23-40, 69-82, 83-92; Zhelubovskaia, *Istoriia Parizhskoi
Kommuny*, pp. 591-4; Kuniskii, *Russkoe obshchestvo i Parizhskaia Kommuna*, pp. 149-50.

56.   Georges Bourgin, 'La lutte du gouvernement français contre la
Première Internationale. Contribution à l'histoire de l'après-
Commune,' *International Review for Social History*, 1939, vol. 4, p. 49.
The Parisian *La Verité* claimed that fifty Russians fought for the
Commune; see *Neue Zürcher Zeitung*, no. 336, July 3, 1871.

57.   Wyczánska, *Polacy w Kommunie*, pp. 253-322. For less reliable esti-
mates see *La Suisse Radicale*, July 29, 1871; *Neue Zürcher Zeitung*, no.
333, July 1, 1871; *Journal de Genève*, Sept. 7, 1871; de Belina
(Mlochowski), *Les Polonais et la Commune de Paris*, p. 122n; *Krasnyi
Arkhiv*, vol. 45, pp. 18-20.

58.   De Belina (Mlochowski), *Les Polonais et la Commune de Paris*, pp. 5-6.
59.   On the Polish Communards the Wyczańska work is invaluable. See
also the 'Insurgés Contumax' dossiers in *APP*; the military archives
at Vincennes (I have used the dossiers of Eugeniusz Kompański,
August Okolowicz, and Victor Jaclard); *Archives Nationales*, BB24
862.5169, Kompanski, Eugène; Irena Koberdowa, *Pierwsza miedzynar-
odówka i lewica wielkiej emigraciji*, Warsaw, 1964; V.A. D'iakov, *Iaroslav
Dombrovskii*, Moscow, 1969. Beginning on January 9, 1876, *Der
Volksstaat* published a series of articles on Dombrowski. According to
the spy Adolf Stempkowski, Tkachev's friend Kasper Turski urged
the Commune to appoint a special Polish tribunal to try the
conservative, 'Hôtel Lambert' Poles; see *TsGAOR*, f. III otd., 3 eksp.,
ed. khr. No. 80/1872, 'Ob obrazovavshemsia v Tsiurikhe revoliutsionnom slavianskom sotsial'no-demokraticheskom obshchestve,' 11.
1-2. According to one report, Dombrowski's last words were, 'Voilà
comment on meurt, et ces hommes m'accusaient de les trahir!' *APP*,
B/A 1,039, *pièces* 40, 75.

60. Quoted in *L'Express,* no. 1038, May 31 - June 6, 1971.
61. Itenberg, *Rossiia i Parizhskaia Kommuna, passim;* Martin Katz, *Mikhail N. Katkov,* The Hague, 1966, pp. 153-6; A.V. Nikitenko, *Zapiski i dnevnik (1804-1877 gg.),* 2nd edition, 2 vols., St Petersburg, 1905, vol. 2, pp. 427-8, 431-2; Reuel', *Russkaia ekon. mysl',* pp. 174-7.
62. The issues of *Viselitsa* (with an introduction by S. Valk) are reproduced in *LN.* vol. 1, pp. 157-64. On Goncharov, who was apparently not related to the creator of *Oblomov,* see *Deiateli,* vol. 2, pt. 1, pp. 294-5.
63. The indictment and a summary of the trial are in B. Bazilevskii (V.Ia. Iakovlev), *Gosudarstvennye prestupleniia v Rossii v XIX veke,* vol. 1, *1825-1876,* Stuttgart, 1903, pp. 411-4. Goncharov broke down while awaiting trial and made a full confession. When Utin publicized Mrs Goncharova's affair with the liberal journalist A.F. Zhokhov, the latter challenged him to a duel. Utin killed Zhokhov. The case was extensively covered in the Russian press; I have used primarily *Golos,* beginning with the issue of Aug. 17, 1872 (Old Style). After the death of Zhokhov, Mrs Goncharova, the first woman defence attorney in Russia, committed suicide. Nor was that the end of the matter. Her younger sister went to Utin's office, intending to kill him, but was unable to do so and shot and killed herself. See A.I. Kornilova-Moroz, 'Perovskaia i osnovanie kruzhka Chaikovtsev,' *KS,* 1926, no. 1(22), p. 26n., and Panteleev, *Vospominaniia,* p. 161n. On the attempts of the writer M.E. Saltykov (Schedrin) and others to defend the Commune, see *LN,* vol. 49-50, pp. 397-428, and Efimova, 'Parizhskaia Kommuna,' pp. 320-1.
64. France, *AMAE,* Russie, 1871 à 1872 Dépêches politiques des Consuls, vol. 9, Odessa, Nos. 12-15; Belgium, *AMAE,* CP, Consulats, vol. 13, Odessa, 1871-80, no. 1; *Tsarskaia diplomatiia i Parizhskaia Kommuna,* p. 105; Switzerland, *Bundesarchiv,* Konsulardienst, Korrespondenz, Odessa, 1848-1917, April 3(15), 1871; *Le Nord,* April 28, May 2, 1871; *Neue Zürcher Zeitung,* no. 194, April 16, no. 207, April 23, no. 290, June 8, 1871; S.L. Chudnovskii, *Iz davnikh let: Vospominaniia,* Moscow, 1934, pp. 37-45. Chudnovskii reported that four people were killed, three wounded by bayonets and seventeen by blunt instruments and stones. Windows were broken in 528 houses, 335 apartments had property destroyed, 151 shops had windows and doors broken, and 401 shops were looted. The anti-Semitic *Golos* reported on Nov. 7, 1872 (Old Style) that in Odessa Jews owned 1,641 shops (including 116 tobacco shops), 866 eating places and 58 'houses of tolerance.' The same source claimed that Jews owned 569 houses on the best streets and that the city received 4,317.15 rubles from Jewish merchants in taxes per annum while spending 10,000 rubles on the Jewish hospital alone. *Golos* maintained that ten of fourteen pharmacists in Odessa were Jews and that almost all the physicians were Jews; the baking and sale of bread were in Jewish hands—and all this, the journal lamented, despite the fact that Odessa had plenty of Armenians, Greeks, 'foreigners' and others in Odessa who were in business.

65.   Reuel', *Russkaia ekon. mysl'*, p. 177n.:   *Neue Zürcher Zeitung,*   no. 232, May 6, 1871.

66.   Tatishchev, 'Sotsial'no-revoliutsionnoe dvizhenie,' pp. 1334-7; M.P. Chubinskii, 'Sud'ba sudebnoi reformy v poslednei treti XIX veka,' in *Istoriia Rossii v XIX veke* (Granat), vol. 6, p. 210; Burtsev, *Za sto let,* pt. 2, p. 80.

67.   The text of the new law (which modified that of April 1865) is in *Le Nord,* July 18, 1872. The legislation grew out of an investigation into the dissemination of illegal and subversive literature; the findings of that enquiry are in *TsGAOR,* 'O vozzvaniiakh poluchaemykh iz-za granitsy.'

68.   Reuel', *Russkaia ekon. mysl'*, p. 214n.

CHAPTER NINE

Après Commune

Not until 1891 did Engels refer to the Paris Commune as the embodiment of the dictatorship of the proletariat, but save for Bakunin few contemporaries would have disputed the claim in 1871. Because the Commune struck at the very heart of its state, social and economic system, the European middle class rallied against the insurrection in a movement resembling a religious crusade. Conservatives feared that the ghosts of the French Revolution had risen again and that the lower classes were taking the old egalitarian formulas and slogans seriously. No one could predict when or where the leaders of the great conspiracy, the men who composed the General Council of the International, might again hurl their 'cosmopolitan' (the standard conservative epithet) forces into battle.[1]

The revolutionaries, adventure-seekers, idealists, profiteers and the merely curious of many nations who had streamed into Paris in March and April of 1871 fled the city during 'Bloody Week.' The triumphant Versailles forces caught many thousands as they tried to slip through the battle lines. Street fighting was still in progress when Jules Favre directed French diplomats in Europe to seek the arrest and extradition of Communards who crossed into foreign countries. With nearly 40,000 people under arrest, the prospects for the total extermination of all traces of the insurrection seemed promising. But one obstacle remained. So long as the International remained alive, the Paris Commune was not dead.[2]

'Like a vast Freemasonry, their society embraces all Europe.' Thus Jules Favre described the International in a June 6, 1871, circular requesting formal agreement on the outlawing of that organization and the extradition of the Communards. Favre declared that 'to hate . . . and punish them is not enough. One must seek out the germ and destroy it.' The Commune was synonymous with the International, which was, he argued, everywhere—even in Russia. The International threatened European civilization, and Favre called upon all Europe to join France in a crusade against it. His circular constituted a plea for a new Holy Alliance.[3]

Russia and Germany, and soon Austria-Hungary, gave their formal blessing to Favre's proposal. It cost nothing and merely reaffirmed existing policy. Smaller powers such as Belgium and Spain rushed to prove their willingness to run the Communards and Internationalists to ground; and if Mazzini and the Pope had anything to say in the matter, Italy would soon follow.[4] But as Castereagh and Canning had thwarted the efforts of Alexander I and Metternich to make the first Holy Alliance a potent organization, so Gladstone now crimped the plans of Alexander II and Thiers. The British government declared that it would treat the Communards as political refugees and grant them asylum.[5]

No one could move London. Berne was perhaps another matter, but in Switzerland not everything depended upon the federal capital. The cantons jealously guarded their autonomy; nowhere was this more true than in Geneva, where a large colony of Communard refugees assembled. Despite the sharp warning of the French ambassador, the president of the Confederation (Charles-Emmanuel Schenk) insisted that the Swiss government did not feel menaced by the International and he reiterated the Swiss intention to treat each refugee individually. Switzerland would extradite common criminals, grant asylum to political refugees.[6]

In Geneva, members of the Russian section of the International and other Russian émigrés worked in the *ad hoc* groups that aided the refugees. The French consul learned that Nicholas Utin was involved in these activities, and fanciful stories about his exploits filled the consul's reports to the foreign ministry. Utin and his colleagues had indeed helped revive the old 'groupe d'initiative et de propagande' (the organization into which Barteneva and Levashyova had alledgedly recruited St Petersburg students) to assist the Communards. French and Russian spies knew of this committee's existence, but they were unable to penetrate it.[7] One of the first individuals whom the 'groupe' helped was Elizabeth Tomanovskaya. She arrived at the end of May. Utin hid her until August, when she registered with the cantonal police as a political refugee. Utin had learned that neither Geneva nor still less Berne would honour the French warrant for her arrest: she was fairly small game, 'Mme Dmitrieff's' reputation notwithstanding. Tomanovskaya remained in Geneva until October 1871; in that month, in a state of extreme emotional depression, she returned to Russia. Fortunately, no one there associated her with the notorious activities of the *pétroleuses*.[8]

Victor Jaclard came to Geneva shortly after his escape and joined his wife, Anna, who had reached the city a couple of months earlier. They soon moved elsewhere in Switzerland and after a few years went to Russia. Benoît Malon came to Geneva for a while, as did Maxime Vuillaume (an editor of *Père Duchêne*), Mme André Léo, 'Mme Paule Mink' (the Polish Communard Paulina Mękarska), and Léon Massenet, brother of the composer Jules. J.-B. Dumay, who had tried to establish the Commune in Le Creusot ('en plein fief Schnieder') also sought refuge in Geneva, as did, later, Jules Guesde, Gustave Cluseret, Henri Rochefort and many others. The Russians in Geneva helped most of these refugees in one way or another. A deeply disturbed and frustrated Russian government looked on, unable to curb the 'criminal' activities of its nationals, and pondered the reports passed on through French diplomatic channels:

> The Russian Utin, imbued with the most extreme revolutionary ideas, and editor of *L'Egalité*, one of the most violent organs of the International, was installed in Geneva by one of the leaders of the organization, Bakunin ... [Utin] has become one of the most active, fiery organizers of that society. This is an unscrupulous young man of outlandish ambition. His talent is mediocre, but he is endowed with a powerful will, and his work is formidable.[9]

Russian Après-Commune: The Trial of the Nechaevists

Its inability to prosecute Utin and the other émigrés angered the Russian government, and Sergei Nechaev's continued evasion of an international police dragnet outraged it beyond measure. A murder indictment against the fugitive remained outstanding, so there was no question, St Petersburg assumed, of any challenge to his extradition, even from a country such as Switzerland with which Russia had no such treaty or convention. First, however, Russian agents had to find him.[10]

The British, as we have seen, gave Russia little assistance in the search for Nechaev even after the publication in London of his *Obshchina*, and this indifference to the revolutionary threat from that quarter irritated the Russians as much as London's refusal to extradite the Communards angered the French. Russian authorities, in official conversations with British diplomats, affected a 'marked disinclination . . . to acknowledge that . . . [communist] ideas are prevalent in their country.' Paradoxically, however, the Russian government did admit that it was paying serious attention to the problem, however minor it was inside Russia. Referring to the forthcoming trial of those accused of consorting with Nechaev, Russian officials claimed (according to a British report) that the Nechaevists were 'bent on enacting a repetition of the Sicilian Vespers. The day of carnage . . . had even been fixed for . . . 19 February 1870.'[11]

The trial of the Nechaevists opened in St Petersburg on July 1, 1871 (Old Style), a date not chosen by chance. The prosecution had long since compiled its case and could have commenced the trial a year or more earlier. But the government hoped to capture the central figure in the drama and place him in the dock alongside his comrades. So the proceedings were repeatedly postponed, and the accused sat in prison, unable to avail themselves of any relief in Russian law (to be sure, the same situation obtained—and does to this day—in France). The great uprising in Paris gave the authorities an excuse to conduct the trial without Nechaev as an exposé of the international revolutionary-socialist conspiracy. It was a contrived argument. Many people in Russia feared revolutionary terror, by which they understood either peasant violence or individual acts such as that of Karakozov, but few (other than the Third Section) took the internal socialist menace seriously. The French ambassador reported that Count Peter Shuvalov and others exaggerated the socialist danger to deter the tsar from pursuing a liberal policy, to obtain more funds for the Third Section and perhaps even to establish it as a separate ministry.[12]

The trial of the Nechaevists was the first public adjudication of political crimes in modern Russian history.[13] The government prepared indictments against eighty-seven people; ten fewer than that actually came before the court. In the absence of Nechaev the prosecutor concentrated upon elucidating the network of conspiracy and intrigue that stretched from Geneva and other Western cities to Moscow and St Petersburg. He repeatedly cited the 'Geneva international revolutionary committee' as the organizational base of Nechaev and his accomplices, and he introduced Nechaev's membership card in Bakunin's 'Russian Section of the Universal Revolutionary Alliance' into evidence. The IWMA emerged as the overall directorate of the several revolutionary societies that were—according to the prosecutor—plotting uprisings all over Europe on the model of the Paris Commune. Few Russian officials knew exactly what the International was, but the very name was sufficiently sinister—the xenophobia of old Muscovy has never died—to serve any purpose; and Nechaev had claimed membership in the organization. The prosecution read the 'Catechism of a Revolutionary' into the record along with other documents, and the trial continued for more than two months.

The prosecution's case demonstrated beyond doubt that the trial was essentially political. The murder of the hapless Ivanov figured very little in the proceedings, but after the government made its interminable point about the danger from the International, that murder alone provided the real basis for the trial. The prosecutor's recitation of anti-socialist slogans could not link the accused with the IWMA and had no bearing whatsoever upon the murder case. And so the 1864 reform of the Russian judicial system now proved all too successful from the government's point of view: the court freed forty of the defendants. The four men who had—with Nechaev—participated in the murder received sentences of up to fifteen years in prison. Two people (Barbara Aleksandrovskaya and Varlaam Cherkezov) were exiled to Siberia. The remainder, convicted on lesser charges, received mild sentences. Peter Tkachev, for example, went to prison for sixteen months, and most of the others received even shorter terms. The trial of the Nechaevists was over. Its greatest accomplishment was to reveal that the government case, apart from the murder, was almost totally without foundation. A few young people with subversive literature did not make a revolution.[14]

The trial revealed some interesting data about the radical youth. They were, for one thing, younger than their counterparts of the preceding decade. The average age of the accused was 25.2 years; only five were over 30. This compares with an average age of 30.9 years for the defendants in the 'Trial of the Thirty-two' (1862-1865) involving members of Land and Liberty. Seven women were among the Nechaevists, none among the accused of the 1860's. Students and intellectuals were less prominent, and the theoretical underpinnings of the Nechaevist movement were markedly inferior to those of Land and Liberty. Terror had become fashionable, social theories cruder and less comprehensive.[15]

The Russian government failed to recognize that the young generation was becoming increasingly disillusioned with the conditions of Russian life. Tsar Alexander and his advisers believed that foreign influence was responsible for the surge of radicalism. The International provided a convenient scapegoat, the Paris Commune an object lesson, and the tsar resolved to take the initiative in the revival of the Holy Alliance. The trial of the Nechaevists was one of the first steps in that direction. That ended in fiasco, with the court freeing more than half the accused and only mildly disciplining the rest, save for the actual murderers. The regime's answer to this untidy situation was, as we saw in the last chapter, to change the law.

The campaign against the IWMA gained ground. Bismarck supported the cause, though his approach lacked the brutal directness St Petersburg preferred. Count Beust of

Austria-Hungary took a relatively moderate stand, and even proposed some labour and social reforms, but the implacable Magyar aristocrat Andrássy soon replaced him. The French Republic rooted out the Communards and their supporters. Only Switzerland and Great Britain remained immune to the wave of reaction.

The International could hardly remain indifferent to the assault. Governments devised pretexts to place socialists on trial in many countries. These frequently backfired (e.g. the trial of the Nechaevists in Russia and the Liebknecht-Bebel 'high treason' affair in Germany) but they continued and they halted the growth of the IWMA. Severe internal tensions also beset the organization. The monumental changes in the European political structure in 1870-1 exacerbated the disagreements over labour's attitude toward the political struggle, and the International debated its response to the new situation.

Nicholas Utin and the London Conference

The International could not hold its scheduled Mainz Congress in 1870 because of the war, and the prospects for a meeting in 1871 were even more bleak. The General Council therefore decided—at Engels's suggestion—to hold a 'private conference' in London in September. It proceeded to select the participants despite protests from the anarchists.[16]

The Council disposed—so it thought— of one major issue prior to the meeting. After two years of uncertainty and confusion, it conceded in July 1871 that the documents concerning the admission into the IWMA of Bakunin's Alliance were genuine. Upon receiving this acknowledgement of its legitimacy, however, the Geneva Alliance announced its dissolution to the General Council. The London conference subsequently declared 'the question of the "Alliance de la Démocratie socialiste" to be settled.'[17] Anarchist organizations, however, had a peculiar regenerative quality: when one disappeared, another often with the same membership, arose to take its place. Before the end of the summer, the old Geneva Alliance was reconstituted as the 'Propaganda and Socialist Revolutionary Action' section of the IWMA.

Nicholas Utin, whom the General Council nominated as one of the two delegates from Switzerland to the London conference, came to England bitterly hostile toward the new section. He succeeded in delaying the admission of the group. These tactics infuriated the Bakunists and their ex-Communard allies and drove them still further into opposition to the General Council. The anarchists and Communards began to form fictive organizations ('Latin Group,' 'Section of Revolutionary Atheism,' 'Section of French Revolutionary Propaganda') and to apply for admission into the International.[18]

The problem of the Alliance's offspring embodied the struggle for control of the IWMA. There were those who saw the organization as a huge working-class political organization led by the General Council, and there were others who regarded it as an insurrectionary force that should abandon 'bourgeois politics' and abolish the Council. Contemporaries referred to the factions as centralists and federalists, authoritarians and anti-authoritarians, collectivist communists and anarchists, Marxists and Bakuninists. Whatever one called them, however, two mutually exclusive philosophies of socialism and the working-class movement had joined battle.

The London conference, which was important in that struggle, was a strange gathering. Because no one knew the French delegate he was admitted but denied the right to vote. No German delegates came. Utin represented the German-speaking workers in Geneva, reflecting the decline of the Russian section and the highly arbitrary method of delegate selection. Paul Robin, a French exile whom Marx and Lopatin had installed on the General Council as a concession to the anarchists, represented Bakunin. But Robin, like the other members of the Council, could not vote in that capacity. Marx, Engels and five other members, however, were corresponding secretaries for countries not otherwise represented, and they did have voting rights.

Some minor resolutions passed easily. The General Council had firm command of the proceedings, and in any event a Congress would have to review and approve or reject everything done in London. The conference adopted two resolutions on the French situation which Utin presented on

Marx's behalf, and it directed Utin to prepare a full report on the Nechaev affair (including the recent trial of the Nechaevists). The meeting expressly and publicly denied that Nechaev had ever had any connection with the IWMA.

Trying to speak for the Bakuninists, Robin could not obtain a hearing and in general was treated shabbily. In some respects the anarchists merited this, for their policies were by any reasonable standard harmful to the cause of labour. But they were indisputably a major force in the IWMA and they convinced many members that the General Council should be abolished for its arbitrary use of its virtually unbridled powers.[19] Utin led the assault on Robin, resorting to ridicule and heavy-handed sarcasm rather than serious arguments. Robin left the conference because the majority refused to hear him. After the conference, the General Council, quite illegally treating Robin's refusal to withdraw a letter of complaint as tantamount to resignation, voted narrowly to expel him from its ranks. This set still another dubious precedent.[20]

Save for its denunciation of Nechaev the General Council hoped to keep the conference secret. Johann Eccarius, however, a German émigré, sold the entire story to *The Scotsman* of Edinburgh, apparently believing that no one read the provincial press. Within a few days accounts of the socialist meeting appeared in newspapers all over Europe. The press noted that a Russian delegate had been present and had discussed the IWMA's prospects in Russia. Nicholas Utin figured by name in some reports, and this confirmed information that the Third Section received from other sources about his activities. It was probably Apollon Mlochowski who wrote from Geneva at about this time,

> One of the biggest figures in the International and in Geneva in particular is Nikolai Isaakovich Utin; if I am not mistaken, judging from his face, he must belong to the pure-blooded Jewish race. Utin counts himself one of the emigrants; but we do not much believe him, although it may be so, because he really does have some unsettled accounts with the late . . . [General M.N.] Muravyov. Be that as it may, this man Utin is extremely dangerous to Russia, and before him in this respect the Bakuninist party (which broke with him) pales. We serve notice that Utin

is getting ready to go to Russia . . . We repeat that Utin is a very influential person in the International Revolutionary Organization; he is one of the main pillars of the International; he knows all the ins and outs, and he, as one of the main members of the Comité du groupe de Propagande, knows everything pertaining to the Russian revolutionary intelligentsia in the International.[21]

This and similar reports fed official Russian prejudices and preconceptions and strengthened St Petersburg's determination to seek an international agreement to combat revolutionism. The government took notice of Utin's claim in London that no country offered such fertile soil for the IWMA as Russia, a claim it considered wholly at variance with the conference's insistence that Nechaev had never belonged to the International and had fraudulently used the organization's name to 'make dupes and victims in Russia.'[22]

Utin returned to Geneva in what he thought was triumph. Like Herman Lopatin and Elizabeth Tomanovskaya before him, he had received a warm welcome in London from the General Council and the Marx family and had been treated as an important representative of the Russian revolutionary movement. But his importance soon faded in Geneva, where the local anarchists and disgruntled Communards accused him of having sold himself to Marx and the 'German dictatorship' in the IWMA.[23]

The former Alliancists, other Bakuninists and the Communard refugees who made common cause with them held a meeting in the Swiss mountain town of Sonvilier on November 12, 1871. Out of this affair came the famous 'Sonvilier Circular' denouncing the London conference and the General Council. The circular stated in part that the Council wished to

introduce into the International the principle of authority; circumstances have seemed to favour this tendency, and it seems to us quite natural that this school, whose ideal is the *conquest of political power by the working class,* should have believed that the International, after the recent course of events, must change its original direction and be transformed into a hierarchical organization directed and governed by a committee. But even though we understand these tendencies and these facts, we do not feel ourselves less obliged to combat them in the name of the social

revolution for which we are working and of which the
programme is: 'emancipation of the workers by the workers
themselves,' independently of all guiding authority, even though
that authority should have been appointed and consented to by
the workers themselves.[24]

A mass meeting of Geneva Internationalists rejected the
'Sonvilier Circular' early in December of 1871. Benoît Malon,
no anarchist but an opponent of the General Council, tried to
defend and explain the document, but the crowd shouted
him down. Utin wrote to Marx that only his own intervention
had saved Malon and two friends from bodily harm.[25]

The London conference had recommended that, if the
anarchists and their opponents in the Romande Federation
(which supported the General Council) could not agree
among themselves, the former should form their own federation. The former Alliancists and some Communards now
decided to follow that advice. A 'Jura Federation' came into
being and provided the organizational base for the new
anarchist attempt to seize control of the entire International.

Anarchist Counterattack: The Zürich Russians

Part of the anarchist counter-offensive involved an attempt to
create a Slavic section of the IWMA in Zürich. The origins of
this group remain obscure. In October 1871, one of the
organizers asked help from Becker, who passed the request on
to Marx. The latter, through Jung, relayed it to Nicholas
Utin. This complex procedure arose out of the suspicion that
the Bakuninists were behind the project. Marx asked for
information on the founders, A. Dubov, Kasper Turski, and
Manuilo Hrvačanin. The last two were genuine: Turski was a
Communard of Polish-Ukrainian-Russian descent, and
Hrvačanin was a Croatian leftist. But 'Dubov' was Sergei
Nechaev.[26] It was Nechaev who had the idea of reviving the
special section for foreigners that the Swiss Internationalists
Herman Greulich and Karl Bürki had established alongside
their regular Zürich section in August 1867. The auxiliary
group was known as 'wild' or 'mixed' because of its composition (in which many East Europeans figured). When war
broke out between France and Prussia in 1870, many Zürich

Internationalists left to join one or another of the armies. Several Slavs were among them, but enough Serbs, Croats and others remained to make the Slav element temporarily dominant in the 'wild' section, which now officially became know as the 'Slav section.' After the war, there had been a few unsuccessful attempts to revive this group.[27]

At the end of the summer of 1871, three young men involved in the Nechaev affair, Valerian Smirnov, Vladimir Holstein and Alexander Oelsnitz, escaped from Russia and came to Zürich, where they at once plunged into émigré politics on the side of Nechaev.[28] The latter, the object of a continuing police search, actually arrived in the Swiss city only after his three disciples came. He found his former associate, M.P. Sazhin, and Kasper Turski (a Communard whom he might have known in Paris) also in Zürich. Nechaev broached his plan to revive the old 'wild' or 'Slav' section of the IWMA. Sazhin wrote to Bakunin asking his opinion; in reply, the old anarchist described his split with Nechaev. These revelations surprised the Zürich group, which Nechaev proceeded to alienate further by announcing his intention to blackmail the Herzen family with stolen documents. Unable to establish his sway over this group (some of whom knew of Lopatin's charges), and unable to move about freely, Nechaev then dropped the project to revive the 'Slav' section.[29] Turski and Smirnov likewise washed their hands of the matter, but the rest, joined by several newcomers, pressed ahead and continued to solicit Bakunin's advice. In the summer of 1872 they finally agreed upon a programme written by Bakunin, and a Slav section came into existence. It never officially entered the International, but it did join the new Jura Federation and that gave it anarchist legitimacy. The new group gave Bakunin its unwavering support in the fight against Marx and the General Council.[30]

Nechaev at the End of the Road

Although they took no part in the actual creation of the Slav section, in the winter of 1871-2 Nechaev and Turski established a revolutionary cell, some members of which were also in that section. The tsarist spy Adolf Stempkowski reported that there were Russians, Serbs and Poles in the secret cell, which had no connection with the International.[31] Along with scores of Russian, German and Swiss agents, Stempkowski had participated in the search for Nechaev since 1870, and early in 1872 he began to close in on his quarry. That he was able to do so reveals incredible *naïveté* and incaution on Nechaev's part: in March of 1868, a 'jury of honour' composed of Polish émigrés in Zürich had found Stempkowski guilty of spying for the Russian government. A similar body convened in Paris a few months later overturned this 'verdict,' but events were to prove the original finding accurate.[32]

The Zürich émigrés and the local socialists shared Nechaev's gullibility where Stempkowski was concerned. The Polish spy had, astonishingly, succeeded in establishing an identity as a political radical. He participated, in the spring of 1872, in the founding of the Zürich Polish Social-Democratic Association. In May, that Association approved a programme and statutes drawn up—according to some evidence—by Kasper Turski. The programme commenced with some bombast that was the common property of the European radical left, speaking of the 'political and economic despotism of the privileged minority over the working masses.' Then came the Bakuninism that constituted the hallmark of the document: a 'free union of workers' associations' would characterize the future society, which a 'general uprising' and a 'social revolution' would create. Land would be the property of 'agricultural communes'; factories would belong to 'worker associations.' The programme rejected Polish nationalism but hinted strongly at revolutionary panslavism: 'We cordially greet and enter into close and solidary union with the rest of our brothers of the great Slavic fraternity who, also being under the yoke of governments we all hate... have the absolute right to independence and national development.' An 'internationalist' paragraph offered aid of an unspecified nature to 'other nations aspiring to freedom,' and the programme concluded, 'Long live the social revolution! Long live the free commune! Long live free and social-democratic Poland!'[33]

We can assume that Stempkowski gave Nechaev the copy of

this programme which the Zürich police found among his effects. And we know that Nechaev could not resist the temptation to infiltrate the Polish Social-Democratic Association, a temptation that was to prove fatal. Changing his abode every few days, Nechaev eventually found himself under the roof of Stempkowski, who, having surmounted the accusations of 1868, was a trusted member of local leftist and Slavic circles. Reading the programme that Stempkowski brought to him, Nechaev recognized it as not social-democratic but Bakuninist. He decided to present a more sweeping revolutionary programme to the Zürich Poles and to draw them into his existing cell. We gather this from the similarity of Nechaev's phraseology to that found in the Association's programme; from the fact that he discussed many of the same problems; from his use of the Polish word *gmina* for 'Commune'; and from the evidence of Stempkowski's reports on the Third Section.

In 1973 the author published in an English translation Nechaev's previously unknown 'Fundamental Theses.'[34] That document, and his other works during the last two years he was at liberty, indicate that, although Nechaev had not wholly divested himself of Bakunin's influence, he had become an elitist revolutionary whose thinking now derived chiefly from Blanquism. He wanted to organize a small, tightly-knit party to carry out a social revolution and establish a socialist (he and everyone else in the period wrote 'social-democratic') republic. Though he still recognized the indispensable role of the masses in the revolution, Nechaev reiterated his belief that an élite party had to play a leading, directing, tutorial role.

To bring about the revolution, the party would propagandize the masses and revolutionize them, in part through acts of violence against the state. These acts were certain to generate reprisals, and those in turn would still further alienate the masses from the state. This cumulative violence would shatter the myth of the state's invincibility. The revolution would be violent, and the new society would consolidate its victory through still more violence against enemies internal and external. The new society could only arise upon the graves of those who had controlled the old.

The existing order maintained itself by violence; only violence would overthrow it.

In Nechaev's view, reason, parliaments and good intentions did not overthrow despotisms. The history of revolution in the West (he did not mention the Russian *jacqueries*) demonstrated, however, that violence alone produces no solutions, no utopias. Therefore, 'competent and experienced men' from the 'honest fraction of the intellectual minority' (i.e. the revolutionary elite) must direct the revolution. This elite would ensure that the goals of the 'insurgent people,' once realized, did not collapse by destroying the enemies of the revolution.

Nechaev anticipated objections. Who would control the elite? What were the limitations on its powers? In the programme of his London *Obschina* (September, 1871) and in the 'Fundamental Theses,' his straightforward answer emanated directly from Blanquist teachings: the elite controlled itself, made its own rules, recognized only such limitations as it chose to impose upon itself. The elite party would not hold elections, after its victory, until it had secured the goals of the revolution; and it alone would determine when that time had come. When it did, candidates would be required to pledge allegiance to the republic; accept state regulation of labour; approve nationalization of land, factories and all means of production; and affirm state responsibility for the rearing and educating of children. The revolutionary new society would take the form (here was an element of pure Bakuninism) of a 'federated union of communes.'

The closing exhortations, appeals to the Zürich Poles, also reflected Bakunin's thinking. Nechaev urged all Slavs to take concerted revolutionary action and spoke of their 'great historical mission' and of their 'union.' Like Bakunin and the Poles, he often spoke of 'social democracy' and claimed to belong to that camp; but this open proclamation of revolutionary panslavism could only alienate and outrage the mass of European social democrats.

Nechaev was an interesting but unoriginal and unsystematic thinker. Elements of old-fashioned Jacobinism and anarchism nibbled at the Blanquism that was now dominant in his revolutionary view. This leaves open to doubt the question whether he actually formulated anything that can accurately be called a theory. Indeed, his views and opinions added up to an unstable amalgam perhaps best described as democratic despotism. Like his successor and fellow Blanquist on the extreme left of the Russian revolutionary movement, Peter Tkachev, Nechaev agreed with the bard that everything resolves itself in power. Power in the hands of king, gentry or middle class was tyranny. Power in the hands of a revolutionary elite professing to act on behalf of the downtrodden masses was freedom.

This of course was merely a crude world-view, and its validity depends upon one's view of history. Clearly, an enormous burden of proof rested upon Nechaev's elite, for the masses, seeking security, would surrender considerable freedom to it. If the elite took that freedom and gave security in the form of chains, what then of the revolution? But Nechaev ruled out any possibility that the revolution would take this course. A true fanatic, he argued that revolutionaries might fail but the revolution would succeed.

We do not know whether Nechaev ever pondered the illogicality of this view. It does seem certain, however, that, had the Zürich émigrés rather than the police found the 'Fundamental Theses,' that document would have become— not necessarily for its intrinsic merit—an important piece of Russian revolutionary literature.

The Russian Diplomatic Campaign

Sergei Nechaev remained at large, the trial of his associates ended ignominiously for the Russian government, labour disorders erupted in Moscow province, and revolutionary propaganda flowed into Russia at an ever-increasing rate. Convinced that the International was responsible for all this, St Petersburg pressed its campaign against the organization.[35] Bismarck and Beust met in Gastein and Salzburg in September 1871, their emperors joined them, and all agreed with the Tsar that communism and the International were dangerous. Bismarck sent Alexander II a note telling him what had transpired, omitting only Beust's anti-Russian sallies. When Andrássy succeeded Beust in the autumn the Tsar was no nearer an international agreement against the socialists: there was speculation in Europe that Andrássy hoped to secure an alliance with Germany against Russia. Re-establishing the Holy Alliance was not so simple as the socialists feared and Alexander II hoped.[36]

The diplomats probed each other's positions and the spies and informers continued to stock police dossiers. In July 1871 a Berlin police official informed the Russians that someone from the Liebknecht-Bebel circle was going to Russia 'with the goal of spreading, among the working class that knew German and Polish, social teachings according to the apostolic system.'[37] Innocent citizens sometimes paid heavily for such unsubstantiated reports. For example, an informer told the Warsaw police that a local section of the 'Social International Society of Communists' planned a wide programme of incendiarism, and he gave the name of a working-man who, he claimed, was a member. The police arrested the unfortunate labourer immediately but failed to uncover any subversive activity on his part. They nevertheless held him in jail for thirty days 'because of the gravity of the accusation,' then released him under surveillance.[38] Spies reported to St Petersburg that sections of the IWMA existed in Odessa, Kaluga and Zhitomir, that the parent organization was recruiting members among the Old Believers (dissenters from Russian Orthodoxy), and that Russia and Polish revolutionaries were counterfeiting tsarist notes. Moreover, someone sent a group photograph of the 'main members of the London section of the International Society' to the Third Section, which made copies and distributed them to police stations throughout the Empire. The central figure in the photograph was Juliusz Balaszewicz ('Potocki'), the Third Section's chief agent in Great Britain.[39]

The counterfeiting charge, unlike the rest of this nonsense, had some foundation. It will be recalled that the Russian government had sent Gabriel Kamensky to Paris in 1865 to investigate such activities. Kamensky had some success, and a few counterfeiters went to prison. Some of them were released around 1870, however, and they went to Switzerland and resumed their former occupation. Kamensky pursued them to Yverdon in the canton of Vaud and was on the point of arresting them when—yielding to the temptation to make a quick fortune—he decided instead to join the operation. Alas for him, the Swiss police soon arrested everyone involved.[40]

The affair touched Nicholas Utin. One of the criminals whom Kamensky was supposed to be chasing, the Swiss citizen Edouard Bongard, worked for *Narodnoe Delo* and was a member of the Russian section. Bongard disappeared. But Apollon Mlochowski, learning of the arrest of Kamensky, convinced the Geneva authorities that he was associated with Utin and Bakunin. The police subjected Utin to a thorough *visite domiciliaire* in January of 1872, having summoned Mlochowski from Paris to take part in it and translate the Russian and Polish papers and documents in Utin's possession. The perusal of Utin's papers by six members of the Geneva police, plus a *juge d'instruction* and Mlochowski, took four days; from this we can get some idea of the importance of an archive that has been lost to history. No evidence of counterfeiting or other criminal activity was uncovered. Utin went free and the chagrined Geneva authorities declined to suggest that their Locarno counterparts investigate Bakunin. But an agent of the Russian secret police (and the Austrian, French, Belgian and perhaps others), Mlochowski, had seen every scrap of paper concerning the IWMA that Utin had in his possession.[41]

A minor *furor* ensued; the General Council issued a statement:

> The Russian Government . . . has taken advantage of the sham conspiracies of men like Netchayeff, who did not belong to the International, to prosecute opponents at home under the pretext of being Internationals. Now it takes another step in advance. Supported by its faithful vassal, Prussia, it commences an intervention in the internal concerns of Western nations by calling upon their magistrates to hunt down in its service the International. It opens its campaign in a Republic, and the Republican authorities hastened to make themselves the humble servants of Russia.[42]

The Utin affair embodied a Russian warning to the Swiss, whose complaisance (Geneva presumably told Berne what was going on) reflected their delicate situation. In January

1872, just prior to the Utin search, press rumours held that Austria-Hungary, Germany and Russia would send a joint expeditionary force into several Swiss cantons to crush the International and the Communard organizations. The conservative press denied these reports in such a manner that they appeared extremely plausible.[43]

In March of 1872 the announcement that Michael Gorchakov, the young, undistinguished son of the Russian foreign minister, would be the new ambassador to Berne intensified the anxiety that many Swiss felt concerning St Petersburg's intentions. The appointment signalled the tightening of communications between the Berne embassy and the foreign ministry in St Petersburg; and the most urgent matter then in Russo-Swiss relations was Swiss toleration of the IWMA and the Communards. Michael Gorchakov informed Swiss diplomats in St Petersburg that he would interpellate the federal government concerning its position in the event the powers agreed to act against the International; this suggests that his father anticipated such an agreement.[44]

The strange appointment—the thoroughly unpopular young Gorchakov had only the most modest intellectual competence—convinced the new Swiss president, Welti, of the truth of the rumours that, up to that time, only Bismarck's opposition had restrained the Russians from taking military action against the Confederation. Welti anticipated a démarche from the Eastern powers; his apprehension increased when the senior Gorchakov accompanied his son (who was *en route* to Berne) as far as Berlin. Gorchakov *fils* presented his credentials early in July 1872 and immediately pressed for an end to Swiss permissiveness toward the IWMA and the Communards. He was to enjoy an early and wholly unexpected success.[45]

The Bakuninist Surge

The tensions that beset the International threatened to destroy the organization. In Germany, where Marx's own mass base lay, the IWMA never had a fully legal existence. If Bismarck were to move to prevent German workers from participating in its meetings outside the country (none came to the London conference, for example), the Southern European and Swiss anarchists might well emerge as the dominant faction. To combat this possibility, the London conference had directed Utin to publish a report on the Nechaev affair (naturally linking the famous renegade to Bakunin), and Marx and others of his friends proceeded to try to document Bakunin's plans to take over the International. Paul Lafargue went to Spain after the Commune and learned that the Bakuninists controlled most IWMA sections in that country. He also discovered that some of Bakunin's followers in Madrid, and the Italian anarchist Giuseppe Fanelli, were trying to seize control of the federal council of the Spanish International, which had recently rejected an anarchist proposal to form a secret Alliance section. The Bakuninists managed to move the federal council to Valencia, where they soon turned it to their own ends. Lafargue then created a new, loyalist federation in the capital which the General Council promptly recognized. In the spring and summer of 1872 Lafargue also obtained documents proving that Bakunin's Alliance continued to exist as a secret, international organization and that it sought to subvert the IWMA by taking it over and giving it a Bakuninist character.[46]

Bakuninism was still stronger in Italy than in Spain. Mazzini had dominated the labour movement until the late 1860's, when Bakunin began to make inroads with both his International Brotherhood and the Alliance. By 1870, about two dozen labour groups with 3,000 members considered themselves members of the Bakuninist wing of the International. The General Council, however, recognized only the original Italian section Bakunin and his friends had established in Naples.[47] Marx and the General Council maintained a precarious foothold in the peninsula through the Turin section, but it came into existence only in October 1871 and one of the founders, the Russian revolutionary V.A. Zaitsev, had close ties to Bakunin.[48]

Representatives of the Italian working-class movement met in Rimini in August 1872, on the eve of the International's Congress in The Hague. They approved a statement criticizing the General Council for propagating the 'authoritarian doctrine of German communism' and declared that they would not go to The Hague. The delegates sent 'affectionate greetings' to the 'indefatigable champion of the social revolution,' Michael Bakunin, and despatched an account of their meeting to the General Council. Engels, as secretary for Italy, replied that only one Bakuninist section (the Neapolitan) actually belonged to the IWMA; therefore, the Rimini meeting hardly constituted an Italian federation: 'It will be for the Congress at The Hague,' he wrote, 'to pass a resolution on such usurpations.'[49]

Months prior to the Rimini meeting, the Belgian federation of the International also embarked upon a course that threatened to embarrass the General Council. Though the federation rejected the anarchist 'Sonvilier Circular's' call for a special Congress to discipline the Council, it nevertheless directed a commission to draft new statutes for that body. Eugène Hins, a Proudhonist who had become a disciple of Bakunin, headed the commission, which produced a recommendation to abolish the General Council. The Belgian federation rejected that plan in July 1872, but the fact that it had to be discussed indicated the seriousness of the split in the IWMA.[50]

Marx and Engels struck back at their enemies in a brochure they called 'Fictitious Splits in the International,' which constituted the General Council's reply to the Jura Federation's Sonvilier document. 'Fictitious Splits' attacked the anarchists on many fronts, from the dual secret-public character of the Alliance to Bakunin's Lyon fiasco, to James Guillaume's call for a Swiss volunteer corps to fight against Prussia in 1870. And Marx and Engels presented the first salvos of their argument that the anarchists were scheming to take power in the IWMA and remove it from the political arena.[51] They were, however, clearly on the defensive. Their supporters in France and Germany had been silenced, at least temporarily. The Swiss International was in turmoil. Southern Europe was solidly Bakuninist. Belgium had flirted dangerously close to the edge of anarchism. The unideological British working-class movement was becoming increasingly dissatisfied with the General Council.

Bakunin replied curtly to 'Fictitious Splits.' He demanded a 'jury of honour' at the forthcoming Congress and cited the

Belgian proposal to abolish the General Council as evidence of widespread disaffection. His hand seemed stronger than ever, the disappointments of the last two years notwithstanding.[52]

Although Bakunin himself remained in Locarno, in the summer of 1872 the headquarters of Bakuninist activity was in Zürich. The local Slavic section of the Jura Federation had grown considerably and was becoming a serious irritant to the loyalist Internationalists in the city. Nicholas Utin appeared in Zürich in July to obtain and publish information about Nechaev and Bakunin in accordance with the London conference's instructions. He was taking quite a risk, for the General Council had little or no support among the local Slavs. In the course of his investigations, Utin fell into the hands of some Russian and Serbian anarchists, who administered a severe beating. His injuries, however, did not prevent him from completing his report and despatching it to the Hague Congress.[53]

Marx and the Russians

Nicholas Utin had performed several services for Marx and the International, and now, in helping to discredit Bakunin and Nechaev, he was rendering another. The task was no doubt—certainly from Marx's point of view—a necessary one, but the zeal with which Utin performed it offended many of the Slavic émigrés and helped destroy his own credibility within the revolutionary movement. It was ironic that Utin's standing fell, along with that of his victims, at a time when there was a significant rise in Marx's popularity among the radical Russians, a popularity Utin had helped to generate. The Russian movement was becoming more sophisticated as the labours of Lopatin, Danielson, Utin and the Russian section began to bear fruit.

We have seen that Herman Lopatin left his unfinished translation of *Capital* with Danielson in St Petersburg when he went to Siberia to liberate Chernyshevsky. When the scheme miscarried and Lopatin went to prison, Danielson took over the translation. He corresponded with Marx about the work, and the two men also discussed political affairs. At

one point Danielson asked Marx about the rumour that
Bismarck and Beust would move jointly against the Interna-
tional. He reported the conclusion of the trial of the
Nechaevists to Marx and noted that the Russian translation
of the *Communist Manifesto* (done, as we have seen, by
Nechaev) had been introduced into evidence.[54]

Danielson worked rapidly, and his translation of *Capital*
went on sale in March 1872. Strangely enough, the first
translation of this most powerful of attacks upon capitalism
appeared in a country that had not really entered the
industrial age. Furthermore, it appeared with the approval of
the censor at a time when the tsarist government was trying
to mount a crusade against the IWMA, in which Marx
played such a major role.[55] Pursuing the old English argument that a book costing five guineas could do no harm, the
censor approved *Capital* without serious reservations. The
original edition, after all, had been circulating in Russia for
several years.[56]

Within six weeks the public had bought a third of the 3,000
copies published. This was a phenomenal sale for such a
work; the first German edition had sold only 700 copies in the
first year. Uniformly favourable reviews appeared. Critics
praised Marx's analysis of capitalism; one, the populist
economist Mikhailovsky, considered the work a manual on
'how *not* to industrialize.' The book fuelled the populist
argument that Russia should try to avoid the capitalist stage
of economic development, but populists searched in vain for
any hint that the author considered this possible.[57]

Though he was naturally pleased, Marx wasted no time in
congratulating himself upon his success in Russia. He wrote
to Danielson at the end of May, 'Ich bin so overworked [*sic*]
and in fact so much interfered with in my theoretical studies,
that, after September, I shall *withdraw* from the *commercial
concern* [the IWMA], which, at this moment, weighs principally upon my own shoulders, and which, as you know, has its
ramifications all over the world.' In a postscript, he asked for
information on the 'mountebank' Bakunin, specifically the
extent of his influence in Russia (he also asked whether his
name had figured in the trial of the Nechaevists).[58] Danielson
replied that Bakunin had little influence and that his

standing was especially low at the time because of his association with Nechaev. He told Marx that M.F. Negreskul (Lavrov's son-in-law) would have exposed Bakunin publicly had he not died before the trial of the Nechaevists (it was not clear from Danielson's letter why someone else could not have performed this task).[59]

In August, Marx asked Danielson for Nechaev's threatening letter to Liubavin concerning the Bakunin translation of *Capital*. Liubavin himself sent the letter, cautioning Marx not to construe it as conclusive proof of Bakunin's perfidy. He admitted, however, that it 'cast a shadow' over Bakunin and agreed that 'our common cause' would profit from his exposure.[60]

Marx now had most of the evidence he needed to go to The Hague in September with a sweeping indictment of the anarchists. Lafargue had sent documents on the Alliance from Spain, Utin had nearly completed his report on Nechaev and Bakunin, and now Liubavin supplied the famous letter from the 'Bureau of Foreign Agents of the Russian Revolutionary Society "The People's Summary Justice".' Anarchist strength in the IWMA was such, however, that no one could be certain how the Congress would interpret Marx's documents. But then the Italians unwisely decided not to send any delegates, thus reducing Bakuninist strength, and Marx and his friends took precautions to ensure the presence of a majority of reliable supporters. The fact that the meeting would take place in a relatively remote corner of Europe also worked to the disadvantage of the anarchists.

The End of Nechaev

Referring to the forthcoming Congress of the International, the Austro-Hungarian minister in The Hague reported in August that 'Bakunin and Nechaev are expected.'[61] This was a common fantasy of police spies and diplomats, who described the Congress as the most important revolutionary gathering since the Paris Commune. But at the moment when his prestige stood highest, when his dream of seizing control of the International seemed attainable, Bakunin could summon neither the will nor the funds to make the journey to Holland. For his part, Nechaev was hiding in Zürich in the summer of 1872 and never thought of going. Russian and other agents were looking for him: the Zürich police ransacked the dwellings of the Slavic students, conducting themselves with a certain lack of delicacy. One Russian citizen complained of the harassment; he could not have known that the local chief of police—not to mention some spies—had a pecuniary interest in finding Nechaev.[62]

Nechaev hid among the local Serbs, Poles and Russians, frequently changing his residence, seeing only a few people, rarely venturing outdoors during daylight hours. He kept several notebooks which he filled with random information; one contained the names of over eight hundred prominent Russians including the Tsar. The purpose of the list remains unknown; possibly these people were marked for execution. Nechaev did not devote all his time to the revolution; he corresponded .with the Parisienne who had become his mistress (Albertine Hottin), displaying for her a consideration and affection out of keeping with the precepts of his 'Catechism.'[63]

The rumours that Nicholas Utin would take revenge for the beating he had suffered disturbed Nechaev.[64] Someone brought him a Russian newspaper article on the assault; he copied it into one of his notebooks. But his concern did not strengthen his guard. In the course of his frequent moves, he eventually—as we have seen—came to the home of Adolf Stempkowski, who not only welcomed him but gave him a job as a sign-painter (according to some reports, this had been Nechaev's father's occupation) and persuaded him to stay several days.

On the afternoon of August 14, 1872, Sergei Nechaev, who had violated one of his strictest rules by spending too many nights under the same roof, broke another and showed himself in daylight. He went with Stempkowski and another man to the outskirts of Zürich. The three were sitting in the Café Müller when police agents entered and seized Nechaev, whose companions did not intervene. Two other patrons of the café, Herman Greulich (leader of the Zürich 'loyalist' Internationalists) and Theodore Remy (J.P. Becker's secretary) also ignored the affair. Greulich and Remy later declared that they did not know Nechaev, and this was probably true. Beyond that, one did not casually interfere with the police. But the presence of two Swiss 'loyalists' in the Café Müller that August afternoon inspired ugly stories, not least because the arrest of Nechaev followed so soon upon the beating of Utin, a friend of Greulich. The rumours of Marxist complicity in the arrest were, however, false; someone apparently planted them in order to cover the tracks of the real Judas, Stempkowski.[65]

In custody, Nechaev displayed a quite human—if unrevolutionary and not according to the 'Catechism'—inability to shed his identity completely, for he again called himself 'Stepan Grazhdanov' (the spelling varied), thus using his true initials (Sergei Gennadievich). He produced a Serbian passport in Grazhdanov's name, Serbs came forward to vouch for him, but few people in Switzerland had any doubts as to the prisoner's identity. The new Russian ambassador, Michael Gorchakov, overjoyed at such a *coup* so early in his assignment, brought enormous pressure upon cantonal and federal authorities to grant immediate extradition. The Russian émigrés, both supporters and opponents of Nechaev, argued against this course of action, seeking first to establish his Serbian identity and then, when that collapsed, to prove his right to political asylum. The cantonal government sent to Serbia and Russia for information, Gorchakov alternately threatened and cajoled, and the émigrés (joined by the Serbian and Polish students) bombarded the press with letters claiming that the arrested man was not Nechaev and that, even if he were, Nechaev's crimes were political and not criminal and therefore did not warrant extradition. On October 9, Nechaev admitted his identity and requested political asylum.[66]

Unfortunately for the captive, the Yverdon counterfeiting trial of Gabriel Kamensky and his new-found friends commenced shortly after the arrest, focussing attention upon the criminal activities of certain foreigners in Switzerland. The conservative press did not fail to suggest a link between the Yverdon gang and Nechaev. The Zürich police chief, J.J. Pfenninger, loudly insisted that the cantons could not tolerate the presence on their soil of common criminals who, to escape extradition, claimed to be opponents of tsarism. He did not mention the reward he expected from St Petersburg for the capture of Nechaev.[67]

Some members of the cantonal government opposed handing Nechaev over to the tsar's justice, but the Gorchakov-Pfenninger argument that the prisoner was a common murderer prevailed. Undoubtedly to the relief of the federal government in Berne, the Zürich council decided to extradite. Before dawn on October 27, 1872, having bound their prisoner heavily, a strong police detachment conducted him to the German frontier, where they handed him over to agents of the Russian gendarmerie. The police arrested and later expelled from Zürich several Polish émigrés who had attempted to interfere with the melancholy cortège, and Vladimir Serebrennikov's plan to free Nechaev failed miserably.[68]

Three years later, Nechaev wrote to the tsar complaining that he did not even know what conditions the Swiss had placed upon his extradition. He would have taken little comfort had he known of Zürich's pious insistence that the Russian government try him only for the murder of Ivanov, and that, if it found him guilty, it levy no penalty more severe than that prescribed by law (deprivation of civil rights and confinement at hard labour).[69]

The trial began in Moscow district court at two o'clock in the afternoon on January 9, 1873 (Old Style). There was a huge crowd but only 280 people could be admitted into the courtroom. Security was extremely severe; tickets of admission had to be shown three times before a spectator reached his seat. A correspondent for a Moscow newspaper described the defendant, who was so nervous that he was removed from the court several times before he finally calmed down enough for the proceedings to begin: 'He looked no more than twenty-five [that was indeed his age], his hair was brown, shortish and combed back; he had a sparse French [sic] beard, short sidewhiskers and long thin moustaches. Nervousness showed in his slightest movement.'[70]

When the indictment was read, Nechaev was asked whether he wanted counsel. He screamed that he did not recognize the jurisdiction of the court, and there were cries of 'Out with him! Out! Out!' from the spectators. Nechaev was removed for a few moments, but when he returned he had not calmed down and he cried out, 'I have ceased to be the slave of your despot! Long live the Zemsky Sobor [Assembly of the Land]!' A jury composed of five merchants, two state officials, two 'bourgeois,' one guildsman, one 'distinguished citizen' and one peasant found Nechaev guilty of murder as charged. When the sentence was pronounced, the chairman of the court asked, 'The accused does not object?' Nechaev answered, 'This is a Shemyakin court [a kangaroo court of Medieval Moscow]. Long live the Zemsky Sobor! Down with despotism!'[71]

The extensive reports that foreign diplomats filed proved that this was not an ordinary murder case, and still further proof came when the Tsar personally ordered that Nechaev not be sent to Siberia, whence he might escape, but held instead, for the rest of his life, in the maximum-security Peter-Paul Fortress in St Petersburg. Such confinement had destroyed more than one strong man. Nechaev, however, stubbornly refused to break. He subverted some of his guards, for a time corresponded freely with the revolutionaries, and early in the 1880's urged a new terrorist group, The People's Will, not to try to liberate him but to concentrate upon assassinating the Tsar. When Alexander fell to the bombs of March, 1881, Nechaev was in a sense an accomplice in the assassination. In November 1882, thirteen years to the day after he killed Ivanov, he died in his cell.[72]

Nechaev's influence lived on, even among—although they heatedly denied it—the Bolsheviks. And his case had serious repercussions at the time upon relations between Berne and St Petersburg. The two governments signed a treaty of extradition in November 1873. The agreement excluded political crimes from extraditable categories, but this was a mere formality, a concession to liberal opinion. The Nechaev precedent demonstrated that the budding new Holy Alliance had closed a major loophole in its defences against revolutionism.[73]

NOTES

1. On June 26, 1870, *Le Nord* observed that 'henceforth cosmopolitanism is the essential character of revolution.' Reactionary states frequently use such language; one has only to recall the Stalinist campaign against 'rootless cosmopolitans.'

2. Bourgin, 'La lutte,' pp. 41-2. On the problem of extradition see Lora L. Deere, 'Political Offenses in the Law and Practice of Extradition,' *American Journal of International Law,* vol. 27, April, 1933, pp. 247-70. Belgium had earlier expelled Victor Hugo; and both Belgian and French governments conveniently forgot that Thiers had been granted political asylum in Belgium in 1850.

3. The text of the Favre circular is in Bourgin, 'La lutte,' pp. 50-6. For the General Council's reaction, see *DFI,* vol. 4 pp. 417-8, and for press comment see *APP,* B/A 440, *pièces* 5560-6. For Russian comment see *Journal de St Petersbourg,* June 2, 1871 (Old Style).

4. R. Hostetter, *The Italian Socialist Movement,* vol. 1 *Origins (1860-1882),* Princeton, 1958, pp. 138-44, 146-50. On Spanish reaction see Belgium, *AMAE,* CPL, Espagne, vol. 18, 1871-2, no. 22; see also *Le Nord,* May 28, 1871.

5. Bourgin, 'La lutte,' pp. 61-2; *Le Nord,* July 6, 1871. The Anglo-French Convention on Extradition of February 13, 1843, excluded political crimes from extraditable categories.

6. Belgium, *AMAE,* CP, Réfugiés, vol. 9, no. 171; *ibid.,* vol. 10. no. 7; *ibid.,* CPL, Suisse, vol. 7, no. 24; Great Britain, F.O. 100 (*Switzerland*), 181, no. 56. Article 2 of the Franco-Swiss extradition convention exempted political refugees from extradition. See the text (ratified in 1870) in *Journal de Genève,* July 31, 1869, and see also *La Suisse Radicale,* Aug. 2, 1871. The French ambassador (Chateaurenard) assured his government that the Swiss people and press despised the Commune; see France, *AMAE,* Suisse, vol. 600, Apr.-Dec. 1871, 81-4, May 26, 1871.

7. Utin, Trusov, Olga Levashyova, Becker and others were members of this secret committee, the records of which are in IISG, *Archive Lucien Descave.* See also *APP,* B/A 431, *pièce* 251. A Russian spy, probably Mlochowski, complained in October of 1871 of his inability to infiltrate the group; see *TsGAOR,* 'Ob ustroistve v Moskve osoboi sekretnoi agentury,' 11. 149-56.

8. *LN,* vol. 62, p. 462; *AEG,* Etrangers Fb 2, 88 no. 1112. The Geneva police validated Tomanovskaya's residence permit on August 14, 1871, for a stay until October 10. See further Knizhnik-Vetrov, *Russkie deiatel'nitsy,* pp. 108-11.

9. France, *AMAE,* Suisse, vol. 600, 95-8, Chateaurenard to Favre, June 15, 1871; see also *ibid.,* Suisse, 1870-1, Genève, vol. 9, 363-6, Dubruel to MAE, Nov. 26, 1871.

10. The best account of the hunt remains Kantor's *V pogone za Nechaevym*.

11. Great Britain, F.O. 65 (Russia), 821, no. 137.

12. Bourgin, 'La lutte,' pp. 84-9. Third Section delusions of grandeur are revealed in *TsGAOR*, 'Ob ustroistve v Moskve osoboi sekretnoi agentury.'

13. It was extensively reported in the Russian press. I have consulted *Pravitel'stvennyi Vestnik, Journal de St- Pétersbourg, Golos, Sudebnyi Vestnik, Sankt-Peterburgskie Vedomosti, Vedomosti Moskovskoi Gorodskoi Politsii* and other newspapers.

14. See Bazilevskii, *Gosudarstvennyia prestupleniia v Rossii v XIX veke*, vol. 1, pp. 289-411 for a resumé of the trial, and see also *Archives Bakounine*, vol. 4, pp. 279-301; *SIE*, vol. II, p. 666; *Le Nord*, July 20, 1871, and following.

15. *SIE*, vol. II, pp. 665-6, 671-2. For a primitive sociological profile of the revolutionaries who were indicted in the period 1871-7, see *APP*, B/A 196, *pièce* 302. This is a report of agent '36' dated Paris, Dec. 1, 1882; like 'de Belina,' '6,' 'Isidore Schmidt' and other names, '36' was probably Apollon Mlochowski.

16. *DFI*, vol. 4, pp. 244-5.

17. IISG, *Jung*, 419 (most sources, following the General Council's inadvertent error, date this Aug. 6 letter four days later); *DFI*, vol. 4, pp. 447-8.

18. *DFI*, vol. 4, pp. 308-9, 447, 544 note 338; IISG, *Jung*, 901, 902; *ibid.*, *Marx-Engels Correspondence*, D 4345; *Der Volksstaat*, Feb. 28, 1872; *APP*, B/A 431, *pièces*, 59-60, 3611-3.

19. Miklós Molnár, *Le déclin de la Première Internationale: La conférence de Londres de 1871*, Geneva, 1963, pp. 54, 59-73.

20. *DFI*, vol. 4, pp. 294-5, 301-3, 308.

21. *TsGAOR*, 'O byvshem studente Nikolae Utine,' 11. 121-7; *ibid.*, 'Ob ustroistve v Moskve osoboi sekretnoi agentury,' 11. 149-56; *ibid.*, 'Ob usilenii nadzora na granitsakh Imperii,' 1. 179. See also *APP*, B/A 434, *pièce* 787; *Neue Zürcher Zeitung*, no. 519, Oct. 10, 1871; *Le Nord*, Oct. 30, Nov. 15, 1871. The French consul-general in Frankfurt-am-Main believed Utin to be Bakunin; see *Archives Nationales*, BB30 487, dr. 5, Commune de 1871. Ressort de Paris. Pièces diverses 1871-2.

22. *DFI*, vol. 4, p. 434.

23. IISG, *Marx-Engels Correspondence*, D 4345; *L'Egalité*, Nov. 5, 1871.

24. *Freymond*, vol. 2, p. 264 (quoted also in Stekloff, *History of the First International*, p. 212). Nicholas Zhukovsky was among the signatories. The Second International, recalling anarchist criticism of the General Council, did not establish such a body and made its 'information bureau' a 'simple office for correspondence and statistics.' We might note the fate of the Second International.

25. *DFI*, vol. 5, p. 61; *Werke*, vol. 33, p. 688.

26. *Werke*, vol. 33, p. 296; IISG, *Marx-Engels Correspondence*, D 4345; DFI, vol. 4,, p. 305.

27. Herman Greulich, *Das grüne Hüsli*, Zürich, 1942, pp. 53-5; IISG,

Becker, D I 866, 867; *Freymond,* vol. 3, notes 166, 245. Russian students in Zürich are listed in Meijer, *Knowledge and Revolution,* pp. 208-17. See further *Die Tagwacht,* Sept. 10, 17, 24, Oct. 1, 8, 15, 1870, where an unidentified Russian (Eugene Utin?) discusses 'The Situation of the Working Class in Russia' at meetings of the Greulich-Bürkli section of the IWMA.

28. Zürich. *Staatsarchiv,* p. 191a, Fremdenpolizei, Einvernahms-Protokolle betr. polit. Flüchtlinge verschiedenen Staaten, 1871, nos. 15, 16, 17. On Smirnov's expulsion from medical school in Moscow see *Le Nord,* Dec. 22, 25, 1869

29. *TsGAOR,* 'Ob obrazovavshemsia v Tsiurikhe rev. Slav. sots'.-dem. obshchestve,' 11. 22-25; Meijer, *Knowledge and Revolution,* pp. 85-6.

30. The programme is in Bakunin, *Pis'ma,* pp. 499-501; see also pp. 501-3 (this may be the programme that Venturi and others thought Bakunin drew up for the group that became the Geneva Russian section). See further Zemfiri Ralli, 'Slavianskaia sektsiia Internatsionala,' in B. Bazilevskii, *Materialy dlia istorii revoliutsionnogo dvizheniia v Rossii v 60-kh godakh,* St Petersburg, 1906 (also published in Paris in 1905), pp. 207-8. The Serbian socialist Svetozar Marković refused to join this section, but Nikola Pašić, future prime minister of Serbia and Yugoslavia, did enter it; see *Freymond,* vol. 3, note 133.

31. *TsGAOR,* 'Ob obrazovavshemsia v Tsiurikhe rev. Slav. sots.-dem. Obshchestve,' 11. 1, 2 (1. 229 identifiies Stempkowski as the author of this report); see also 11. 22-5.

32. On the Zürich 'trial' see *Kolokol* (Geneva), Apr. 1, 1868, p. 86, and on the Paris sequel see 'Wyrok sadu bratniego w Paryzu w sprawie Adolfa Stepkowskiego,' in Zürich, *Staatsarchiv,* P 190 fasz. 1.

33. The documents of the Towarzystwo Polskie Socialno-Rewolucyjne w Zurychu are in Zürich, *Staatsarchiv,* 'Auslieferung des Sergius Netschajeff,' no. 56-11.

34. W. McClellan, 'Nechaevshchina: An Unknown Chapter,' *Slavic Review,* Sept. 1973, pp. 546-53.

35. The Russian government took seriously a spy's report that Karl Marx 'intends to come to Russia for evil purposes.' See *TsGAOR,* 'O rev. Internatsionalnom obshchestve,' 1. 106. In May 1872 the German-born Julius A.M. Marx was arrested in Odessa; he was only released when it was established that he was a merchant from England. See *ibid.,* 11. 264-6. The historian Donald MacKenzie Wallace suffered the same indignity in 1873; see his *Russia,* 5th edition, London, 1877, vol. 1, pp. 319-23. See also B.S. Itenberg, *'Iuzhnorossiiskii soiuz rabochikh'—pervaia proletarskaia organizatsiia v Rossii,* Moscow, 1954, p. 21.

36. Henryk Wereszycki, *Sojusz trzech cesarzy: Geneza 1866-1872,* Warsaw, 1965, pp. 318-9, 330.

37. *TsGAOR,* 'O rev. Internatsionalnom obshchestve,' 1. 85.

38. *Ibid.,* 11. 87, 116.

39. *Ibid.,* 11. 119-20, 139, 182, 237. Balaszewicz had some contact with

Marx; see *Werke*, vol. 33, pp. 349-50, and *Krasnyi Arkhiv*, vol. 6, pp. 254-5.

40. König, *Die polnischen Banknotenfälscher*, pp. 11, 16n., 19, 40, 75-7 (König was Kamensky's defence counsel); *DFI*, vol. 5, pp. 111-2; Switzerland, *Bundesarchiv*, Polizei-Abt., 'Auslieferungen 1849-1925,' G. Kamensky, russischer Staatsrath.

41. An unsigned manuscript in Valerian Smirnov's papers notes the significance of Mlochowski's perusal of Utin's effects: IISG, *Smirnov*, map. 2 no. 2. On the historical importance of those papers, see *TsGALI*, f. 1691 (L.F. Panteleev), Op. no. 1, ed. khr. no. 94, 1. 12. See further on the search *AEG*, Juridictions Pénales P., Jan. 1872, 'Contrefaçon de billets de banque. *Inculpé:* Outine Nicholas.' In 1878, the French police agent '6' recalled that the Swiss magistrate had asked him to translate the Utin papers; thus one can positively identify '6' as Mlochowski. See *APP*, B/A 196, *pièce* 419. See also König, *Die polnischen Banknotenfälscher*, pp. 57-8, 80-3.

42. *DFI*, vol. 5 pp. 111-2 (see also pp. 104-6).

43. There were also reports that a force of Communards would invade the French Midi; these originated in the French consulate in Basle. See France, *AMAE*, Suisse, vol. 600, nos. 31-2, 33. *Le Monde* constantly complained of Swiss toleration of the IWMA and speculated about intervention by the powers; see especially June 12, 24, 30, October 28, 1871. Reviving the rumours of Russo-German intervention, *Le Courrier Français* (Paris) claimed early in 1872 that those powers would move to thwart a Communard invasion of France; see the report from that newspaper in *Nouvelliste Vaudois*, Jan. 22, 1872.

44. Switzerland, *Bundesarchiv*, 'Sozialistische Arbeiterinternationale,' *pièce* 12.

45. Belgium, *AMAE* CPL, Suisse, vol. 7, nos. 105, 108; *ibid.*, CPL, Russie, vol. 11, 1871-3, no. 71; *Journal de Genève*, June 23, 1872.

46. Maximiano García Venero, *Historia de los movimentos sindicalistas españoles, 1840-1933*, Madrid, 1961, pp. 171-220; Marx-Engels-Lafargue, 'L'Alliance,' pp. 404-11; Max Nettlau, *La Première Internationale en Espagne (1868-1888)*, Dordrecht, 1969, pp. 92-159; *Werke*, vol. 33, pp. 348, 364-6, 424-5, 436-42; *DFI*, vol. 5, pp. 446-9; A. Gonsales, *Istoriia ispanskikh sektsii Mezhdunarodnogo Tovarishchestva Rabochikh, 1868-1873*, Moscow, 1964, ch. 3.

47. A. Romano, *L'Unità italiana e la Prima Internazionale* (vol. 2 of his *Storia del Movimento Socialista in Italia*), 2nd edition, Bari, 1966, pp. 309-43; Hostetter, *The Italian Socialist Movement*, vol. 1, ch. 6; Bakh, *Pervyi Internatsional*, pt. 2, pp. 442ff.

48. IISG, *Becker*, D III 193; *ibid.*, *Jung*, 901; *DFI*, vol. 5, pp. 86, 394-5; *Werke*, vol. 33 pp. 371-5, 395-6, 443, 490, 513; I.V. Grigor'eva, *Rabochee i sotsialisticheskoe dvizhenie v Italii v epokhu I Internatsionala*, Moscow, 1966, pp. 94-5, 164-198. On Zaitsev see *Krasnyi Arkhiv*, vol. 52, pp. 283-6, and *Deiateli*, vol. 1, pt. 2, pp. 135-6.

49. *DFI*, vol. 5, pp. 451-2.

50. *Archives Bakounine*, vol. 2, pp. 305-6; *Werke*, vol. 33, pp. 339, 376, 451, 465, 485, 491, 497.
51. *DFI*, vol. 5, pp. 356-409; see also *MERR*, p. 235.
52. *Archives Bakounine*, vol. 2, pp. 123-5.
53. IISG, *Jung*, 657; *ibid.*, *Smirnov*, afz. stk. IV, Smirnov to Buturlin, Aug. 11, 1872; *TsGAOR*, 'O byvshem studente Nikolae Utine,' 11. 121-7;; Koz'min, *Russkaia sektsiia*, pp. 359-60; Max Nettlau, *Michael Bakunin*, vol. 2, London, 1899, note 3191.
54. *MERR*, pp. 211-12 (see also pp. 196-7); *Werke*, vol. 33, p. 478.
55. *MERR*, pp. 233-4.
56. *Ibid.*, pp. 244-5; 'Karl Marks i tsarskaia tsenzura,' pp. 6-10; *Werke*, vol. 33, p. 477.
57. Resis, *'Das Kapital* Comes to Russia,' pp. 228-37; Billington, *Mikhailovsky*, pp. 66-7; *MERR*, pp. 246-9.
58. *Werke*, vol. 33, pp. 477, 543. Engels had earlier tried unsuccessfully to get information about Bakunin from Lavrov; see *ibid.*, pp. 354, 380.
59. *MERR*, p. 245.
60. *Ibid.*, pp. 257-60.
61. Austria-Hungary, *HHStA*, IB 1872, no. 649.
62. IISG, *Smirnov*, afz. stk. IV, Smirnov to Buturlin, Aug. 11, 1872; *APP*, B/A 431, *pièce* 339; *TsGAOR*, 'Ob obrazovavshemsia v Tsiurikhe rev. Slav. sots.-dem. obshchestve,' 11. 89-90.
63. Zürich, *Staatsarchiv*, 'Auslieferung des Sergius Netschajeff.' Citing no proof, Boris Nikolaevsky claimed that Nechaev and Turski shared a room in Zürich: 'Pamiati poslednego 'iakobintsa'-semidesiatnika. (Gaspar-Mikhail Turskii),' *KS*, 1926, no. 2(23), p. 216.
64. *TsGIA* (Moscow), f. 1737 (V.N. Smirnov), 1. 2.
65. IISG, *Smirnov*, map. 59, Smirnov to Buturlin, Mar. 4 [1873]. Another Judas was the Serb Nikolić, who held a high rank in the Russian secret police; one surely exaggerated report has him receiving thousands of acres of land in Ekaterinoslav province for his role in the capture of Nechaev; see Aleksei Tveritinov, *Ob ob'iavlenii prigovora N.G. Chernyshevskomu, o rasprostranenii ego sochinenii na frantsuzskom yazyke v zapadnoi Evrope i o mnogom drugom*, St Petersburg, 1906, p. 90. A newspaper with which Greulich had quarrelled, *Die Zürcher-Presse*, claimed that Greulich accepted a 2,000 franc 'denier de Judas' from the Russians for betraying Nechaev; this was false. See *Journal de Genève*, Feb. 5, 1873.
66. Zürich, *Staatsarchiv*, 'Auslieferung des Sergius Netschajeff,' *pièces* 24, 58, 63, 73, 75, 94. See also Kantor, *V pogone*, pp. 136-44; Haas, 'Njetschajew und die schweizer Behörden,' pp. 363ff; IISG, *Smirnov*, afz stk. IV, Smirnov to Buturlin, Sept. 13, 1872.
67. *La Suisse Radicale*, Oct. 17, 1872; *Neue Zürcher Zeitung*, no. 560, Nov. 3, 1872. Stempkowski told the Third Section in July that Pfenninger would probably co-operate if given a reward; see *TsGAOR*, 'Ob obrazovavshemsia v Tsiurikhe rev. Slav. sots.-dem. obshchestve,' 11. 89-90.
68. On the manoeuvering of Michael Gorchakov and his spies see

V.N. Firstova, 'Tsarskaia diplomaticheskaia missiia v Berne i russkaia emigratsiia,' *Voprosy Istorii*, 1973, no. 6, pp. 205-6. On Serebrennikov's hopes to free Nechaev see *TsGIA* (Moscow), f. 1737, 1. 1, V.E. Varzar to V.N. Smirnov.

69.   Kantor, *V pogone*, pp. 128-35; *Krasnyi Arkhiv*, vol. 4, p. 253; *Neue Zürcher Zeitung*, nos. 555-6, 558-61, Oct. 31-Nov. 3, 1872; IISG, *Smirnov*, afz. stk. IV, Smirnov to Buturlin, Oct. 27, 1872; *Die Tagwacht*, Nov. 2, 1872.

70.   *Russkie Vedomosti* (Moscow), Jan. 9, 1873 (Old Style).

71.   *Ibid.*, Jan. 14, 16, 19, 1873 (Old Style).

72.   Great Britain F.O. 65 (Russia), 851, no. 47; *ibid.*, no. 865; Bazilevskii, *Gosudarstvennyia prestupleniia v Rossii*, vol. 1, pp. 415-56; *Neue Zürcher Zeitung*, nos. 59, 63, 65, 94, Feb. 2-21, 1873; P. Shchegolev, ed., 'S.G. Nechaev v Alekseevskom raveline,' *Krasnyi Arkhiv*, vol. 4, pp. 222-72; *ibid.*, vol. 5, pp. 172-212; *ibid.*, vol. 6, pp. 77-123; [L. Deich], 'S.G. Nechaev v Alekseevskom raveline v 1873-83 gg.,' *Byloe*, vol. 1, no. 7, July 1906, pp. 151-70; 'Obriad publichnoi kazni nad S.G. Nechaevym,' *Krasnyi Arkhiv*, vol. 1, pp. 280-1.

73.   For a copy of the treaty see Great Britain, F.O. 100 (Switzerland), no. 67, Nov. 30, 1873.

CHAPTER TEN

The End of the First International

The arrest of Nechaev caused little stir outside Switzerland and Russia. The wide notoriety which he enjoyed earlier had faded in the wake of the monumental upheaval that was the Paris Commune, and this helps explain the ease with which Switzerland (technically, Zürich) extradited him. European working-class and socialist circles were much more interested, in August 1872, in the impending Congress of the International than in Nechaev. Most eager of all for this meeting were the anarchists, whose strength was growing steadily in most European countries save Russia and Serbia, where the loyalists retained control of the International. But those two countries then carried little weight in the organization and had no well-defined working-class movements.

The revolutionary momentum that had built up in Europe since the Polish Rebellion of 1863 spent itself in the fury of the Commune and a period of reaction set in. This favoured the anarchists, whose 'abstentionism' gave people who needed one an excuse for their political frustrations. The|anarchists, grouped around the figure of Bakunin, fully expected to take control of the IWMA at the 1872 Congress, and this presented Marx and the General Council with a painful dilemma. Failure to convene a Congress for the third consecutive year would almost certainly wreck the International and deliver the rubble to Bakunin, yet the anarchists

213

also might very well seize control in an open meeting. What was to be done? Marx and his allies decided to liquidate the first working-class political party in history in order to achieve two ends: (1) keep it out of anarchist hands, and (2) thwart the revived Holy Alliance.

The Hague Congress

Sixty-five delegates from fifteen countries assembled in the Dutch capital on Sunday, September 1, 1872; their numbers were unquestionably inferior to those of the international corps of police spies, not to mention the journalists. A Belgian agent assured Brussels that Bakunin had arrived, and the Habsburg ambassador to the The Netherlands even reported the 'text' of instructions Bakunin had given an associate.[1] A British correspondent reported that on Sunday afternoon 'a mob assembled around the Hotel Pico, where many Communists were known to be staying, and performed a pantomime of shooting and cutting throats, such as to the spectator was at least suggestive.' Other observers claimed that the citizens of the city railed at the delegates with cries of 'Oranje boven!' and 'Vive le roi!' A Swiss newspaper considered an attempt to reconcile Marx and Bakunin imminent. A Dutch journal referred to Marx's wife, his daughter Laura and the wife of another delegate as 'tricoteuses.' The Third Section reported that Nicholas Utin attended the Congress (he did not).[2]

The Congress opened on Monday; disputes over credentials paralyzed it until Wednesday evening. James Guillaume, Bakunin's spokesman, challenged the right of the General Council members—including Marx, who was attending his first Congress—to sit as voting delegates. The General Council challenged the Spanish Alliancists and others. Everyone disputed the credentials of William West, an American who hoped to speak for the spirited if erratic reform movement of the sisters Tennessee Claflin and Victoria Woodhull. In the end only Nicholas Zhukovsky (who claimed to represent the 'Propaganda and Socialist Revolutionary Action' section of Geneva) and William West were denied the right to participate.[3]

The first public meeting took plaçe on Thursday, September 5. Marx read the General Council's report which the Congress—to the surprise of many—unanimously accepted. In the afternoon, the Blanquists, some of whom were moving closer to a Marxist position, submitted a resolution to place the question of the 'militant organization of the revolutionary forces of the proletariat and of the political struggle' on the agenda of the next Congress. The Blanquists assailed the anarchists, who in their turn called for the abolition of the General Council.

Thus, after three days of squabbling, the assembly confronted the great issue of the proletariat's role in politics. The International, some appearances to the contrary, had fought economic rather than political battles during the eight years of its existence; it had not really been active in legal politics anywhere. The anarchists wanted to maintain this record, or lack of one, and shut off any alternatives; this was why Guillaume proposed the liquidation of the General Council and the renunciation of strikes as political weapons. Marx and the General Council, on the contrary, wished to place the IWMA firmly and irrevocably on record in favour of working-class political action. Though the time had come to terminate the organization's existence, they wanted to pass on to the national working-class parties that would succeed it a legacy of political activism.

Guillaume argued that the General Council had never built any barricades, had never 'organized or conducted a class war,' and had become unnecessary, parasitical, and constrictive. Adolf Hepner, editor of *Der Volksstaat* while Wilhelm Liebknecht was in prison, ridiculed this stand:

> Are these good people so unscientific as to believe that one can make revolutions? Do they still not know that revolutions arise only in a natural way and are stages of historical development? Have these people not even surpassed the barricadology?[4]

The Marxists easily won on this issue. On the question of the General Council's powers, Marx observed that

> whether we concede and ascribe to the General Council the prerogatives of a Negro Prince or Russian Tsar, its power is naught once it ceases to represent the majority of the I.W.[M.]A.;

the General Council has no army, no budget, but only a moral force and always will be impotent unless it has the consent of the entire Association.[5]

This was all true, but Marx did not point out that the Council almost certainly no longer commanded the allegiance of a majority. He and his friends nevertheless argued for increased powers for it, deliberately applying cosmetics to a moribund body, adding to the legend of the International.

After the Marxist resolution on the Council prevailed, Marx and Engels, to the surprise of most delegates, proposed to move the body to New York. Engels explained that 'party frictions' had compromised its work in London, and beyond that 'a certain ossification' had occurred. He recalled that Marx had proposed in 1870 to move the Council to Brussels. Alluding to the government's campaign against the IWMA, Engels declared that no city in Europe could ensure the safety of the Council; therefore, the only alternative was New York, a 'cosmopolitan' centre in a country that had a vigorous working-class movement.[6]

What Engels did not say was that removal to New York would keep the General Council out of anarchist hands. Such a move would also prevent it from falling to the Blanquists. When Marx, Engels and their friends announced—again to great surprise—their intention to resign from the Council, the Blanquists, led by Edouard Vaillant, saw an opportunity to seize control. They had supported the Marxists up to this point in the Congress, but now they sided with the anarchists in resisting the proposal to transfer the seat of the Council. The Marxists won by a mere three votes, and a larger majority then confirmed New York as the new site.[7]

Not until 10 p.m. on Saturday, September 7, did the Congress turn to the last major piece of business on the agenda, the report of the committee that had investigated Bakunin's Alliance. The document contained some wondrous conclusions: (1) a secret Alliance opposed to the International had existed, but 'there is insufficient proof of its continued existence'; (2) Bakunin 'has tried to establish, and perhaps has succeeded in establishing, a society in Europe named 'Alliance' with rules entirely different from those of the

I.W.[M.]A. in social and political respects'; (3) Bakunin had engaged in fraud; (4) Bakunin 'or his agents have had recourse to threats lest he be compelled to meet his obligations.'[8] The obvious alternatives, that the Alliance did or did not currently exist, did not emerge from this report. The Spanish Alliancists had earlier admitted that the organization did exist but claimed they no longer belonged to it. Paul Lafargue brought documents from Madrid which proved the Alliance did exist as a secret organization. James Guillaume denied that he had ever belonged to any secret group. J.P. Becker, who had helped Bakunin found the original *public* Alliance, sat by now as the Marxists assailed his former friend. The Congress (or rather the packed Marxist majority) attached great significance to the Nechaev letter to Liubavin about the Bakunin translation of *Capital,* but this was utterly irrelevant to the issue at hand.

The investigating committee made several recommendations: (1) to expel Bakunin from the International; (2) to expel Guillaume and Adhémar Schwitzguébel (a Swiss Bakuninist) from the organization 'in the conviction that they still belong to the society Alliance'—the existence of which the same committee had been unable to establish; (3) to expel several other Internationalists not present (including Benoît Malon) for having engaged in conspiracies detrimental to IWMA interests; (4) to accept the claim of the Spanish Alliancists and Nicholas Zhukovsky that they no longer belonged to the Alliance and to 'waive charges against them.'[9]

Roch Splingard, the one anarchist member of the committee, dissented from the report and recommendations and asked for an enquiry into the methods Marx used to obtain the Nechaev letter. The anarchist Charles Alerini accused the Congress of conducting an 'inquisition' and demanded that the session be opened to the public. James Guillaume refused to defend himself on grounds of principle.

The affair demanded a conclusion. The proprietor of the hall insisted that the delegates (who had paid rent only until September 7) leave on the stroke of midnight. Some had already departed. The Bakuninist minority of fifteen delegates quickly read into the record their protest against the conduct of the Congress. They expressed their desire to avoid a split in the IWMA but declared that they would in the future have only 'administrative relations' with the General Council. By a wide margin, the Congress then expelled Bakunin and Guillaume from the International; the motion to oust Schwitzguébel narrowly failed. Schwitzguébel protested this absurdity, inviting the delegates to treat him as they had men with whom he was in complete accord. The Congress ignored this plea for logical action. On the grounds that the expulsion of Bakunin and Guillaume had set a sufficiently instructive example, the delegates did not even vote on the expulsion of Malon and 'other conspirators.' Finally, they agreed to publish the documents concerning the Alliance (including the Lafargue and Utin reports), to hold the next Congress in Switzerland, and to appoint a committee of Marx, Engels and four of their friends to draw up the minutes of the Hague Congress. The victors became the historians of their triumph: *vae victis*![10]

The End of the First International

With the aid of the Blanquists, the Marxists had kept the International out of anarchist hands. In so doing, they did, in a formal sense, destroy the organization, which no one expected to survive in the United States (there, even the lower classes were fiercely suspicious of 'cosmopolitanism').[11] But the common assumption in historical literature that the conflict between Marxists and anarchists wrecked the IWMA is at best half correct. The first great political organization of the working class lay on its deathbed months before the Hague Congress, sent there by the blows of the intense reaction that followed the Paris Commune. (The Marxists, of course, argued at The Hague and later that it had played out its historical role.)

The old International died of these two major illnesses, of which the reaction was the more severe. The new International, if Marx and Engels had their way, would be subject to fewer torments, for they had succeeded in keeping the old one out of the wilderness of 'political abstention.' In a June, 1873, letter to August Bebel, Engels noted that

old Hegel has already said: a party proves itself a victorious party by the fact that it *splits* and can stand the split. The movement of the proletariat necessarily passes through different stages of development; at every stage one section of people lags behind and does not join in the further advance; and this alone explains why it is that actually the 'solidarity of the proletariat' is everywhere realised in different party groupings which carry on life and death feuds with one another . . . [12]

The International was all the stronger, Engels claimed, because it had expelled the 'rotten elements.'

If one accepts Engels's view, it was obviously the legend and the myth of the International that profited from the expulsions and the 'splits,' for the organization itself was clearly dying, in part because the elements the Marxists cut out of it were important and powerful. A French newspaper reported in October of 1872 that Bakunin dared not leave Switzerland because the Russian government wanted to hang him, the Saxon to shoot him, and several others wanted him behind bars; a man of such stature obviously had to be reckoned with. Another journal, in an article entitled 'Bakunin: Apostle of Universal Destruction,' noted the names of some newspapers he had inspired: *Petrol, La Canaille, Satan, The Atheist, The Thief, Antichrist, Spartacus, International, The Communard.* This list was far from complete.[13]

A contrived majority at The Hague expelled Bakunin from the International, but it could not—nor did it try—to make the membership accept its actions. The Bakuninists convened their own meeting in the Swiss mountain town of Saint-Imier on September 15 and 16, 1872, and declared themselves the true International. Within a short time, most of the old national federations followed the Spanish, Italian and Swiss Jura organizations into the anarchist fold. The Bakuninists were, as one historian wrote, 'much more energetic' than the Marxists in the decade following the Hague Congress; they held congresses annually until 1877, excepting only 1875.[14] Bakunin himself attended none. He wrote to a Geneva newspaper in September of 1873 to announce his withdrawal from politics. Few believed him; and indeed, the next year the old man left his Locarno sanctuary to take part in still another comic-opera uprising in Bologna. But he was not even a shadow of his former self. The legend rather than

the shell inspired those who now called themselves Bakuninists. He died in Berne on July 1, 1876. A fitting epitaph had
been spoken in 1848 by a French official who gave him a
passport and 3,000 francs 'to go and revolutionize Germany.'
The official said, 'S'il y avait trois cent Bakounine en France,
la France ne serait pas gouvernable.'[15]

For their part, the Marxists held only one more Congress
after 1872 and they wished they had not done that. At the
Geneva Congress of 1873, J.P. Becker manufactured whole
delegations out of thin air, made inane speeches and proposals, and generally embarrassed serious socialists. Marx commented that the only good resolution to come out of Geneva
was the decision not to hold another Congress for at least two
years.[16] Friedrich Sorge, leader of the new General Council,
liked neither the Geneva escapades nor the cavalier treatment
Marx and Engels accorded him, and he finally resigned. A
contrite Engels wrote to him,

> With your resignation the *old* International comes to an end.
> And that is good. The organization belonged to the era of the
> Second Empire, when the Europe-wide oppression made it
> necessary for the reawakening labour movement to maintain unity
> and abstain from internal disputes. That was a time when the
> common cosmopolitan interests of the proletariat could come to
> the fore. Germany, Spain, Italy, and Denmark had just entered
> or were entering the movement. The theoretical character of the
> movement was in all Europe, or among the masses at any rate,
> still very unclear. German communism still did not exist as a
> labour party; Proudhonism was too weak to impose its follies;
> Bakunin's new rubbish had not yet entered his own head; and
> even the leaders of the English trade unions . . . thought they
> could participate in the movement . . . . The first great success
> had to break up this naive togetherness of all factions. That success
> was the Commune . . . . But when, through the Commune, the
> International became a moral force in Europe, the quarrel
> immediately erupted. Every tendency wanted to exploit that
> success for itself. The inevitable collapse came. Jealousy of the
> rising strength of the only people who were prepared to continue
> further work along the lines of the old comprehensive program-
> me—the German communists—drove the Belgian Proudhonists
> into the arms of the Bakuninist adventurers. The Hague Congress
> was, in fact, the end for both parties.[17]

A small conference in Philadelphia in July 1876 officially pronounced the dissolution of the Marxist International.[18]

The New Holy Alliance

The Hague Congress was still in the process of arranging the interment of the International when the three eastern monarchs, who had the same goal, met in Berlin to discuss that and other issues. By all accounts their assembly was the more splendid, though perhaps no less awkward. At a dinner on September 7, the tsar proposed the 'welfare of the valiant Prussian army.' His aides later explained that he had not said 'German' army (as he had earlier in St Petersburg) for fear of giving needless offence to the French. The distinction surely escaped Franz Josef.[19]

Not many contemporaries—and only a few historians—drew a connection between the meetings in The Hague and Berlin. A German newspaper commented upon the rendez-vous of the rulers, 'That the son, the grandson and the nephew of the three monarchs who conquered at Leipsic should be exchanging friendly assurances in . . . [Berlin] is a lesson which we may hope may not be thrown away upon France.'[20] The three monarchs did indeed hope to isolate France, but there was manifestly no immediate danger from that defeated and demoralized nation. The chief concern of Bismarck, who dominated the Berlin gathering, was to protect the new Germany. To do that he chose the safest, surest course to bring the tsar and the Austrian emperor around to his position: he manipulated the fear of revolution that pervaded their regimes.[21]

The Russian government had repeatedly urged the necessity of a general monarchical agreement to combat revolution. This obsession, and his concern over the changes in the political map of Europe, had prompted Alexander II to suggest that Kaiser Wilhelm invite him to the long-planned meeting between the two Central European rulers in September. The tsar declared that, although the International little threatened Russia, he would be glad to co-operate with the Germanic powers against it. What form this co-operation might take was unclear: any offer to send Russian armies

marching westward was unlikely to be received with enthusiasm. But because of several favourable developments
on the eve of the Berlin meeting (passage of new laws
against subversion in Russia, co-operation of the Central
European states against the socialists, the arrest of Sergei
Nechaev), Alexander and his foreign minister, A.M. Gorchakov, decided at the last moment not to present protocols
dealing with the International and the extradition of
political criminals which they had drafted. The Berlin
encounter, they reasoned, could discuss principles rather
than policies.[22]

That suited Bismarck perfectly. He had no illusions about
the monarchs, all of whom, he told the British ambassador,
'think themselves greater statesmen than they are.' Nor did he
care for that master of elegant French gibberish, Gorchakov,
who had, Bismarck jibed, brought along 'is best pens and his
blackest ink . . . to dictate his views on an ideal Europe.' The
Reichskanzler had not favoured the tripartite meeting, but he
believed he could bend it to his will.[23] What he wanted, a
prominent historian has written, was a 'demonstration of
reconciliation and friendship . . . an exhibition of monarchical solidarity in the face of subversive and revolutionary
movements.'[24] And that was what he got. Another historian
wrote in 1931,

> There was also the ever-increasing danger to the conservative
> monarchical Powers constituted by the socialist International, a
> movement which at that time had newly come into existence, a
> social revolutionary change which influenced Bismarck and the
> rulers of the three Eastern powers to a far higher degree than was
> realized until recently . . . . For the first time [following the
> opening of some archives] it can be proved that this common
> danger acted as one of the closest bonds between the rulers . . . [25]

All the parties agreed that they should do something about the
International. Andrássy (who had succeeded Beust) suggested
that the rulers prohibit IWMA Congresses on their territories;
it was not immediately clear when the socialists planned such
meetings. Gorchakov loftily declared that, thanks to her
excellent police, Russia was not threatened by the socialists.
She would, however, co-operate against them 'in the interest

of order and morality in Central Europe.' He expressed the hope that the British government would join the continental powers in studying the 'great question of labour and capital . . . and [the] facilities afforded both to the workmen and to their employers to bring about a speedy and equitable settlement of their just grievances.'[26]

The Berlin meeting produced no clear policy concerning the International. Gorchakov, indeed, later expressed satisfaction that the parties had not set anything down on paper. Some kind of convention might however been signed had not Bismarck studiously avoided meeting with Andrássy and Gorchakov at the same time. The chancellor did not oppose an agreement, but he considered a formal document inconvenient, an invitation to republicans, socialists, liberals and even moderate conservatives to charge the monarchs with resurrecting the notorious Carlsbad Decrees of 1819. A community of views existed, and in Bismarck's view, that was enough.[27]

But the international revolutionary menace, and Bismarck's determination to protect the new Reich, remained. To combat revolution and defend Germany, Bismarck made 'France' his code word for revolution. Revolutionary upheaval invariably seemed to originate in that country; therefore, a military convention aimed at isolating France would achieve both his goals. He did not secure that convention in Berlin because he considered the time unripe. He had to win the monarchs over to his view slowly, allowing them to perform the ritual of 'personal diplomacy' to the point where, in doing Bismarck's bidding, they believed themselves the architects of grand strategy.[28]

The Three Emperors' League

Late in 1872 Count Peter Shuvalov, chief of gendarmes and head of the Third Section, went on a secret mission to several European capitals to seek an informal agreement on common measures against the International. The tsar and Gorchakov had been content to let the matter rest on the Berlin understanding, but Shuvalov insisted that the urgent danger of the situation required his personal intervention.

No diplomat, Shuvalov made a fool of himself and achieved nothing.[29]

The following May, Bismarck and General Moltke accompanied the kaiser to St Petersburg, where the first of the bi-lateral meetings agreed upon in Berlin took place. Bismarck had by then seen the recommendations of a joint Austro-Hungarian and German conference on the 'social question,' which had proposed a common agreement against the IWMA, and it is possible that he was ready to sign such a document in the Russian capital. Lord Loftus, the British ambassador to Russia, reported speculation about this issue and noted that the alleged pact would establish the 'principle of rendering the sentence of a Tribune in one country operative in the other.' There is no proof that such an understanding—let alone a signed agreement—ever existed, and even if it did no one (possibly excepting Shuvalov) took it seriously. Loftus reported that Gorchakov dismissed the matter as unworthy of notice. Such an agreement would have been superfluous: the Nechaev affair showed that Germany and Russia were perfectly capable of co-operating against revolutionism without any formal agreement. There was no need to arouse public opposition to such incredible measures as unified judicial proceedings.[30]

What might have been done in secret remains secret; it is no mystery that Bismarck obtained the military convention he wanted. On May 6, 1873, Moltke and his Russian counterpart, Count F.F. Berg, signed an agreement that required Germany and Russia to come to each other's aid with 200,000 troops should either suffer attack from a third European power. The two rulers involved ratified the document that same day. They and their chief advisers were the only witnesses to the birth of the modern alliance system.[31]

A month later, Alexander II went to Vienna to try to complete the forging of the new Holy Alliance that was to become known as the *Dreikaiserbund,* or Three Emperors' League. The official excuse for his visit was his attendance at the Vienna Exposition. Those who noted his 'morose and preoccupied' demeanour, however, doubted his enthusiasm for the spectacle. The last time he had attended such an affair, in Paris in 1867, Berezowski had very nearly succeeded

in killing him.[32] And fantastic reports indicated that Internationalists, anarchists, terrorists, Communards, Russian and
Polish émigrés and others were streaming into the Austrian
capital, all with the express intention of assassinating the tsar.
French spies reported that Bakunin had issued explicit orders
for the deed. Austrian agents declared that Raoul Rigault,
procurator of the Paris Commune, would attend the Exposition (Rigault was executed on May 24, 1871).[33]

The galling 'Habsburg ingratitude' also contributed to the
tsar's dark mood. The wounds of Austrian perfidy during the
Crimean War still rankled (witness Alexander's Berlin toast
to the Prussian army) and the future was uncertain. But the
danger to law and order and stability dictated that Alexander
and Franz Josef close ranks. The several meetings between
the two rulers were correct, if hardly cordial. Alexander's
official biographer devoted one sentence to the encounter in
Vienna.[34] The tsar asked his host to add his signature to the
military convention just concluded in St Petersburg. The
unyielding Russophobe Andrássy, however, did not wish to
tie Austrian and Hungarian hands in relations with a nation
he hated. At his insistence, Franz Josef signed a much less
binding agreement. The two sovereigns agreed only to consult
should a third power threaten the peace of either; if joint
military action seemed appropriate, they would made *ad hoc*
arrangements. The text of the agreement reflected Bismarck's
influence:

> Their Majesties are determined to prevent anyone from succeed-
> ing in separating them on those principles which they regard as
> alone capable of assuring and, if necessary, of imposing the
> maintenance of peace in Europe against all upheavals no matter
> what their origin.[35]

Bismarck had actually pursued an ambivalent policy toward the *rapprochement* between Russia and Austria-Hungary;
tension between them had some advantages for Germany.
That, however, involved an entire complex of issues. For the
moment, the chancellor had achieved his goals. As one
historian has accurately stated, 'At bottom the League of the
Three Emperors was a new Holy Alliance against revolution
in all its forms.'[36] When Kaiser Wilhelm, in October 1873,

adhered to the Vienna agreement between the tsar and Franz Josef, Bismarck declared that the tripartite pact superseded the Russo-German convention. The three monarchs of the East had proclaimed their solidarity in the face of the revolutionary tide that had so often swept across Europe from France. And in so doing, Austria-Hungary and Russia had given Germany the security her chancellor wanted.

By any standard the formation of the Three Emperors' League was a sign of weakness, not strength, of fear, not confidence. The real dangers to the old monarchies came from quarters the rulers and their ministers did not recognize. A defeated France presented no immediate danger that could justify the League. The International was dead and only awaited formal burial. The socialists had proved incapable of overturning governments. Anarchists and terrorists could only hurl bombast and occasionally bombs. The International had embodied some ominous portents, and the Commune foreshadowed one possible fruit of nationalistic wars. But what really threatened the old order was the arrogant assumption of its chief agents that they could propose and dispose in the manner of seventeenth-century absolute monarchs. The rulers and their ministers concluded secret alliances, dragooned populations, settled the fate of nations and turned an indifferent eye toward the great movements for national dignity and social justice. This would be their undoing.

NOTES

1.   Belgium, *AMAE*, CPL, Pays-Bas, vol. 18, 1872, no. 86; Austria-Hungary, *HHStA*, IB 1872, no. 761.
2.   *The Times* (London), Sept. 7, 1872 6:3; *Neue Zürcher Zeitung*, no. 445, Sept. 1, 1872; Austria-Hungary, *HHStA*, IB 1871, no. 756; H. Gerth, ed., *The First International. Minutes of the Hague Congress of 1872 with Related Documents*, Madison, Wisconsin, 1957, 'Barry Report,' p. 282; *TsGAOR*, 'O byvshem studente Nikolae Utine,' 11. 121-7.
3.   *Guillaume*, vol. 2, pp. 330-2; Gerth, *The First International*, pp. 175-7; *The Times*, Sept. 10, 1872, 10:4.
4.   *Guillaume*, vol. 2, pp. 338-41; Gerth, *The First International*, pp. 208, 217-18.
5.   Gerth, *op. cit.*, pp. 211-2 (Sorge's transcription).
6.   *Ibid.*, pp. 213-4, 276-9, 286-7.

7. *Ibid.,* pp. 214-6, 279-81, 292-3; Stekloff, *History of the First International,* pp. 234-5, 241; *Guillaume,* vol. 2, pp. 339-40. The Congress elected a new, all-American General Council.

8. Gerth, *op. cit.,* pp. 225-6, 284; Carr, *Bakunin,* pp. 449-51; *Guillaume,* vol. 2, pp. 343-6.

9. Gerth, *op. cit.,* pp. 226-9, 244-85; *Guillaume,* vol. 2, p. 344.

10. Gerth, *op. cit.,* pp. 229-35, 284-94; *Guillaume,* vol. 2, pp. 349-51.

11. See Samuel Bernstein, *The First International in America,* New York, 1962; Herman Schlüter, *Die Internationale in Amerika,* Chicago, 1918; J.R. Commons, *The History of Labor in the United States,* vol. 1, New York, 1921; Bakh, *Pervyi Internatsional,* pt. 2, pp. 528-61.

12. Marx and Engels, *Correspondence 1846-1895,* London, 1934, p. 327.

13. *Moniteur universel* (Paris), quoted in *Le Nord,* Oct. 30, 1872; *APP,* B/A 944, *pièce* 126.

14. On these meetings see Stekloff, *History of the First International,* pp. 287-303, 329-39; Iu.M. Steklov, 'Internatsional posle Gaagskago kongressa,' *Golos Minuvshego,* 1913, no. 11, pp. 95-121; Georg Stieklow, *Die Bakunistische Internationale nach dem Haager Kongress,* Stuttgart, 1914 (these works are, of course, all by the same author). The documents of the anarchist meetings are in *Freymond,* vol. 4.

15. *APP,* B/A 944, *pièce* 60. The official was the Minister of Agriculture, Flocon. See also Carr's superb account in *Bakunin,* pp. 461-508, and also *Journal de Genève,* Sept. 25, 1873.

16. *Freymond,* vol. 4, pp. 5-244; Stekloff, *History of the First International,* pp. 279-82.

17. *Werke,* vol. 33, pp. 641-2.

18. *Freymond,* vol. 4, pp. 405-12; *TsGAOR,* f. 109 (f. III otd.), no. 144, chast' 135, eksp. 3, 'O begstve kniazia Petra Kropotkina iz Nikolaevskago voennago gospitalia,' 11. 90-3.

19. *The Times,* Sept. 7, 1872, 5:1; Sept. 9, 1872, 3:1; Sept. 27, 1872, 8:1; *Le Nord,* Sept. 13, 14, 1872; *Le Monde,* Sept. 9-10, 12, 1872.

20. *Die Spener Zeitung,* quoted in *The Times,* Sept. 12, 1872, 9:1.

21. Traditional (and in my view erroneous) historiography has stressed Bismarck's desire to isolate France as the motivating factor behind his creation of the *Dreikaiserbund.* Among those who have propagated this view are Renouvin, Bourgeois, Albrecht-Carrié, C.J.H. Hayes, W.H. Dawson, Mowat, Holborn, Japikse, Näf, Rachfall, Nolde, Potemkin, R.J. Sontag and A.J.P. Taylor.

22. Tatishchev, *Imperator Aleksandr II,* vol. 2, pp. 89-92; *Die Grosse Politik,* vol. 1, nos. 121, 123; M. Busch, *Bismarck, Some Secret Pages of His History,* 2 vols., London, 1898, vol 2, pp. 81-82; A. Meyendorff, 'Conversations of Gorchakov with Andrássy and Bismarck in 1872,' *Slavonic Review,* vol. 8, Dec. 1929, p. 400; W.L. Langer, *European Alliances and Alignments, 1871-90,* New York, 1964, p. 21. See further France, *AMAE,* CP, vol. 246, Russie, 246-8; A. Gontaut-Biron, *Mon ambassade en Allemagne (1872 à 1873),* 3rd edition, Paris, 1906, p. 157; A. Dechamps, *Le Prince de Bismarck et l'entrevue des trois empereurs,* 2nd edition, Paris-Brussels, 1872, pp. 13-4, 63; Fritz Leidner, *Die*

aussenpolitik Oesterreich-Ungarns vom Deutch-Französischen Kriege bis zum Deutsch-Oesterreichischen Bündnis, 1870-1879, Halle, 1936, p. 33.

23.   W. Taffs, 'Conversations between Lord Odo Russell and Andrássy, Bismarck and Gorchakov in September, 1872,' *Slavonic Review,* vol. 8, no. 4, p. 704; see also *Documents diplomatiques français,* vol. 1, no. 151.

24.   Langer, *European Alliances and Alignmemnts,* p. 21.

25.   A.F. Pribram, *England and the International Policy of the European Great Powers, 1871-1914,* Oxford, 1931, pp. 7-8.

26.   Meyendorff, 'Conversations,' p. 404; Taffs, 'Conversations,' p. 705; *Documents diplomatiques français,* vol. 1, no. 156; P.A. Valuev, *Dnevnik,* 2 vols., Moscow, 1961, vol. 2, pp. 507-8.

27.   *Documents diplomatiques français,* vol. 1, no. 156; *The Times,* Sept. 16, 1872, 5:1.

28.   *Le Nord,* Sept. 9-28, 1872; *Le Monde,* Sept. 9-10, 12, 1872; *The Times,* Sept. 12, 13, 27, 1872.

29.   Belgium, *AMAE,* CPL, Russie, vol. 11, no. 73; France, *AMAE,* Russie, vol. 248, July-Dec. 1873, 120-121; Great Britain, F.O. 65 (Russia), 855, no. 425; *Journal de Genève,* Jan. 18, 31, 1873; Valuev, *Dnevnik,* vol. 2, pp. 315-6; Samuel Bernstein, 'The First International and the Great Powers,' *Science and Society,* vol. 16, no. 3, Summer 1952, p. 271.

30.   Great Britain, F.O. 65 (Russia), 853, no. 223. On the talks in Central Europe on the 'social question' see Austria-Hungary, *HHStA,* IB 1873, no. 59.

31.   The text is in *Die Grosse Politik,* vol. 1, no. 127. See also Tatishchev, *Imperator Aleksandr II,* vol. 2, pp. 94-100.

32.   France, *AMAE,* Russie, vol. 247, 274-9. On the Exposition see J.M. Hart, 'Vienna and the Centennial,' *The International Review,* vol. 2 no. 1, January 1875, pp. 1-24.

33.   For Bakunin's 'instructions' (a forgery) to assassinate the tsar see *APP,* B/A 438, *pièces* 3760-3761. See further Austria-Hungary, *HHStA,* IB 1873, no. 59; *ibid.,* no. 270; *ibid.,* No. 232; *ibid.,* PSMA 1873, no. 274. See also Switzerland, *Bundesarchiv,* 'Sozialistische Arbeiterinternationale,' *pièces* 16, 17, and France, *AMAE,* Russie, vol. 248, 116-31.

34.   Tatishchev, *Imperator Aleksandr II,* vol. 2, pp. 100-1.

35.   The text is in *Die Grosse Politik.* Langer (*European Alliances,* p. 24) and Bernstein ('The First International,' p. 270) have also quoted the passage given here.

36.   Langer, *European Alliances,* p. 25. Bernstein ('The First International,' p. 270) noted that the Vienna agreement constituted 'the old Holy Alliance refurbished.' Langer, Bernstein and Pribram understood the true nature of the *Dreikaiserbund* as primarily an alliance against revolution. None of the three, however, pursued their accurate and crucial insight, and their views on the subject have made less of an impact than they should have upon modern historiography.

CHAPTER ELEVEN

Conclusion

The true social democrat is an elusive creature. In so far as political labels have any meaning, however, it seems clear that the majority of the Russians in the First International clearly merit the designation of social democrats, and they, rather than Plekhanov and his group, were the first Russians to bear that title. The overwhelming majority were of course émigrés, but they were a vital force in the revolutionary movement. As one prominent émigré of a later generation pointed out,

> It is superficial and erroneous in the highest degree to imagine the Russian political emigration of the Tsarist period as something wrenched out of Russian realities and alien to them. The emigration of this period was not a broken-off chunk of the Russian revolutionary intelligentsia, but a vitally necessary constituent element.[1]

Of what did the social democracy of the Russians in the First International consist? First, the Russians—save for Bakunin and a few others—supported the General Council, which throughout the life of the International was social democratic and Marxist. Secondly, they resolutely fought the opponents of social democracy, namely, the anarchists. Thirdly, the Russians carried out the instructions of the General Council, published its documents, and urged the

young generation in Russia to study and emulate social
democracy. Finally, they propagandized Marx's teachings.
Although most of these Russians persisted in including the
peasantry in the working class, they basically used the
terminology and categories of social democracy, and thus
they—and not the Plekhanov group—first implanted social-
democratic slogans and myths in Russia. Despite all the
obstacles that confronted those who took the message of social
democracy to Russia, new concepts, new terminology, new
organizations and finally a wholly new direction came to the
Russian revolutionary and working-class movements. Already
in the mid-1870's, the South Russian Union of Workers in
Odessa and the Northern Union of Russian Workers in St
Petersburg came into existence as unquestionably proletarian, quasi-social-democratic organizations.[2]

When these organizations came into being, the International was already dead, but the notorious 'lag' that seemed
to dictate Russian imitation of Western ideas and movements
a generation later had been shortened to less than a decade.
The Russian proletariat, unlike its counterparts in the West,
required no lengthy period of oppression to sharpen and
refine its class consciousness. One of the most striking features
of the Russian working-class was the maturity of its class
consciousness from the very beginning of its existence. In the
last decades of the nineteenth century the Russian workers
won the reputation of being the most satanically intractable
and undisciplined labour force in the world. We can only
explain this by pointing to the fact that social democracy
appeared in Russia at precisely the moment—the late 1860's
and early 1870's—when the working-class itself was in the
process of formation.

Were the Russian social democrats of this early period also
Marxists? Our answer must be in the negative, with a caveat.
Eponymic identifications were less common a century ago
than they have subsequently become. Earlier, people called
themselves 'disciples' or 'students' of this or that thinker; it is
well known that not even Marx was prepared to say, 'I am a
Marxist.' The majority of the Russians in the International
were disciples of Marx, but disciples can err. The Russian
followers of Marx did not always fully comprehend his

teachings, and sometimes they did not perceive the applicabi-
lity of those teachings to Russian conditions (and indeed, who
could have said in 1917 that backward, agrarian Russia
would become the first state to call itself 'Marxist'?). One
could perhaps say that they accepted some special theories of
Marxism but remained ignorant of the general theory.

Does this refute our contention that the Russians were
social democrats? It does not, if only we apply to them the
same standards by which we judge, for example, the Germans. No one would challenge Wilhelm Liebknecht's standing as a social democrat, yet Liebknecht frequently uttered
nonsense that Bakunin gleefully used against the Marxists,
and he often edited—sometimes ridiculously—materials that
Marx and Engels send him for publication in *Der Volksstaat*.
Liebknecht's friend and colleague August Bebel was one of
social democracy's foremost champions, yet there were times
when he acted and spoke like Lassalle's first minister. J.P.
Becker was frequently—as we have seen—a source of great
distress to Marx and Engels, yet no one has ever called him
anything but a social democrat.[3] Therefore, simple justice
obliges us to identify the Russians who supported Marx in the
First International (Utin, Lopatin, Tomanovskaya, Trusov,
the Bartenevs, Levashyova and others) as social democrats,
the admittedly eclectic nature of their political and ideological views notwithstanding.

As we indicated at the outset of this study, the populist
surge in Russia in the mid-1870's did much to becloud the
work of those Russians who espoused social democracy in the
First International. In the years 1873-5 (especially the 'mad
summer' of 1874), and as a direct result of the continental
reaction, hundreds of young idealists swarmed into the
Russian countryside in the *v narod* ('to the people') movement.
These young people, unlike their countrymen in the International, were still seeking uniquely Russian solutions to
social problems. Many thought that those solutions lay
in the peasant commune—that hoary institution which the
peasants hated and the government employed as a coercive
and fiscal agency to replace the landlords after the emancipation. The *narodniki* idealized the commune because they
hated and feared the alternatives, of which the most ominous

was capitalism. As Theodore Dan pointed out, 'the profound peculiarity of Russian democratic thought lies in this, that from its very inception it never for a moment idealized capitalism and was not drawn to it, but, on the contrary, sharply criticized it.'[4]

And so the young people went into the countryside, seeking to take the message of socialism—by which they primarily understood Chernyshevsky's teachings—to the peasants and convince them that they and their communes had been socialist all along. They told the peasants that their traditions of mutual aid, periodic redistribution of the land and joint responsibility for state obligations (traditions that varied widely even within the strictly Russian portions of the Empire) had not only prepared but indeed had ordained them to be socialists. The Russian muzhik did not understand all this. He frequently trounced the young crusaders before turning them over to the police. The peasant believed in land, not socialism; in bread, not words; in the immaculate justice of the tsar, not rebellion against his authority. In the preaching of the city slickers he saw a provocation, perhaps another landlord scheme to deprive him of what little land he had.[5]

The *v narod* movement was only a diversion that brought into temporary eclipse the more modern, sophisticated, *international* tendency within the Russian revolutionary movement. Far from destroying this tendency, the diversion ultimately proved its superiority. The populist frenzy of the 1870's, upon which historians have showered much erudite attention, was an intellectually sterile attempt to recapture an imaginary, romantic past. The Russian social democrats re-emerged in the 1880's and forged a movement that culminated in the formation, at the end of the century, of the Russian Social-Democratic Labour Party.

We have so far in these concluding remarks ignored Bakunin and Nechaev. Standing outside the mainstream of the Russian revolutionary movement, Bakunin unfurled the black flag of anarchism in the West and summoned all who would heed him to the great uprising that would produce the stateless millennium. This exhortation seemed to some of the frustrated and impatient to offer real hope. Anarchism has long exercised a powerful influence upon people who insist upon destroying all evils and curing all ills in one great stroke, but it remains something in the nature of suggesting the guillotine for a headache. Bakunin made converts in the West by the thousand and indeed helped to destroy the International, but he never had much standing in Russia, in part because of his association, late in his life, with Sergei Nechaev.

We have seen that Nechaev's 'practical' revolutionism did harm to the revolutionary movement and that his attempts to compete with the social democrats in the realm of theory came to naught. Nechaev was a forceful, dynamic individual, a true man of action. He was also an unscrupulous swindler and a ruthless egocentric. Like Bakunin, though on a lesser scale, he was able to recruit to his service those who were naïve, frustrated and incapable of formulating and pursuing a coherent revolutionary programme. Only in the realm of organization and tactics did he have anything to offer, and there his influence remained less significant than that of his successor on the extreme Russian left, Peter Tkachev.

This has been a study in Russian history, the story of the birth of an historic alliance between the Russian proletariat and European social democracy, and yet we have spent little time in Russia. Our quest has taken us to some of the great capitals and spas of Western Europe, to dingy Belgian and French mill and pit towns, to obscure Swiss mountain villages. Only in passing have we returned to the Russian countryside of infinite beauty, boundless promise, incomprehensible melancholy. Many of the Russians around whom our story has revolved were forced to live out their political lives abroad. But they never forgot Russia and never rested comfortably outside its borders. Most returned: some in secrecy, others in ignominy, a few, ultimately, in triumph. This book has sought to rescue them from obscurity.

NOTES

1. Theodore Dan, *The Origins of Bolshevism,* New York, 1964, pp. 90-1n.
2. On the South Russian Union of Workers, which Eugene Zaslavsky and others formed in 1875, see B.S. Itenberg's excellent *'Iuzhno-rossiiskii soiuz rabochikh'—pervaia proletarskaia organizatsiia v Rossii,* Moscow, 1954. On the more important Northern Union of Russian Workers, which Stepan Khalturin, Victor Obnorsky and others founded in the capital in 1878, see E.A. Korol'chuk, *'Severnyi soiuz russkikh rabochikh' i revoliutsionnoe dvizhenie 70—kh godov XIX v. v Peterburge,* Leningrad, 1946, and *SIE,* vol. 12, pp. 658-60.
3. On many occasions Marx and Engels lamented the harm done to social democracy by their friends. For one example, see Engels's March 18/28, 1875, letter to Bebel (usually appended as an annex to 'Critique of the Gotha Program') complaining that he and Marx were taken to task by Bakunin (in *Statehood and Anarchy*) for 'every ill-advised word Liebknecht has said and written since the founding of *Demokratisches Wochenblatt* [1868].' See *Werke,* vol. 34, p. 129.
4. *The Origins of Bolshevism,* p. 10.
5. We have referred in this study to the works of Venturi, Pipes, Wortman, Billington, Pomper and others. The reader should also consult Andrzej Walicki's essay in Ghita Ionescu and Ernest Gellner, eds., *Populism,* London, 1969, pp. 62-96. There is, of course, an enormous literature in Russian.

Epilogue

After the Hague Congress of the International, the Russian revolutionary émigrés split into three major factions. One went with Marx, another with Bakunin, and a third began to take form around Peter Lavrov. Ever the healer and unifier, Lavrov tried to reconcile his countrymen and indeed the International at large. He published a new journal which he tried to use to bridge the gulf between Marxists and Bakuninists; this journal, *Vpered!* (Forward!), succeeded *Narodnoe Delo—La Cause du Peuple* as a Russian voice in the International. As he helped to build the myth of the Paris Commune, so Lavrov contributed to the legend of the First International.[1]

Lavrov approved of the *v narod* movement, but he himself was only partly a populist. He recognized that conditions in Russia necessitated an appeal to the rural masses, but he never lost sight of the 'historical mission' (as the Marxists put it) of the proletariat, and he called the International that class's greatest triumph. Lavrov evolved a sophisticated socialist theory that owed something to Herzen, Chernyshevsky, Marx and even Bakunin:

> Lavrov took Marx as his guide not only in political economy, as the mass of Russian socialists did, but also in sociology, at that time [the 1870's] a rarer phenomenon .... How then to explain his decisive and resolute entry into the great international family

235

of socialists-revolutionaries . . . 'under the badge' of Marx? . . . .
That in Marx's teaching which struck Lavrov was its close
connection with the then most vital labour trends.[2]

Lavrov continued to associate with Marx and Engels in the
1870's and 1880's although he was never a member of their
inner circle. He pursued his own path to socialism and
arrived at social democracy coloured by agrarian socialism
and a tinge of insurrectionism. He was a 'gradualist' who
generally opposed Peter Tkachev and others of the Blanquist
persuasion who argued for an elitist revolution. But his was
not a blind and unyielding opposition. At Blanqui's funeral
in January 1881 he offered his hand to the followers of
'l'Enfermé':

> I salute you [Blanqui] in the name of *our* quintessential
> revolutionary, Bakunin, who preceded you into the silent tomb
> . . . . Hail, martyr for your convictions, in the name of another
> martyr, the master of the entire young Russian socialist genera-
> tion, Chernyshevsky, who, deep in the wildest Siberian province,
> has for fifteen [actually seventeen] years been atoning for the
> power of his intelligence and his influence on the Russian youth.
> His name figures these days in the pages of the journal that
> throws in the world's face its provocative cry, 'Ni Dieu ni
> maître!'[3]

Tkachev had by the end of the 1870's become one of Blanqui's
most ardent disciples, and when *Ni Dieu ni Maître* was
founded in 1880 he and the ex-Communard and associate of
Nechaev, Kasper Turski, were among the collaborators. The
first issue of Blanqui's last journal noted that it would publish
Chernyshevsky's *What Is To Be Done?* [4]

Compromise was not part of the Jacobin-Blanquist tradition
that motivated Tkachev. The man who had initiated Sergei
Nechaev into the mysteries of communism escaped to the
West in 1873 and settled first in Switzerland. He collaborated for a time on *Vpered!* but he quarrelled with Lavrov
and the two men parted. Tkachev called for the creation of
a highly centralized, tightly disciplined revolutionary elite,
whose goal was the immediate seizure of power. He proclaimed this in an article attacking Lavrov's insistence upon
propaganda, organization and preparation (i.e. 'gradualism')

and he expounded upon his position in a journal he founded in Geneva in 1875, *Nabat* (The Tocsin).[5]

Friedrich Engels defended Lavrov against Tkachev's attack, and a minor polemic ensued as Tkachev responded with an 'Open Letter.' Though he did not agree with Lavrov on all points, Engels found his views much more compatible than those of Tkachev, who in his view hovered on the brink of anarchist adventurism. In a series of articles in *Der Volksstaat,* Engels called attention to what he described as the immaturity of Tkachev's thought and the impracticability of his revolutionary exhortations. Tkachev had sought to make Chernyshevsky's theory of the pretermission of the capitalist stage a revolutionary tactic; in so doing, he tended to minimize the strength of the Russian gentry and to exaggerate the revolutionary instincts of the peasantry and the capabilities of the radical opposition. The force of Engels's attack obliged Tkachev to re-examine his position, and he indeed became a much more consistent Blanquist.[6]

One prominent Soviet historian, M.N. Pokrovsky, called Tkachev the 'first Russian Marxist.'[7] He clearly was not remotely that, but Pokrovsky's comment suggests that, toward the end of his life, Tkachev took a position that did indeed bring him closer to Marx. Much as did Edouard Vaillant, Marx's associate in 1871 and 1872, Tkachev tried to blend Blanquist insurrectionism with Marxist social and political teachings. The resulting amalgam was, as M.G. Sedov has written, the 'Russian variant' of Blanquism.[8]

Tkachev began to lose his mental equilibrium early in the 1880's. He drank heavily, quarrelled with his ever-narrowing circle of friends, spurned Lavrov's conciliatory gestures and had several unsavoury encounters with the police. He died an alcoholic in January 1886. Nevertheless, the Russian émigrés honoured him for his services to the cause of revolution. Incapable of bearing a personal grudge, Lavrov spoke at Tkachev's grave-side in Ivry Cemetery outside Paris. George Plekhanov, who with four friends had founded the Marxist 'Liberation of Labour' group in Geneva three years earlier, was also present.[9]

Lavrov outlived Tkachev by fourteen years and was like him a social democrat, although basically non-sectarian. His views coincided with Marx's at many points, but we cannot accept the claim of an early Soviet historian (Steklov) that 'Lavrovism' was the 'Russified form' of Marxism.[10] On the other hand, B.P. Kozmin's untenable view of Lavrov as a 'representative of the extreme right wing of Russian utopian socialism, an expression of the interests of the petty manu-facturer' is explicable only in terms of Stalinist historiog-raphy.[11] Lavrov died early in February 1900. Victor Jaclard attended the grave-side ceremony, as did other Communards, including Paul Lafargue and Edouard Vaillant. A large and imposing procession had followed the coffin to Montparnasse Cemetery (how Tkachev, and the historian Kozmin, would have sneered at that: even *burial* in bourgeois ground!). On each subsequent annniversary of his death for at least a decade the police maintained a watch over Lavrov's grave. They were particularly apprehensive in 1905, fearing that the socialists would attempt to inflame the usual crowd with speeches condemning 'Bloody Sunday' (January 22) in St Petersburg.[12]

Lavrov had played a major role in sustaining Marx's re-examination of his views about Russia. That process had begun in the late 1860's under the influence of earlier émigrés. Marx developed a passionate interest in the Russian peasant commune and frequently discussed it with his Russian visitors and friends. As we have noted earlier, in 1881 he wrote three drafts of a letter to Vera Zasulich (a colleague of both Lavrov and Plekhanov) in which he attempted to analyze the future of the commune.[13] He reached no firm conclusions, but his efforts indicated that he no longer dismissed as wholly fanciful the insistence of all Cherny-shevsky's disciples upon a role for the commune in a socialist Russia.

Shortly after completing the final draft of his letter to Zasulich, Marx joined Engels in composing a message to a 'Slavonic Meeting' called in London to celebrate the tenth anniversary to the Paris Commune. The revolutionary organ-ization *Narodnaya Volya* (The People's Will) had assassinated Alexander II on March 13, and the German socialists took note of the connection between that deed and the great insurrection:

When the Commune of Paris succumbed to the atrocious massacre organized by the defenders of 'order,' the victors little thought that ten years would not elapse before an event would happen in distant Petersburg, which maybe after long and violent struggles, must ultimately and certainly lead to the establishment of a Russian Commune.[14]

In 1883, the year of Marx's death, Engels told Lavrov that Russia was 'the France of the present century; to her belongs by right the revolutionary initiative of the *new social order.*' And under the influence of the émigrés and of developments inside Russia, Marx and Engels came to believe, in the 1870's and 1880's, that revolution in Russia was indeed nearer than they had earlier thought.[15] In the 1870's the first working-class, socialist organizations appeared in Odessa and St Petersburg, and from that beginning the movement spread rapidly. The message of social democracy, which some of the Russian émigrés had been sending to the homeland from Geneva and London since 1868, had reached the Russian workers.[16]

The fate of the other leading Russian social democrats of the period of the First International is quickly told. Herman Lopatin, though at liberty from 1873 until 1879, was in and out of tsarist prisons until 1887, when at last the authorities found one—Schlüsselberg—that could hold him. He remained a disciple of Marx and in the 1880's tried to resurrect The People's Will as a mass political party (he was unsuccessful). Shortly thereafter he went to prison for eighteen years. The Revolution of 1905 freed him, but the man of sixty no longer had any enthusiasm for revolutionary labours. He lived to see the Bolshevik Revolution and died at the end of 1918.

Nicholas Danielson continued to correspond with Marx and Engels until their deaths. Under the impact of the reactionary reign of Alexander III (1881-94), however, he modified his earlier social-democratic views and moved toward routine liberal populism. The man who had been instrumental in bringing *Capital* to Russia ended his days as an apologist for liberalism. He too witnessed the Bolshevik revolution and died in July 1918. Nicholas Liubavin apparently left the revolutionary movement and went to work for the Compagnie Russe-Américaine; his fate is unknown.[17]

Nicholas Utin and what Michael Confino has accurately called his 'group of Marx's partisans'[18] saw their influence plummet after the arrest of Nechaev and the expulsion of Bakunin and Guillaume from the International. Having alienated many of the émigrés in Switzerland by their extreme hostility toward Bakunin, they lost many of their Swiss and French friends when they continued (in part at Marx's urging) to attack the Communards. Utin left the movement and offered Lavrov *Narodnoe Delo's* printing press, but he set so many conditions (including the exclusion of all Bakuninists) that the offer was declined. In 1874 the Russian government issued a summons to nineteen émigrés, including Lavrov, Utin, Lopatin, Bakunin and Trusov, to return to Russia at once or face prosecution (just how and where the judicial proceedings might take place was not clear). Presumably the authorities believed that the Nechaev example would lead the individuals in question to fear extradition and return. The tactic did not succeed; the émigrés ignored the ominous invitation. Lavrov and Utin declined, for different reasons, to sign a joint response to the summons. Lavrov wrote to Lopatin that Utin 'refuses primarily on the grounds of his separation from the emigration and his refusal to see anything of value in it; he expounds upon his motives at length, and badly.'[19]

After living for a time in Zürich the Utins moved to London, where Nicholas apprenticed himself to a well-known British civil engineer and earned a licence and election to the prestigious Institution of Civil Engineers (1876). They returned to the Continent and lived in Liège, where Marx visited them in September 1876, a month in which he described Utin as 'one of my dearest friends.'[20] In 1877 Nicholas Utin went to Romania to work for Baron S.S. Poliakov, who was building a railway to transport the Russian army to the Turkish front. With Poliakov's support, he wrote a fawning letter to the Third Section requesting an imperial pardon and permission to return to Russia to serve tsar and country. He reminded the authorities that he had won a gold medal at the university, admitted to having kept some bad company for a while, denied participating in the

Polish Rebellion of 1863 and claimed that he had spent his years abroad in study and honest labour. The request was granted; the Utins returned home. Peter Lavrov, alluding to his own sad experience with Lev Tikhomirov, the best-known revolutionary apostate of the period, wrote later that Utin was 'one of the early cases of renegadism in the ranks of Russian socialists, but alas!, not the last.'[21]

Nicholas Utin never won any prizes for virtue, political or otherwise, but Lavrov's indictment was too severe. Unlike Tikhomirov, Utin—his letter notwithstanding—did not return to serve the tsar but merely to work as an engineer (he helped construct the first steel bridge across the Volga). One can only speculate on his thoughts as he walked along the Neva embankment in St Petersburg and gazed across the dark waters at the cold, sunless Peter-Paul Fortress, where Sergei Nechaev sat staring at the walls that would confine him all his days. Did Utin feel any sympathy? Had he really helped Greulich and Remy bring the Nechaev affair to an end? We shall never know. But the restless Utin returned to the West late in 1878 or early in the following year, having found life in Russia less attractive than he had anticipated.

The Utins lived again for a few months in Liège, then moved to Brussels, where they remained until December 1881. They apparently did not see Karl Marx during that time, and the year 1882 found them back in Russia. For the last two years of his life Nicholas Utin worked in the Urals as a mining engineer. There is little information on his activities in this period. Nadezhda Krupskaya, Lenin's wife, reported years later that her father and Utin frequently corresponded. Utin died in the mountains in December 1883, nine months after the death of his friend, Karl Marx. Natalie took his body to St Petersburg for burial, composed herself, then continued to work on a thinly-disguised novel about the lives of the émigrés of the 1860's and 1870's.[22]

Elizabeth Tomanovskaya, as we have seen, returned to Russia in October of 1871. Her husband had died during her absence. After a couple of years, she married the manager of her estates, one Davydovsky. The new husband proved to be a criminal type; he organized a 'Knave of Hearts' club for the express purpose of robbing rich Muscovites at gambling. The police discovered the plot (officially called the 'Affair of the Forty-eight Accused and the Fifty-Six Criminal Deeds') and arrested the principals. Davydovsky and his associates went to Siberian prisons for long terms. Elizabeth, who had raised several thousand rubles for her husband's unsuccessful defence, loyally followed him—and later bore him two children—to the remote eastern reaches of the Empire.[23]

Her revolutionary past did not pursue 'Madame Dmitrieff' to Russia. She lived for a time in Siberia and upon Davydovsky's release from prison moved with him to Krasnoyarsk. In 1903 she returned to the village in northwest Russia where she had spent her youth. A young woman who had served her father saw her then, and in 1970 that woman related the encounter to a French historian who had come to the Soviet Union seeking traces of the famous *pétroleuse.*[24]

Anna and Victor Jaclard lived in various towns in Switzerland before going to Russia in 1874. Doubtless with the aid of Anna's father, General Korvin-Krukovsky, the couple set up housekeeping in St Petersburg and Jaclard completed his medical studies. Both Anna and Victor wrote occasionally for the Russian press, and Victor contributed articles on Russian topics to left-wing Parisian journals. After the declaration of an amnesty for the Communards, the Jaclards returned to Paris. Victor worked politically with Georges Clemenceau (his old friend from medical school in the early 1860's), with Henri Rochefort, Peter Lavrov and others. Several times he stood as a candidate for political office but never had any success in Paris. In 1889 he was elected a municipal councillor in the working-class suburb of Alfortville.

Anna Jaclard died suddenly in 1887. Clemenceau and Louise Michel, among others, joined her husband at the brief civil ceremony in Neuilly Cemetery. Anna had asked on her deathbed that there be no speeches and her request was honoured; and soon even Victor Jaclard ceased to visit her grave.[25]

Jaclard continued to work on Clemenceau's *La Justice* and on other newspapers and to participate in the socialist movement. He was present at the founding of the Second International.[26] In July 1894 he married Joséphine Eugénie Desprès, who was born in 1868, the year Jaclard met Bakunin and Utin and the others at the Berne Congress of the League of Peace and Freedom. Mademoiselle Desprès brought to the marriage, according to the police, 'a rather handsome dowry,' and Jaclard's standard of living noticeably improved.[27]

Toward the end of the 1890's, however, signs of mental deterioration began to appear, and Jaclard's increasingly erratic behavior alienated many old friends and associates. In 1902 his wife had to commit him to a mental hospital; he died the following year. Only about thirty people followed the cortège to Père Lachaise Cemetery, where Joséphine Jaclard-Desprès deposited her husband's ashes in the Columbarium. Clemenceau was not present. Jean Jaurès and Charles Longuet sent word that they were detained in the provinces. Jean Longuet, substituting for his father, made a brief speech. Several Poles and one or two Russian socialists were present. The incidents that frequently attended the funerals of prominent socialists did not materialize; Victor Jaclard was a forgotten man.[28]

Swiss justice finally apprehended another former member of the Russian section of the International, Edouard Bongard, and sent him to prison in 1874 for counterfeiting. Anton Trusov lived on in Geneva and Lausanne, working as a printer, and apparently returned to Russia in the 1880's.[29] Olga Levashyova broke off her revolutionary ties and lived out her days comfortably on Lac Léman. Catherine and Victor Bartenev returned to Russia in 1872, and Catherine remained active in the revolutionary movement. She went to Paris in 1889, where she served as one of the secretaries at the congress that founded, on the anniversary of the French Revolution, the Second International.[30] Peter Lavrov, George Plekhanov, Paul Akselrod and other Russians were also there.[31]

NOTES

1. Boris Sapir, 'The Origin of Vpered!,' in *Vpered!, 1873-1877*, vol. 1, pp. 239-50; IISG, *Lavrov*, no. 848; *ibid., Jung*, 746, 747a. Lavrov's 'Ocherk razvitiia Mezhdunarodnago assotsiatsii rabochikh' appeared in *Vpered!* (Zürich), vol. 1, 1873, part 1, pp. 110-77, and vol. 2, 1874, pp. 74-121. The work also appeared as *Ocherki po istorii Internatsionala*, Petrograd, 1919.

2.   Rusanov (Kudrin), *Sotsialisty zapada i Rossii*, pp. 268-9.
3.   *APP*, B/A 1,144, 'Lawroff ou Lawrow, Pierre,' unnumbered, from *Le Citoyen* (Paris), Jan. 7, 1881. Louise Michel also spoke, saying, 'We salute you, Blanqui, in the name of the whole world, in the name of the social revolution, in the name of the Russians, who are stronger than we are.' See *APP*, B/A 869, 'Blanqui. Année 1880 et 1881,' unnumbered, from *La Vérité* (Paris), Jan. 7, 1881.
4.   *Ni Dieu ni Maître* (Paris), no. 1, Nov. 20, 1880. The novel appeared in November and December of 1880 in a Tkachev-Turski translation.
5.   IISG, *Lavrov*, Lavrov to Lopatin, no. 53, May 9, [1874]; B.P. Koz'min, 'P.N. Tkachev i P.L. Lavrov (Stolknovenie dvukh technii russkoi revoliutsionnoi mysli 70-kh godov),' *Voinstvuiushchii materialist*, book 1, 1924, pp. 291-338.
6.   See Engels's articles in *Werke*, vol. 18, pp. 540-66, 584, 663, 664, and Tkachev's 'Open Letter to Mr. Friedrich Engels' in Tkachev, *Izbrannye sochineniia*, vol. 3, pp. 88-9. See further M.G. Sedov, 'Nekotorye problemy istorii blankizma v Rossii.' A recent unsatisfactory study in English is A.L. Weeks, *The First Bolshevik: A Political Biography of Peter Tkachev*, New York, 1968.
7.   Quoted in Reuel', *Russkaia ekon. mysl'*, p. 149n.
8.   *Geroicheskii period*, p. 26.
9.   Tkachaev's dossier in the Paris police archives (*APP*, B/A 1,285, 'Tkatcheff, Pierre,' unnumbered) indicates several arrests for drunkenness and one for 'outraging public decency.' In the latter instance Tkachev displayed some imagination. He first claimed to be 'Monsieur Gannet,' then, at the station-house, insisted that he was 'Monsieur Joffrin,' a Paris municipal councilman.
10. *Istoricheskoe podgotovlenie russkoi sotsial'-demokratii*, p. 28.
11. *Ot 'deviatnadtsatogo fevralia' k 'pervomu marta'*, pp. 112-5.
12. Lavrov's dossier in the Paris police archives (*APP*, B/A 1,144) contains police agent reports and newspaper clippings, all unnumbered. Present at the 1905 ceremony were Georges Clemenceau, Maurice Maeterlinck, Lucien Lévy-Bruhl, Edouard Vaillant (by then a deputy) and many other notables. The expected disorders did not materialize. Anatole France, Jean Jaurès, Jacques Maritain and others protested against what they thought were the plans of the government to use the 1905 Lavrov demonstration (a peaceful one) as an excuse to expel the Russian refugees from France.
13. *Werke*, vol. 19 pp. 384-406.
14. IISG, *Marx-Engels Correspondence*, K 641; *Karl Marx Chronik*, p. 383.
15. V. Zel'tser, 'Marks-Engel's i Lenin o kapitalizme i revoliutsii v Rossii,' *Istoriia proletariata SSSR*, no. 1-2(13-14), 1933, pp. 88-9, 95.
16. On the dissemination of revolutionary and socialist propaganda in Russia in this period see O.D. Sokolov, 'Revoliutsionnaia propaganda sredi fabrichnykh i zavodskikh rabochikh v 70-kh godakh XIX veka,' *Iz istorii rabochego klassa i krest'ianstva SSSR*, Moscow, 1959, pp. 3-49; B.S. Itenberg, 'Sviazi peredovykh rabochikh Rossii s revoliutsionnym dvizheniem zapada (70-e gody XIX v.),' *Voprosy Istorii*,

1956, no. 9, pp. 17-30; B.S. Itenberg, 'Rasprostranenie izdanii russkoi sektsii I Internationala'; N.G. Sladkevich, 'K. Marks i peredovoe studenchestvo Peterburgskogo universiteta 60-80-kh godov XIX veka,' *Ocherki po istorii Leningradskogo Universiteta,* vol. 1, Leningrad, 1962, pp. 106-17; K.L. Seleznev, 'I Internatsional i revoliutsionnoe dvizhenie v Rossii v XIX veke,' *Istoriia SSSR,* 1964, no. 4, pp. 3-28.

17. On Nicholas Liubavin see *Journal de Saint-Pétersbourg,* no. 115, May 12, 1871 (Old Style).

18. Confino, ed., 'Journal de Natalie Herzen,' p. 140n.

19. IISG, *Lavrov,* no. 67. See further *ibid.,* Lavrov to Lopatin, unnumbered. June 27, [1874], and *ibid.,* no. 68. See also *ibid., Smirnov,* map 54, no. 4; *ibid.,* afz. stk. IV, Smirnov to Buturlin, late December 1872; *ibid., Lavrov,* no. 848, Utin to Lavrov, Dec. 22, 1872; *APP,* B/A 438, 3716, Geneva agent report, Nov. 25, 1872. The summons is in Switzerland, *Bundesarchiv,* Schweizerisches General Konsulat in St Petersburg, 1874, diverses; see also Koz'min *Russkaia sektsii,* pp. 361-2. See further *TsGAOR,* 'O byvshem studente Nikolae Utine,' 1. 108. In May 1873 the Russian government summoned most of its subjects who were studying in Zürich home. Many reluctantly complied, and in Russia, they played a significant role in the *v narod* movement.

20. Institution of Civil Engineers (London), *Proposition Papers,* Nov. 14, 1876; *Werke,* vol. 34, p. 201.

21. *TsGAOR,* 'O byvshem studente Nikolae Utine,' 11. 101, 105-6; see also 1. 102. See further *Obshchee Delo—La Cause Générale* (Geneva), no. 47, March 1882. For Lavrov's comments see 'Narodniki 1873-1878 goda,' *Materialy dlia istorii russkago sotsial'no-revoliutsionnago dvizheniia,* vol. 10, Geneva, 1895, p. 28.

22. Brussels, Service de Population, *Registre de la Population, 1876,* W. 78-76; *TsGAOR,* 'O vozvrativshemsia iz za granitsy gosudarstvennom prestupnike Nikolae Utine,' 1. 10; see also 11. 11-13. Utin wrote a report, 'Serginsko-Ufaleiskie gornye zavody.' which the Panteleev brothers press published in St Petersburg in 1882. On Utin and Konstantin Krupsky, see V.A. D'iakov and I.S. Miller, *Revoliutsionnoe dvizhenie v russkoi armii i vosstanie 1863 g.,* Moscow, 1964, p. 124, citing V.N. Shul'gin, 'Vospominaniia,' *Oktiabr',* 1957, no. 11, pp. 89-90. See also *List of Members of the Institution of Civil Engineers* London, Aug. 20, 1883, and Jan. 2, 1884. Natalie lived at least until 1913. Her novel, *Zhizn' za zhizn',* appeared in *Vestnik Europy,* nos. 4-6, 1885.

23. *MERR.* pp. 335-6; Sazhin, *Vospominaniia,* pp. 75-6, 78-9; Kuniskii, *Russkoe obshchestvo i Parizhskaia Kommuna,* pp. 106-7.

24. N.P. Efremova, 'Elizaveta Dmitrieva—geroinia Kommuny,' *Voprosy Istorii,* 1972, no. 3, p. 215. The date of Elizabeth's death is unknown.

25. *APP,* B/A 1, 123, *pièces* 209-210.

26. *Ibid., pièce* 240.

27. *Ibid., pièces* 272-275.

28. *Ibid., pièces* 280-299.

29. A.Ia. Kiperman, 'Raznochinskaia politicheskaia emigratsiia v pere-piske tsarskikh diplomatov,' *Istochnikovedcheskie raboty,* vyp. 2, Tambov, 1971. p. 42.

30. I. Knizhnik-Vetrov, 'E.G. Barteneva—sotsialistka i pisatel'nitsa,' *KS,* 1929, no. 11(60), pp. 43ff.

31. S.T. Arkomed (pseudonym for Georg Karadzhan), *Za rubezhom: istoricheski zametki. Period studenchestva ot 1886 g. do 1890 g.,* pt. 1, Tiflis, 1929, pp. 56-58.

Bibliography

Archival Collections

Austria-Hungary, *Haus-, Hof-, und Staatsarchiv.* Primarily Präsidialsektion des Ministeriums des Aeussern (PSMA) and Informationsbureau (IB).

Belgium, *Archives du Ministère des Affaires Etrangères.*

Brussels, City of, Service de Population, *Registre de la Population, 1876,* W 78-76.

France, *Archives du Ministère des Affaires Etrangères.*

―――― *Archives Nationales.*

―――― Bibliothèque Nationale, Division des Manuscrits, *Slave 109.*

―――― Ministère de la Guerre, Etat-Major de l'Armée, *Archives Historiques.*

Geneva, City and Canton of, *Archives d'Etat de la République et Canton de Genève.*

Great Britain, Foreign Office, F.O. 65 (Russia); F.O. 100 (Switzerland).

International Institute of Social History. Primarily *Becker, Jung, Lavrov, Marx-Engels Correspondence, Smirnov.*

Paris, City of, *Archives de la Préfecture de Police.*

Switzerland, *Bundesarchiv.*

Union of Soviet Socialist Republics, *Biblioteka imeni Lenina, Otdel' Rukopisei; Tsentral'nyi Gosudarstvennyi Istoricheskii Arkhiv v Moskve; Tsentral'nyi Gosudarstvennyi Arkhiv Literatury i iskusstva; Tsentral'nyi Gosudarstvennyi Arkhiv Oktiabrskoi Revoliutsiii.*

Zürich, City and Canton of, *Staatsarchiv.*

Published Primary Sources

――――, *Rabochee dvizheni v Rossii v XIX veke,* vol. 2, part 1, Moscow, 1950.

Andréas, B., *Le Manifeste Communiste de Marx et Engels. Histoire et bibliographie, 1848-1918,* Milan 1963.

―――― and M. Molnár eds., 'L'Alliance de la démocratie socialiste: procès verbaux de la section de Genève,' in J. Freymond, ed., *Etudes et documents sur la Première Internationale en Suisse,* Geneva, 1964.

247

Bakounine, T., and J. Catteau, 'Contribution à la biographie de Serge Nečaev. Correspondance avec Nathalie Herzen,' *CMRS*, vol. 7, no. 2.

[Bakunin, M.A.] *Archives Bakounine,* edited by A.M. Lehning, vols. 2, 3 and 4, Leiden, 1965, 1967, 1971.

—— 'Discours prononcés au Congrès de la Paix et de la Liberté à Berne (1868) par MM. Mroczkowski et Bakounine,' Geneva, 1869.

—— *Izbrannye sochineniia,* vol. 1, 2nd edition, Peterburg (*sic*)-Moscow, 1922; vol. 2, 2nd edition, Peterburg-Moscow, 1922; vols. 3-4, Peterburg-Moscow, 1920; vol. 5, Peterburg-Moscow, 1922.

—— 'Intrigi gospodina Utina,' in V. Polonskii, ed., *Materialy dlia biografii M.A. Bakunina,* vol. 3, *Bakunin v Pervom Internatsionale,* Moscow-Leningrad, 1928.

—— *Pis'ma M.A. Bakunina k A.I. Gertsenu i N.P. Ogarevu,* 1st edition Geneva, 1896, 2nd edition, St Petersburg, 1906 edited by M.P. Dragomanov.

Bazilevskii, B. (V.Ia. Iakovlev), ed., *Gosudarstvennye prestuplennia v Rossii v XIX veke,* vol. 1, *1825-1876,* Stuttgart, 1903.

—— ed., *Materialy dlia istorii revoliutsionnago dvizheniia v Rossi v 60-kh gg.,* Paris, 1905, and St Petersburg, 1906.

Bismarck, Otto von, *Gedanken und Erinnerungen,* 3 vols. in 1, Stuttgart, n.d.

Bogucharskii, V., *see* Bazilevskii.

Burtsev, V., and S.M. Kravchinskii (Stepniak), *Za sto let (1800-1896),* London, 1897.

Chernyshevskaia-Bystrova, N.M., *Letopis' zhizni i deiatel'nosti N.G. Chernyshevskogo,* Moscow-Leningrad, 1933.

Chernshevskii, N.G. *Polnoe sobranie sochinenii,* vol. 16, Moscow 1953.

—— *What Is to Be Done?,* New York, 1961.

Chudnovskii, S.L., *Iz davnikh let: Vospominaniia,* Moscow, 1934.

Confino, M., ed., 'Autour de "L'Affaire Nečaev." Lettres inédites de Michel Bakunin et de German Lopatin,' *CMRS,* vol. 8, no. 3.

—— 'Bakunin et Nečaev. Les dèbuts de la rupture,' *CMRS,* vol. 7, no. 4.

—— 'Bakunin et Nečaev. La rupture,' *CMRS,* vol. 8 no. 1.

—— *Violence dans la violence. Le débat Bakounine-Nečaev,* Paris, 1973.

Congrès international des étudiants, *Compte rendu official et intégral de la première session, tenue à Liège les 29, 30, 31 octobre et 1er novembre 1865,* Brussels, 1866.

Dombrowski, J., *Trochu comme organisateur et général en chef,* Lyon 1871.

Elpidin, M., *Bibliograficheskii katalog. Profili redaktorov i sotrudnikov,* Carouge (Geneva), 1906.

France, Assemblée Nationale, *Enquête parlementaire sur l'insurrection du 18 mars,* 2 vols., Versailles, 1872.

—— Ministère des Affaires Etrangères, Commission de publication des documents relatifs aux origines de la Guerre de 1914, *Documents diplomatiques français (1871-1914),* 1re série, 1871-1900, vol. 1, (*10 mai 1871–30 juin 1875*), Paris, 1929.

Freymond, J., ed., *La Première Internationale. Recueil de documents,* 4 vols., Geneva, 1962-71.

Fribourg, E.E., *L'Association internationale des travailleurs,* Paris, 1871.

Friedrich III, *Tagebücher von 1848-1866,* Leipzig, 1929.

Germany, Auswärtiges Amt, *Die Grosse Politik der Europäischen Kabinette, 1871-1914*, vol. 1, *Der Frankfurter Friede und seine Nachwirkungen, 1871-1877*, Berlin, 1927.

Gerth, H., ed., *The First International. Minutes of the Hague Congress of 1872 with Related Documents*, Madison, Wisconsin, 1957.

Goncourt, Edmond and Jules de, *Journal: Mémoires de la vie littéraire, 1864-1878*, vol. 3, Paris, 1956.

Gontaut-Biron, A., *Mon ambassade en Allemagne (1872 à 1873)*, 3rd edition, Paris, 1906.

Greulich, H., *Das grüne Hüsli*, Zürich, 1942.

Guillaume, J., *L'Internationale, Documents et souvenirs (1864-1878)*, 4 vols., Paris, 1905-10.

Herzen, A., *My Past and Thoughts*, 4 vols., London, 1968.

——— (Gertsen), *Sobranie sochinenii*, 31 vols., Moscow, 1954-66.

Herzen, N., 'Journal,' *CMRS*, vol. 10, no. 1, edited by M. Confino.

Institute of Marxism-Leninism of the Central Committee of the Communist Party of the Soviet Union, *Documents of the First International*, 5 vols., Moscow, 1963-??

——— *Gaagskii kongress Pervogo Internatsionala, 2-7 sentiabria 1872 g.: Protokoly i dokumenty*, Moscow, 1970.

——— *K. Marks, F. Engel's i revoliutsionnaia Rossiia*, Moscow, 1967.

——— *Literaturnoe nasledstvo K. Marksa i F. Engel'sa. Istoriia publikatsii i izucheniia v SSSR*, Moscow, 1969.

——— *Pervyi Internatsional i Parizhskaia Kommuna: Dokumenty i materialy*, Moscow, 1972.

Institution of Civil Engineers (London), *List of Members of the Institution of Civil Engineers*, London, 1883, 1884.

——— *Proposition Papers*, London 1876.

Jura Federation, *Mémoire présenté par la Fédération jurassienne de l'Association Internationale des Travailleurs à toutes les fédérations de l'Internationale*, Sonvilier, 1873.

Lavrov, P.L. *Filosofiia i sotsiologiia: izbrannye proizvedeniia*, 2 vols., Moscow, 1965.

——— *Historical Letters*, Berkeley and Los Angeles, 1967, edited by J. Scanlan.

——— *Izbrannye sochineniia na sotsial'no-politicheskie temy v vos'mi tomakh*, vol. 1, Moscow, 1934.

——— 'Narodniki 1873-1878 goda,' in *Materialy dlia istorii russkago sotsial'no-revoliutsionnago dvizhenniia*, Geneva, 1895.

——— *Ocherki po istorii Internatsionala*, Petrograd, 1919.

——— 'Pis'ma P.L. Lavrova k E.A. Shtakenshneider,' *Golos Minuvshego*, 1916, nos. 7-8, 9.

——— *Protsess 21-go s prilozheniem biograficheskoi zametki o G.A. Lopatine*, Geneva, 1888.

——— *18 marta 1871 goda*, Geneva, 1880.

Lemonnyer, J., *Les journaux de Paris pendant la Commune. Revue bibliographique complète de la presse parisienne du 19 mars au 27 mai*, Paris, [1871].

Lenin, V.I., 'What the "Friends of the People" Are and How They Fight the Social-Democrats,' *Collected Works*, vol. 1, Moscow, 1963.

Lissagaray, P., *History of the Commune of 1871*, London, 1886.

Lopatin, G.A., *Avtobiografiia*, Petrograd, 1922, edited by A. Shilov.

Maitron, J., et al, eds., *Dictionnaire biographique du mouvement ouvrier français,* deuxième partie, *1864-1871*, 6 vols., Paris, 1964-7.

Marx, K., and F. Engels, *Correspondence 1846-1895*, London, 1934.

—— *Pis'ma K. Marksa i F. Engel'sa k Nikolaiu -onu*, St Petersburg, 1908.

—— *Werke*, 39 vols. and supplements, Berlin, 1959-1967.

Marx-Engels-Lenin Institute (Moscow), *Karl Marx: Chronik seines Lebens,* Moscow, 1934.

Masanov, I.F., *Slovar' psevdonimov russkikh pisatelei, uchenykh i obshchestvennykh deiatelei,* vol. 1, Moscow, 1956.

Meyendorff, A., 'Conversations of Gorchakov with Andrássy and Bismarck in 1872,' *Slavonic Review*, vol. 8, no. 23.

Michel, L., *La Commune*, Paris, 1898.

Mins, L., ed., *Founding of the First International*, London, 1939.

Nikitenko, A., *Moia povest' o samom sebe i o tom, 'chemu svidetel' v zhizni byl.' Zapiski i dnevnik (1804-1877 gg.)*, 2nd edition, 2 vols., St Petersburg, 1905.

Panteleev, L., *Vospominaniia*, Leningrad, 1958

Passek, T., *Iz dal'nykh let*, 2 vols., Moscow, 1963.

Plekhanov, G., *Sochineniia*, vol. 5, Moscow, n.d., vol. 24, Moscow-Leningrad, 1927.

Ralli, Z., 'Mikhail Aleksandrovich Bakunin. Iz moikh vospominanii,' *Minuvshie gody*, 1908, no. 10.

—— 'Sergei Gennad'evich Nechaev (Iz moikh vospominanii),' *Byloe*, vol. 1, no. 7.

—— 'Slavianskaia sektsiia Internatsionala,' in Bazilevskii, *Materialy*.

Richard, A., 'Bakounine et l'Internationale à Lyon, 1868-1870,' *Revue de Paris*, no. 5, Sept.-Oct. 1896.

Sapir, B., ed., *Vpered!, 1873-1877. Materialy iz arkhiva Valeriana Nikolaevicha Smirnova*, 2 vols., Dordrecht, 1970.

Sazhin, M. ('Arman Ross'), *Vospominaniia, 1860-1880-kh gg.*, Moscow, 1925

Serebrennikov, S., 'Zapiska Semena Serebrennikova o Nechaeve,' *KS*, 1934, no. 3 (112)

—— 'Arest Semena Serebrennikova v Zheneve,' Geneva, 1870

Taffs, W., 'Conversations between Lord Odo Russell and Andrássy, Bismarck and Gorchakov in September, 1872,' *Slavonic Review*, vol. 8 no. 24.

Tkachev, P.N., *Izbrannye sochineniia na sotsial'no-politicheskie temy v chetyrekh tomakh*, vol. 1, Moscow, 1932, vol. 3 Moscow, 1933.

Tsentrarkhiv, *Tsarskaia diplomatiia i Parizhkaia Kommuna 1871 goda*, Moscow-Leningrad, 1933.

Tuchkova-Ogareva, N., *Vospominaniia*, Moscow, 1959.

Uspenskaia, A., 'Vospominaniia shestidesiatnitsy,' *Byloe*, 1922, no. 18.

Utina, N., 'Zhizn' za zhizn'', *Vestnik Evropy*, 1885, nos. 4-6.

Valuev, P., *Dnevnik*, 2 vols., Moscow, 1961.

Vergès A., *Le coin du voile: trahison et défection au sein de la Commune*, Geneva, 1872.

Vsesoiuznoe obshchestvo politicheskikh katorzhan i. ssyl'no-poselentsev, *Deiateli revoliutsionnogo dvizheniia v Rossii: Bio-bibliograficheskii slovar'*, vols. 1, 2, 3, 5, in 10 parts, Moscow, 1927-34.

Vuillaume, M., *Mes cahiers rouges au temps de la Commune*, Paris, 1871.

Wyczańska, K., *Polacy w Komunie Paryskiej 1871 R.*, 2nd edition, Warsaw, 1971.

Zasulich, V., 'Nechaevskoe delo (posmertnaia rukopis'),' in *Gruppa 'Osvobozhdenie Truda' (Iz arkhivov G.V. Plekhanova, V.I. Zasulich i L.G. Deicha)*, no. 2, Moscow, 1924.

———— 'Vospominaniia V.I. Zasulich,' *Byloe*, 1919, no. 14.

Secondary Sources

———— *Materialy dlia biografii P.L. Lavrova*, Petrograd, 1921.

———— *P.L. Lavrov. Sbornik statei*, Petrograd, 1922.

Antonov, V., *Russkii drug Marksa: G.A. Lopatin*, Moscow, 1962.

Arkomed, S. T. (Georg Karadzhan), *Za rubezhom: istoricheskie zametki. Period studenchestva ot 1886 g. do 1890 g.*, part 1, Tiflis, 1929.

Bakh, I., ed., *Pervyi Internatsional*, in 2 parts, Moscow, 1964-5.

———— ed., *Pervyi Internatsional v istoricheskoi nauke*, Moscow, 1968.

Baron, S.H., *Plekhanov, The Father of Russian Marxism*, Stanford, 1963.

Barrué, J., *Bakounine et Netchaiev*, Paris 1971.

Bartier, J., 'Etudiants et mouvement révolutionnaire au temps de la Première Internationale. Les congrès de Liège, Bruxelles et Gand,' in *Mélanges offerts à G. Jacquemyns*, Brussels, 1968.

Bazarov, V. (V.A. Rudnev), et al, *Karl Marks (1818-1883). K dvadtsatipiati-letiiu so dnia ego smerti (1883-1903)*, St Petersburg, 1908.

Bel'chikov, N., 'Rublevoe obshchestvo,' *Izvestiia AN SSSR, otd. obshchest-vennykh nauk*, no. 10, 1935.

de Belina (A. Mlochowski), *Les Polonais et la Commune de Paris*, Paris-Versailles-Brussels, 1871.

Bernstein, S., 'The First International and the Great Powers,' *Science and Society*, vol. 16, no. 3.

———— *The First International in America*, New York, 1962.

Billington, J., *Mikhailovsky and Russian Populism*, Oxford, 1958.

Bocharova, L., 'Russkaia sektsiia I. Internatsionala i ee sotsial'no-ekonomicheskaia platforma,' unpublished *kandidat* dissertation, Moscow State University, 1955.

Bourgin, G., 'La lutte du gouvernement français contre la Première Internationale. Contribution à l'histoire de l'après-Commune,' *International Review for Social History*, vol. 4, 1939.

Braunthal, J. *History of the International, 1864-1914*, London, 1966.

Briggs, A., and J. Saville, eds., *Essays in Labour History*, London, 1960.

Busch, M., *Bismarck, Some Secret Pages of His History*, 2 vols., London, 1898.

Cannac, R., *Aux sources de la révolution russe: Nechaiev du nihilisme au terrorisme,* Paris, 1961.

Carr, E.H., *Michael Bakunin,* New York, 1961.

—— *The Romantic Exiles,* London, 1968.

Cherkezov, V., 'Znachenie Bakunina v internatsional'nom revoliutsionnom dvizhenii,' in Bakunin, *Izbrannye sochineniia,* vol. 1, 2nd edition, Petrograd-Moscow, 1922.

Chubinskii, M., 'Sud'ba sudebnoi reformy v poslednei treti XIX veka,' *Istoriia Rossii v XIX veke* (Granat), vol. 6, St Petersburg, n.d.

Claretie, J., *Histoire de la révolution de 1870-1871,* Paris, 1872.

Cole, G.D.H., *A History of Socialist Thought,* vol. 2, *Marxism and Anarchism, 1850-1890,* London, 1957.

Commons, J., *The History of Labour in the United States,* vol. 1, New York, 1921.

Dan T., *The Origins of Bolshevism,* New York, 1964.

Dechamps, A., *Le Prince de Bismarck et l'entrevue des trois empereurs,* 2nd edition, Paris-Brussels, 1872.

Deere, L.L., 'Political Offenses in the Law and Practice of Extradition,' *American Journal of International Law,* vol. 27.

[Deich, L.], 'S.G. Nechaev v Alekseevskom raveline v 1873-1883 gg.,' *Byloe,* vol. 1, no. 7.

D'iakov, V., *Iaroslav Dombrovskii,* Moscow, 1969.

—— and I. Miller, *Revoliutsionnoe dvizhenie v russkoi armii i vosstanie 1863 g.,* Moscow, 1964.

Diuvel' [Düwel], V., 'Chernyshevskii v nemetskoi rabochei pechati (1868-1889),' *LN,* vol. 67.

Dohm, B., *Marx und Engels und ihre Beziehungen zu Russland,* Berlin, 1955.

Dommanget, M., *Blanqui et l'opposition révolutionnaire à la fin du Second Empire,* Paris, 1960.

Efimova, Z., 'Parizhskaia Kommuna i organ russkoi revoliutsionnoi demokratii "Iskra",' *Istoricheskie zapiski,* vol. 59.

Efremova, N., 'Elizaveta Dmitrieva—geroinia Kommuny,' *Voprosy Istorii,* 1972, no. 3

Filippov, R., *Ideologiia Bol'shogo obshchestva propagandy (1869-1874),* Petrozavodsk, 1963.

—— *Revoliutsionnaia narodnicheskaia organizatsiia N.A. Ishutina—I.A. Khudiakova (1863-1866),* Petrozavodsk, 1964.

Firstova, V., 'Tsarskaia diplomaticheskaia missiia v Berne i russkaia emigratsiia,' *Voprosy Istorii,* 1973, no. 6.

Flerovskii, N. (V. Bervi), *Polozhenie rabochego klassa v Rossii,* Moscow, 1938.

Freymond, J., and M. Molnár, 'The Rise and Fall of the First International,' in M. Drachkovitch, ed., *The Revolutionary Internationals,* Stanford, 1966.

Gambarov, A., *V sporakh o Nechaeve,* Moscow-Leningrad, 1926.

García Venero, M., *Historia de los movimentos sindicalistas españoles, 1840-1933,* Madrid, 1961.

Geffroy, G., *L'Enfermé,* 2 vols. in 1, Paris, 1926.

Gonsales, A., *Istoriia ispanskikh sektsii Mezhdunarodnogo Tovarishchestva Rabochikh, 1868-1873,* Moscow, 1964.

Gorev, B., and B. Koz'min, eds., *Revioliutsionnoe dvizhenie 1860-kh godov*, Moscow, 1932.

Gorokhov, V., *I-i Internatsional i russkii sotsializm. 'Narodnoe Delo'—Russkaia sektsiia Internatsionala*, Moscow, 1925.

Grigor'eva, I., *Rabochee i sotsialisticheskoe dvizhenie v Italii v epokhu I Internatsionala*, Moscow, 1966.

Gruner, E., *Die Arbeiter in der Schweiz im 19. Jahrhundert*, Berne, 1968.

Haas, L., 'Njetschajew und die schweizer Behörden,' *Schweizerische Zeitschrift für Geschichte*, vol. 17.

Haimson, L., *The Russian Marxists and the Origins of Bolshevism*, Cambridge, Mass., 1955.

Halkin, L., *Le Premier Congrès International des étudiants à Liège en 1865*, Liège, 1866.

Hart, J.M., 'Vienna and the Centennial,' *The International Review*, vol. 2, no. 1.

Hostetter, R., *The Italian Socialist Movement*, vol. 1 *Origins (1860-1882)*, Princeton, 1958.

Howard, M., *The Franco-Prussian War*, New York, 1962.

Ionescu, G., and E. Gellner, eds., *Populism*, London, 1969.

Itenberg, B., *'Iuzhno-rossiiskii soiuz rabochikh'—pervaia proletarskaia organizatsiia v Rossii*, Moscow, 1954.

—— 'Parizhskaia Kommuna i P.L. Lavrov (Novye dokumenty),' *Istoriia SSSR*, 1971, no. 2.

—— 'Parizhskaia Kommuna i russkie revoliutsionery 70-kh gg. XIX veka,' *Istoriia SSSR*, 1961, no. 2.

—— *Pervyi Internatsional i revoliutsionnaia Rossiia*, Moscow, 1964.

—— 'Rasprostranenie izdanii Russkoi sektsii I Internatsionala v revoliutsionnom podpol'e Rossii,' *Voprosy Istorii*, 1962, no. 10.

—— 'Russkie revoliutsionery—Uchastniki Parizhskoi Kommuny,' Institut istorii AN SSSR, *Parizhskaia Kommuna 1871 g.*, vol. 2, Moscow, 1961.

Ivanov, L.M., ed., *Rabochii klass i rabochee dvizhenie v Rossii, 1861-1917*, Moscow, 1966.

Jaeckh, G., *Die Internationale*, Leipzig, 1904.

Jellinek, F., *The Paris Commune of 1871*, New York, 1965.

Kantor, R., *V pogone za Nechaevym*, Leningrad, 1925.

Karataev, N., ed., *Ekonomicheskaia platforma russkoi sektsii I Internatsionala*, Moscow, 1959.

Katz, M., *Mikhail N. Katkov*, The Hague, 1966.

Keep, J.L.H., *The Rise of Social Democracy in Russia*, Oxford, 1963.

Kimball, A., 'The First International and the Russian Obshchina,' *Slavic Review*, vol. 32, no. 3.

—— 'The Russian Past and the Socialist Future in the Thought of Peter Lavrov,' *Slavic Review*, vol. 30, no. 1.

Kiperman, A., 'Raznochinskaia politicheskaia emigratsiia v perepiske tsarskikh diplomatov,' *Istochnikovedcheskie raboty*, vyp. 2, Tambov, 1971.

Kirpotin, V., *Dostoevskii v shestidesiatye gody*, Moscow, 1966.

Klevenskii, M., ed., *Pokushenie Karakozova. Stenograficheskii otchet po delu D. Karakozova, I. Khudiakova, N. Ishutina i drugikh*, 2 vols., Moscow-Leningrad, 1928-30.

Knizhnik-Vetrov, I., 'E.G. Barteneva—sotsialistka i pisatel'nitsa,' *KS*, 1929, no. 11(60).

―――― 'Geroinia Parizhskoi Kommuny 1871 g. E.L. Tumanovskaia [sic] ('Elizaveta Dmitrievna.),' *Letopisi marksizma*, 1928, no. 7-8.

―――― 'P.L. Lavrov ot pervykh publitsisticheskikh vystuplenii do izdanii 'Vpered' (1857—mart 1872),' in Lavrov, *Izbrannye sochineniia*, vol. 1.

―――― *Russkie deiatel'nitsy Pervogo Internatsionala i Parizhskoi Kommuny (E.L. Dmitrieva, A.V. Zhaklar, E.G. Barteneva)*, Moscow-Leningrad, 1964.

―――― 'Uchastnik Parizhskoi Kommuny 1871 g. V.A. Potapenko,' *KS*, 1929, no. 5(54).

Koberdowa, I., *Pierwsza miedzynarodnowka i lewica wielkiej emigraciji*, Warsaw, 1964.

König, K., *Die polnischen Bankotenfälscher in der Schweiz*, Berne, 1875.

'Kommunisticheskii manifest' i tsarskaia tsenzura,' *Istorik-marksist*, 1928, no. 2(66).

Kornilova-Moroz, A., 'Perovskaia i osnovanie kruzhka Chaikovtsev,' *KS*, 1926, no. 1(22).

Korol'chuk, A., *'Severnyi soiuz russkikh rabochikh' i revoliutsionnoe rabochee dvizhenie 70-kh godov XIX v. v Peterburge*, Leningrad, 1946.

Koz'min, B., et al, eds., *Istoriko-revoliutsionnaia khrestomatiia*, vol. 1, Moscow, 1923.

―――― *Iz istorii revoliutsionnoi mysli v Rossii*, Moscow, 1961.

―――― 'Kto byl pervym perevodchikom na russkii iazyk 'Manifesta Kommunisticheskoi Partii'?,' *LN*, vol. 63.

―――― *Nechaev i nechaevtsy*, Moscow-Leningrad, 1931.

―――― *Ot 'deviatnadtsatogo fevralia' k 'pervomu marta'*, Moscow, 1933.

―――― 'P.N. Tkachev i P.L. Lavrov (Stolknovenie dvukh techenii russkoi revoliutsionnoi mysli 70-kh godov),' *Voinstvuiuschii materialist*, 1924, book 1.

―――― *'Revoliutsionnoe podpol'e v epokhu 'Belogo terrora'*, Moscow, 1929.

―――― *Russkaia sektsiia Pervogo Internatsionala*, Moscow, 1957.

―――― 'A.A. Serno-Solov'evich v I Internatsionale i v zhenevskom rabochem dvizhenii,' *Istoricheskii sbornik*, 1936, book 5.

―――― *P.N. Tkachev i revoliutsionnoe dvizhenie 1860-kh godov*, Moscow, 1922

Kuniskii, S., *Russkoe obshchestvo i Parizhskaia Kommuna*, Moscow, 1962.

Langer, W.L., *European Alliances and Alignments, 1871-1890*, New York, 1964.

―――― 'Red Rag and Gallic Bull: The French Decision for War, 1870,' in *Europa und Uebersee. Festschrift für Egmont Zechlin*, Hamburg, 1961.

Leffler, A.C., *Sonya Kovalevsky*, London, 1895.

Lehning, A., *The International Association, 1855-1859*, Leiden, 1938.

Leidner, F., *Die Aussenpolitik Oesterreich-Ungarns vom Deutsch-Französischen Kriege bis zum Deutsch-Oesterreichischen Bündnis, 1870-1879*, Halle, 1936.

Lenskii, Z., 'Pol'skoe vozstanie 1863 g.,' *Istoriia Rossii v XIX veke* (Granat), St Petersburg, n.d., vol. 3.

Levin, L., *'Manifest Kommunisticheskoi Partii' v Rossii*, Moscow, 1956.

Levin, Sh., *Obshchestvennoe dvizhenie v Rossii v 60-70-e gody XIX veka*, Moscow, 1958.

Malia, M., 'What Is the Intelligentsia?', *Daedalus,* vol. 89, no. 3.

Mason, E., *The Paris Commune,* New York, 1930.

McClellan, W., 'Nechaevshchina: An Unknown Chapter,' *Slavic Review,* vol. 32, no. 3.

Meijer, J., *Knowledge and Revolution: The Russian Colony in Zuerich (1870-1873),* Assen, 1955.

Meschkat, K., *Die Pariser Kommune von 1871 im Spiegel der sowjetischen Geschichtsschreibung,* Berlin, 1965.

Miller, M., 'Ideological Conflicts in Russian Populism: The Revolutionary Manifestoes of the Chaikovsky Circle, 1869-74,' *Slavic Review,* vol. 29, no. 1.

Molnár, M., *Le déclin de la Première Internationale: La Conférence de Londres de 1871,* Geneva, 1963.

Molok, A., *Germanskaia interventsiia protiv Parizhskoi Kommuny 1871 goda,* Moscow, 1939.

N.N., 'Graf Bismark—organizator russkoi politicheskoi agentury zagranitsei,' *Byloe,* 1907, no. 6(18).

Nauchitel', M., *G.A. Lopatin v Sibiri,* Irkutsk, 1963.

Nettlau, M., 'Bakunin und die russische revolutionäre Bewegung in den Jahren 1868-1873,' *Archiv Für die Geschichte des Sozialismus und der Arbeiterbewegung,* vol. 5, 1915,

—— *Michael Bakunin,* 3 vols. in 2, London, 1898-9.

—— *La Première Internationale en Espagne (1868-1888),* Dordrecht, 1969.

Nevskii, V., 'Karl Marks i russkoe revoliutsionnoe dvizhenie (Epokha 60-80 godov XIX v.),' *Istoriia proletariata SSSR,* no. 1-2(13-14), 1933.

Nicolaievsky, B., and O. Maenchen-Helfen, *Karl Marx, Man and Fighter,* Philadelphia, 1936.

—— 'Pamiati poslednego 'iakobintsa'-semidesiatnika. (Gaspar-Mikhail Turskii),' *KS,* 1926, no. 2(23).

—— 'Secret Societies and the First International,' in M. Drachkovitch, ed., *The Revolutionary Internationals, 1864-1943,* Stanford, 1966.

Pipes, R., 'Narodnichestvo: A Semantic Enquiry,' *Slavic Review,* vol. 23, no. 3.

—— 'Russian Marxism and Its Populist Background: The Late Nineteenth Century,' *Russian Review,* vol. 19, no. 4.

Polevoi, Iu., *Zarozhdenie marksizma v Rossii, 1883-1894 gg.,* Moscow, 1959.

Pomper, P., *Peter Lavrov and the Russian Revolutionary Movement,* Chicago, 1972.

Prawdin, M., *The Unmentionable Nechaev,* London, 1961.

Pribram, A., *England and the International Policy of the European Great Powers, 1871-1914,* Oxford, 1931.

Rapoport, Iu., *Iz istorii sviazei russkikh revoliutsionerov s osnovopolozhikami nauchnogo sotsializma (K. Marks i G. Lopatin),* Moscow, 1960.

Resis, A., '*Das Kapital* Comes to Russia,' *Slavic Review,* vol. 29, no. 2.

Reuel', A., '*Kapital*' *Karla Marksa v Rossii 1870-kh godov,* Moscow, 1939.

—— *Russkaia ekonomicheskaia mysl' 60-70-kh godov XIX veka i marksizm,* Moscow, 1954.

Romano, A., *L'Unità italiana e la Prima Internazionale, 1861-1871,* 2nd edition, Bari, 1966.

Rusanov, N. (N.E. Kudrin), *Sotsialisty zapada i Rossii,* St Petersburg, 1908.
—— 'P.L. Lavrov (Ocherk ego zhizni i deiatel'nosti),' *Byloe,* 1907, no. 2(14).
Ryndziunskii, P., *Krest'ianskaia promyshlennost' v poreformennoi Rossii (60-80-e gody XIX v.)*, Moscow, 1966.
Samorukov, N., 'Obshchestvenno-politicheskaia deiatel'nost' G.A. Lopatina (1845-1918),' *Voprosy Istorii* 1951, no. 3.
Sapir, B., 'The Origin of Vpered!,' in Sapir, ed., *Vpered!, 1873-1877,* vol. 1.
Scanlan, J., 'Peter Lavrov: An Intellectual Biography,' in Lavrov, *Historical Letters* (Scanlan edition).
Schlüter, H., *Die Internationale in Amerika,* Chicago, 1918.
Sedov, M., *Geroicheskii period revoliutsionnogo narodnichestva,* Moscow, 1966
—— 'Nekotorye problemy istorii blankizma v Rossii (Revoliutsionnaia doktrina P.N. Tkacheva),' *Voprosy Istorii,* 1971, no. 10.
Seignobos, C., *Le déclin de l'Empire et l'établissement de la 3e République,* Paris, 1921.
Seleznev, K., 'I Internatsional i revoliutsionnoe dvizhenie v Rossii v XIX veke,' *Istoriia SSSR,* 1964, no. 4.
Shchegolev, P., ed., 'S.G. Nechaev v Alekseevskom raveline,' *Krasnyi Arkhiv,* vol. 4, 1923, vol. 5, 1924, vol. 6, 1924.
Shpadaruk, I., *Russkaia sektsiia I Internatsionala i ee sotsiologicheskie vozzreniia,* Minsk, 1970.
Sladkevich, N., 'K. Marks i peredovoe studenchestvo Peterburgskogo universiteta 60-80-kh godov XIX veka,' *Ocherki po istorii Leningradskogo Universiteta,* vol. 1, Leningrad, 1962.
Sokolov, O., 'Novye materialy o rasprostranenii idei I Internatsionala v Rossii,' *Voprosy Istorii,* 1959, no. 1.
—— 'Revoliutsionnaia propaganda sredi fabrichnykh i zavodskikh rabochikh v 70-kh godakh XIX veka,' *Iz istorii rabochego klassa i krest'ianstva SSSR,* Moscow, 1959.
Stieklov (Steklov, Stekloff), G. (Iu.M. Nakhamkis), *Die Bakunistische Internationale nach dem Haager Kongress, Stuttgart,* 1914.
—— *History of the First International,* London, 1928.
—— *Istoricheskoe podgotovlenie russkoi sotsial'-demokratii,* St Petersburg, 1906.
—— 'Internatsional posle Gaagskago Kongressa,' *Golos minvshego,* 1913, no. 11.
Stewart, N., *Blanqui,* London, 1939.
Svatikov, S., 'Studencheskoe dvizhenie 1869 goda. (Bakunin i Nechaev),' *'Nasha Strana'—Istoricheskii sbornik,* 1907, no. 1.
Tagirov, R., 'Iz istorii russkoi sektsii Mezhdunarodnogo Tovarishchestva Rabochikh (Russkaia sektsiia i evropeiskoe revoliutsionnoe dvizhenie),' *Uchenye zapiski Kazanskogo gosudarstvennogo Pedagogicheskogo Institute,* vol. 2, no. 2, 1956.
—— 'Russkaia sektsiia Mezhdunarodnogo Tovarishchestva Rabochikh i Rossiia,' *Uchenye zapiski Kazanskogo gosudarstvennogo Pedagogicheskogo Instituta,* vol. 7, 1949.
Tatischev, S., *Imperator Aleksandr II,* 2 vols., St Petersburg, 1903.
Thomas, E., *The Women Incendiaries,* New York, 1966.

Troitskii, N., *Bol'shoe obshchestvo propagandy*, Saratov, 1963.

Tveritinov, A., *Ob ob'iavlenii prigovora N.G. Chernyshevskomu, o rasprostranenii ego sochineii na frantsuzskom iazyke v zapadnoi Evrope i o mnogom drugom*, St Petersburg, 1906.

Utin, N., 'Serginsko-Ufaleiskie gornye zavody,' St Petersburg, 1882.

Venturi, F., *Roots of Revolution*, New York, 1966.

Viktorov-Toporov, V., 'Svetozar Markovich,' *Golos minuvshego*, vol. 1 no. 3.

Vuilleumier, M., 'Le gouvernement de Versailles, les autorités suisses et les proscrits de la Commune en 1871,' *Le Mouvement sociale*, no. 38, Jan. March 1972.

—— 'L'Internationale à Genève et la Commune de Paris (1871),' in *Mélanges offerts à M. Paul-E. Martin*, Geneva, 1961.

Weeks, A., *The First Bolshevik: A Political Biography of Peter Tkachev*, New York, 1968.

Wereszycki, H., *Sojusz trzech cesarzy: Geneza 1866-1872*, Warsaw, 1965.

Woehrlin, W., *Chernyshevskii: The Man and the Journalist*, Cambridge, Mass., 1971.

Wortman, R., *The Crisis of Russian Populism*, Cambridge, 1967.

Wysotzki, K., et al, *Die polnische Fälscherbände und die russischen Staatsräthe und deren Agenten*, Zürich, 1874 (P. Tkachev and M. Elpidin, translators, *Fal'shivye monetchiki ili agenty russkago pravitel'stva*, Geneva, 1875).

Zelnik, R., *Labour and Society in Tsarist Russia, 1855-1870*. Stanford, 1971.

Zel'tser, V., 'Marks-Engel's i Lenin o kapitalizme i revoliutsii v Rossii,' *Istoriia proletariata SSSR*, No. 1-2(13-14), 1933.

Zhelubovskaia, E., et al, *Istoriia Parizhskoi Kommuny 1871 goda*, Moscow, 1971.

Contemporary Periodicals

Note: Dates in parentheses indicate years consulted, not necessarily inclusive dates of publication.

Der Bund (Berne, 1870).

Bulletin de la Fédération Jurassienne de l'Association Internationale des Travailleurs (Sonvilier, Le Locle and La Chaux-de-Fonds, 1872-1875).

Le Constitutionnel (Paris, 1870-1871).

Le Cri du Peuple (Paris, 1871).

Demokratisches Wochenblatt (Leipzig, 1868-1869).

L'Egalité (Geneva, 1868-1872).

Le Figaro (Paris, 1870-1871).

La Flandre (Ghent, 1868).

Gazette de Lausanne (1867-1872).

Golos (St Petersburg, 1872-1873).

L'Indépendance Belge (Brussels, 1868-1869).

L'Internationale (Brussels, 1869-1873).

L'Internationale (Geneva, 1868).

Izdaniia obshchestva Narodnoi Raspravy (Geneva, 1869-1870).
Journal des Débats (Paris, 1873).
Journal de Gand (Ghent, 1868-1869).
Journal de Genève (1863-1873).
Journal de Saint-Pétersbourg (1871).
Journal Officiel de la République Française (Paris, March-May 1871).
Kolokol (Herzen: London and Geneva, 1857-1868; Nechaev: Geneva, 1870).
La Liberté (Brussels, 1868-1862).
La Marseillaise (Paris, 1869-1870).
Le Monde (Paris, 1870-1872).
Narodnoe Delo (Geneva, 1868-1870).
Neue Zürcher Zeitung (Zürich, 1863-1873).
Ni Dieu ni Maître (Paris, 1880-1881).
Le Nord (Brussels, 1866-1873).
Nouvelliste Vaudois et Journal National Suisse (Lausanne, 1866-1872).
Obshchee Delo—La Cause Générale (Geneva, 1877-1879).
Obshchina. (La Commune. Die Commune) (London, 1871).
Pravitel'stvennyi Vestnik (St Petersburg, 1871)
Rizhskii Vestnik (Riga, 1871)
Russkie Vedomosti (Moscow, 1873).
Sudebnyi Vestnik (St Petersburg, 1871).
La Suisse Radicale (Geneva, 1868-1872).
Die Tagwacht (Zürich, 1869-1872).
The Times (London, 1863-1873).
Vedomosti Moskovskoi Gorodskoi Politsii (Moscow, 1871).
Der Volksstaat (Leipzig, 1869-1876).
Der Vorbote (Geneva, 1866-1871).
Vpered! (Zürich and London, 1873-1877).

Index